A COMMENTARY

ON THE

DOCTRINE

— AND —

COVENANTS

A COMMENTARY ON THE

DOCTRINE

— AND —

COVENANTS

VOLUME ONE

Stephen E. Robinson
H. Dean Garrett

DESERET BOOK COMPANY
SALT LAKE CITY, UTAH

Library of Congress Cataloging-in-Publication Data

Robinson, Stephen Edward.

A commentary on the Doctrine and Covenants / Stephen E. Robinson and H. Dean Garrett.

p. cm.

Includes bibliographical references.

ISBN 1-57345-784-1

1. Doctrine and Covenants—Commentaries. I. Garrett, H. Dean. II. Title.

BX8628 .R65 2000

289.3'2—dc21

00-040441

Printed in the United States of America   54459-6675

10   9   8   7   6   5   4   3   2   1

CONTENTS

CONTENTS

PREFACE

This commentary on the Doctrine and Covenants of The Church of Jesus Christ of Latter-day Saints is offered in the hope that it will help Church members understand the original meaning of the revelations in their original context. But language is a difficult and sometimes even confusing tool. President Brigham Young said concerning Doctrine and Covenants 58:

"When revelations are given through an individual appointed to receive them, they are given to the understandings of the people. . . . After a lapse of years, [these revelations] become mystified to those who were not personally acquainted with the circumstances at the time they were given. . . . The revelation which I have read was perfectly plain, and could readily be understood by all the brethren then in Jackson County, Missouri, and in Kirtland, Ohio, as easily as you can understand me when I talk about digging canals, building dwellings, tabernacles, temples, and storehouses, or when I talk about drawing sand and clay, burning lime, &c. . . . When Joseph received this revelation, it was as plain to the understanding of the Saints, as are my instructions when telling you what to do" (in Cook, *Revelations,* xi).

We therefore conclude that written scripture may be frozen in time and must sometimes be thawed out by turning back the clock and adjusting our understanding for the years that have elapsed since it was given. Yet, no one has the right to declare or define doctrine for the Church and its members except the prophet (see D&C 43:5–7). Therefore, these volumes represent our best efforts to learn and explain the meaning of the revelations, and we may be mistaken on any point.

Nothing in this commentary should be understood as authoritative for Latter-day Saint belief except the scriptures that are cited. Every effort has been made to express and interpret the doctrines correctly, but in the long run, our efforts remain private views, shared with the reader for whatever they may be worth. We caution against relying too heavily upon the opinions expressed in this or any other commentary. No commentary is greater than the scriptural text it attempts to explain, nor can it encompass, limit, or define the full meaning of the scriptural text. Although we hope that the present work, which is itself indebted to the insights, opinions, and research of many previous writers, will be an aid to readers who seek to better understand the Doctrine and Covenants, it is still only an aid or a support. The scriptural text is always primary and always contains more than can be brought out and explained by any commentary.

If this commentary encourages a more full study of the Doctrine and Covenants itself, then our objectives will have been met. The Doctrine and Covenants stands as a witness to the restoration of the gospel of Jesus Christ through the Prophet Joseph Smith and his successors in The Church of Jesus Christ of Latter-day Saints. In it are the teachings that will lead an individual to exaltation through the atonement of Jesus Christ. It is a witness of the mission of the Savior and of his role as the head of the Church that bears his name. It testifies to the world that the heavens are open and that God reveals his will to the world today through his living prophets.

We are grateful for the restoration of the gospel of Jesus Christ. In it is the hope of eternity and the peace of mortality.

ACKNOWLEDGMENTS

We acknowledge with gratitude the assistance of many who have aided in the production of this commentary. Larry E. Dahl and Keith W. Perkins, two fine Church historians and gospel scholars, read the manuscript carefully and offered invaluable suggestions. We express appreciation to Richard Daleboot, Gordon Stokes, Janiece Johnson, Tammy Woods, and Kirk Anderson for reading portions of the manuscript. And we are grateful to our wives and children, who have encouraged and challenged us to complete this project.

DOCTRINE AND COVENANTS

INTRODUCTION

The Doctrine and Covenants is a marvelous book of scripture. It bears strong testimony to the whole world that the heavens are open, and that the God of heaven, who loves his children, reveals his mind and will to the world through living prophets. It testifies of Jesus Christ and his role as Savior and Redeemer of the world. The Doctrine and Covenants is the capstone of the Restoration, and it contains the doctrines and commandments that will help an individual to receive all the promises that God has given to his Saints.

A dynamic, open book, the Doctrine and Covenants represents neither a complete nor a closed canon. It contains revelations and reports of revelations received through presidents Joseph Smith, Brigham Young, Wilford Woodruff, Joseph F. Smith, and Spencer W. Kimball. The revelations are part of the history of The Church of Jesus Christ of Latter-day Saints and are best understood in the context of that history. The revelations are the foundation of the Church in these last days and benefit the world, "showing that the keys of the mysteries of the kingdom of our Savior are again entrusted to man" (headnote to D&C 70).

The Lord instructed Joseph Smith that "this generation shall have my word through you" (D&C 5:10). From the time Joseph entered the grove of trees on that spring morning of 1820 until his death at the hands of a mob at Carthage Jail 27 June 1844, he received many important revelations and communications from the heavens. Early members of the Church, however, did not have ready access to this growing store of revelations. Some individuals copied certain revelations by hand and read them to the Saints when they traveled to various meetings. Elder Orson Pratt recorded that he and others often had access to the manuscripts when boarding with the Prophet, and they read them repeatedly before the revelations were printed. "And so highly were they esteemed by us, that we committed some to memory; and a few we copied for the purpose of reference in our absence on missions; and also to read them to the saints for their edification."[1]

As the Church expanded to Ohio and then to Missouri, the need for ready access to the revelations increased. The Prophet expressed his concern regarding the importance of the Lord's instructions being available to the members of the Church: "It is very difficult for us to communicate to the Church all that God has revealed to us, in consequence of tradition; for we are differently situated from any other people that ever existed upon this Earth."[2] The solution to this challenge, the eventual publication of the Doctrine and Covenants, the "capstone" of our religion[3]—has had a tremendous effect on the LDS Church.

PUBLICATION OF THE REVELATIONS

The process of making the revelations available to the Saints began in July 1830. After receiving what today is recorded in sections 24, 25, and 26 of the Doctrine and Covenants, the Prophet Joseph began to arrange and copy the revelations, which had been received from time to time. The work of recording the revelations continued through 1830 and 1831. Both Oliver Cowdery and John Whitmer, who resided with him, assisted in this process.

W. W. Phelps, a recently converted Church member who was called to assist Oliver Cowdery in the work of printing for the Church (D&C 55:4), helped in publishing the revelations. Phelps was a printer and newspaper editor by trade and, therefore, possessed invaluable skills to assist in the task. After being introduced to the Book of Mormon as early as 1830, he arrived in Kirtland about the middle of June 1831, where he was baptized and expressed a desire to do the will of God. The Prophet Joseph, preparing for a journey to Jackson County, Missouri, invited Brother Phelps to join him on this trip.

This was the Prophet's first visit to Missouri and was historic in that Independence was identified by revelation as Zion (D&C 57:3). Their journey greatly affected Phelps. While in Missouri, Phelps was commanded to "be planted in this place, and be established as a printer unto the church" (D&C 57:11). Phelps was told that "if the world receive his writings," he could use the profits "in righteousness, for the good of the saints" (D&C 57:12).

In a conference held in Ohio during September 1831, Phelps received instructions to travel to Cincinnati and purchase a printing press. He was to continue on to Independence and begin the publication of a monthly paper to be called *The Evening and the Morning Star.* This newspaper was to declare "the meaning of the revelations of God from the earliest times to the present, but more especially those revelations which God has given in the present dispensation." [4] After building a printing office and creating the W. W. Phelps Printing Company in Independence, Phelps published in the *Star* twenty-three sections of the future Doctrine and Covenants.

The decision to publish the revelations in the newspaper was made in relation to a larger decision: the leaders of the Church desired to publish the revelations in book form. At a conference held at Hiram, Ohio, in early November 1831, the decision was made to publish ten thousand copies (later adjusted to three thousand) of the Book of Commandments. The quality of the revelations and the language to be used in the revelations was then discussed. When some of the elders present objected to the language of the revelations, a revelation was received challenging them to improve the language or to find any unrighteousness in the revelations (D&C 67). After William E. McLellin failed to improve the revelation he considered the least of those under consideration for publication, the decision to publish the book was confirmed.

Shortly after this conference, the Literary Firm was organized as the publishing arm of the Church.[5] The proceeds from the printing were to compensate Joseph Smith, Oliver Cowdery, Sidney Rigdon, John Whitmer, and Martin Harris for the "diligence of our brethren, . . . in bringing to light by grace of God these sacred things."[6] The Lord indicated that the appointed stewards over the literary concerns of the Church had claim upon the Church for assistance with their temporal needs, so "that the revelations may be published, and go forth unto the ends of the earth; that they also may obtain funds which shall benefit the church in all things" (D&C 72:20–21). The Firm was to publish not only the Book of Commandments but also the New Translation of the Bible, the Church hymnal, children's literature, a church almanac, and newspapers.

At the November conference, the elders present bore testimony that "they were willing to attach to these commandments which should shortly be sent to the world . . . that they knew that they were of the Lord."[7] Sidney Rigdon raised concerns about "the errors or mistakes which are in commandments and revelations, made either by the translation in consequence of the slow way of the scribe at the time of receiving or by the scribes themselves."[8] The conference resolved that "Br Joseph Smith Jr correct those errors or mistakes which he may discover by the holy Spirit while reviewing the revelations & commandments & also the fulness of the scriptures."[9] The Prophet indicated that his time was occupied closely in reviewing the commandments and sitting in the conference for nearly two weeks.[10] Some of that time might have been spent making copies of the revelations. The copying work needed to be done quickly, because Oliver Cowdery and John Whitmer had been called to take the manuscripts and money to Missouri in mid-November. After the book containing the revelations had been dedicated to the Lord by the Prophet, Cowdery and Whitmer left Kirtland about 20 November 1831 and arrived in Independence around 5 January 1832.

On 1 March 1832, the Prophet received a revelation instructing the Saints to organize a branch of the Firm in Independence "to the glory of your father who is in heaven that you may be equal in the bonds of heavenly things yea and earthly things."[11] The Prophet Joseph and a party of men also journeyed to Missouri in the spring of 1832 to establish the Firm.[12] They traveled to Wheeling, Virginia, to purchase paper for the press, sailed to Cincinnati, and then traveled overland to Jackson County, arriving at the beginning of April. On 30 April 1832, the Literary Firm of Missouri held a meeting in which a decision was made "that three thousand copies of the book of Commandments be printed [of] the first edition."[13] The members of the Literary Firm also gave to Phelps, Cowdery, and Whitmer the responsibility to "review the Book of Commandments & select for printing such as shall be deemed by them proper, as dictated by the Spirit & make all necessary verbal corrections."[14] They were also instructed to keep the revelations available only to those involved in the printing until the Book of Commandments was printed. The Prophet left Independence on 6 May 1832 to return to Kirtland, leaving the job of printing in the hands of Phelps, Whitmer, and Cowdery.[15]

On Tuesday, 29 May 1832, a conference was held in the offices of *The Evening and the Morning Star.* John Whitmer read "several appropriate commandments," after which Brothers Phelps and Cowdery made remarks "in relation to rules & regulations of the office & the important duties devolving upon those whom the Lord has designated to spread his truths & revelations in these days to the inhabitants of the earth. After which the Bishop [Partridge] proceeded Solemnly to dedicate the building for Printing & all materials appertaining thereto unto the Lord."[16]

By December 1832, the Book of Commandments was in press. That the proofs had to be sent back to Kirtland for the approval of the Prophet complicated the editing and printing process. Joseph Smith recorded that he spent time "writing and correcting revelations."[17] Also, because of the unavailability of a bookbinder or materials for binding the books in Independence, plans were made to distribute them unbound.[18]

During this time, W. W. Phelps deposited a copy of the title with the U.S. District Court for Missouri, and on 13 February 1833, the copyright of the Book of Commandments was secured. The editors of *The Evening and the Morning Star* expressed frustration concerning the slowness of the printing process. The May 1833 edition stated the Book of Commandments "will be published in the course of the present year, at from 25, to 50 cents a copy. We regret that in consequence of circumstances not within our control, this book will not be offered to our brethren as soon as was anticipated. We beg their forbearance, and solicit an interest in their prayers, promising to use our exertions with all our means to accomplish the work."[19] It appears that they were close to completing the work by the middle of June. Sidney Rigdon wrote a letter to W. W. Phelps on 25 June 1833, followed by another one a week later, instructing Phelps not to bind the books in Missouri but rather to ship them to Kirtland to N. K. Whitney & Co.[20]

The delay in completing the printing of the Book of Commandments proved quite costly to the Saints. This period of time was marked by growing tension between the Mormons and the old settlers in Missouri. Economic, political, and social as well as religious differences led to conflict between these groups, including mob action. In this atmosphere, a Reverend Pixley had written several articles to eastern newspapers attacking the Mormons' relationship with the Indians. On the first of July he wrote "Beware of False Prophets." The Saints called it a "slanderous tract . . . which he carried from house to house, to incense the inhabitants against the Church, to mob them, and drive them away."[21] The editor of *The Evening and the Morning Star* responded to the tract in the July issue. The mob reacted to this editorial by drawing up a manifesto attacking the Mormons and affirming that they would use any means to remove the Mormons from the county. The mob met on Saturday, 20 July 1833, and demanded that the Saints stop using the printing establishment in Jackson County, close the store, and cease all mechanical labors. When the Saints refused to concede to these demands, the mob attacked the W. W. Phelps printing establishment and destroyed the printing press and most of the copies of the Book of Commandments that had been printed.[22]

For a time, efforts to publish the revelations ended, though the resolve to print the book remained strong. Nine days after the destruction of the press, W. W. Phelps wrote to the brethren in Kirtland, declaring: "Although the enemy has accomplished his design in demolishing the printing establishment they cannot demolish the design of our God, for his decree will stand & his purposes must be accomplished."[23]

The center for printing the Book of Commandments was now changed to Kirtland. On 11 September 1833, a meeting of the Literary Firm in Kirtland decided that the press should be reestablished under the auspices of the F. G. Williams Co. to continue publishing *The Evening and the Morning Star* as well as starting a new publication to be called *The Latter-Day Saint Messenger and Advocate*. One overriding purpose of the two newspapers was to make available to the members the revelations being prepared for publication in book form. Plans had already been made to erect a printing office in Kirtland in response to the direction of the Lord. He commanded that a lot in Kirtland be "dedicated unto me for the building of a house unto me, for the work of the printing of the translation of my scriptures, and all things whatsoever I shall command you" (D&C 94:10). On 10 October a frame printing office (thirty feet by thirty-eight feet) was started. Completed by the end of November, it was used as a printing office in the upper story and as the office of the First Presidency in the lower story.[24]

At the beginning of October 1833, Oliver Cowdery left for New York with eight hundred dollars to buy a new printing press. He returned with it in late November, and on 6 December 1833 the Prophet wrote: "Being prepared to commence our Labours in the printing business I ask God in the name of Jesus to establish it for ever and cause that his word may speedily go for[th to] the Nations of the earth to the accomplishing of his great work in bringing about the restoration of the house of Israel."[25] By 18 December 1833, the printing of *The Evening and the Morning Star* was resumed in Kirtland.[26]

Obtaining funds sufficient for printing the Doctrine and Covenants was a problem. On 15 June 1835, the Prophet wrote a letter to the brethren of the Church, indicating that the Firm was beginning "to prepare and print the new translation of the Bible, together with all the revelations which God has been pleased to give us in these last days." The brethren were asked "to donate and loan us all the means and money you can that we may be enable[d] to accomplish the work as a great means towards the Salvation of Men."[27]

At a special meeting in Norton, Ohio, on 19 April 1834, Sidney Rigdon was set apart to assist Oliver Cowdery in arranging the Book of Commandments. Elders began the task of raising funds. On 24 September 1834, a committee was appointed to "arrange the items of the doctrine of Jesus Christ, for the government of the Church of Latter-Day Saints."[28] The committee consisted of the First Presidency (Joseph Smith, Sidney Rigdon, and Frederick G. Williams) and Oliver Cowdery. Because of the many errors contained in the first publication of the revelations in *The Evening and the Morning Star,* Oliver Cowdery was instructed to reprint the *Star* for the purpose of correcting mistakes in the first printing of the revelations in the Missouri publication.[29] To make these corrections, it appears that Cowdery used the same manuscript the committee used in preparing the new edition, now to be titled the Doctrine and Covenants. By October 1834, the reprints of the Missouri *Star* containing the corrected revelations began to appear.

In the meantime, the committee labored through the end of 1834 and the beginning of 1835, completing their work and preparing the manuscript for publication in book form. In May 1835, W. W. Phelps and John Whitmer arrived in Kirtland from Missouri. Both were put to work in the printing business immediately. Whitmer was appointed editor of the *Messenger and Advocate*; Phelps was to assist in preparing the Doctrine and Covenants. The book was in press by June 1835.

At a special conference of the Church held in Kirtland on 17 August 1835, the book of revelations was presented to the Church membership for acceptance. This conference took the form of a solemn assembly in which the priesthood members sat by quorum and was presided over by Sidney Rigdon and Oliver Cowdery.[30] The business of ordaining members to the different quorums was conducted. During the second session of the conference, the business of accepting the revelations was conducted. Oliver Cowdery "arose with the Book of Doctrine and Covenants (284 pages) contain[in]g the faith articles and covenants of the Latter-Day Saints, then proceeded to take the vote of the whole House commencing with the President of Zion."[31] After presidents W. W. Phelps, John Whitmer, and John Smith had responded, the presidency of Zion declared that "they would receive the Book as the rule of their faith & practice and put themselves under the guidance of the same and also that they were satisfied with the committee that were chosen to compile it, as having discharged their duty faithfully."[32]

Next the high council voted in favor of the book. President Phelps read the testimony of the Twelve Apostles favoring the book. The members of the Quorum of the Twelve were away on missions. The presidents of the "70 Apostles" then indicated that the members present were unanimously in favor of the book and the committee work. The bishoprics of Kirtland and Zion next gave their approval of the Doctrine and Covenants. The quorums of elders, priests, teachers, and deacons each expressed their acceptance of the book and the committee's action. At that point, a vote of all members, male and female, was taken and "they gave a decided voice in favor of it & also of the committee. There being a very large portion of the Church present."[33] At that time, President Phelps read a "Chapter of Rules" for marriages among the Saints, which the Church voted to receive and attach to the book. President Cowdery then read an article on "laws in general & church governments" which was also accepted by the Church and attached to the book. At this point, the conference ended.[34]

The entire compilation was sent to Cleveland, Ohio, for binding.[35] Bound copies of the book were available from the second week of September and were distributed by the missionaries to some of the branches at a cost of one dollar per copy.

CONTENTS OF THE DOCTRINE AND COVENANTS

The contents of the Doctrine and Covenants differed from that of the Book of Commandments. Whereas the Book of Commandments contained only revelations, the Doctrine and Covenants contained a section on theology and a section of revelations. The section on theology was called Lectures on Faith, seven lectures given to the School of the Elders. The section of revelations in the Doctrine and Covenants differed also from the Book of Commandments. Some of the revelations in the Book of Commandments were combined into one section in the Doctrine and Covenants. For example, chapters 17 through 21 in the Book of Commandments were combined into what is now section 23 of the Doctrine and Covenants. Other revelations, many of which had been received since the compilation of the Book of Commandments, were included in the Doctrine and Covenants: the Book of Commandments contained 66 revelations; the Doctrine and Covenants, 102.[36]

Also in the new publication were minutes of the high council meeting of 24 September 1834 authorizing the completion of the book as well as the minutes of the meeting of 17 August 1835 accepting the book. The testimony of the Quorum of the Twelve Apostles was included. A preface written by the committee was placed at the beginning of the book.

REACTIONS TO THE BOOK

The publication of the Doctrine and Covenants affected the doctrinal understanding of members of the Church. A review of the history and the journals of that time shows that the Doctrine and Covenants became the standard by which the teachings and beliefs of the people were measured. In announcing the forthcoming publication of the Doctrine and Covenants, the editor of the *Messenger and Advocate* declared: "It may be well, for the information of the churches abroad, to say, that this book will contain the important revelations on doctrine and church government now extant, and will, we trust, give them a perfect understanding of the doctrine believed by this society. Such a work has long been called for, and if we are prospered a few weeks, shall have this volume ready for distribution."[37]

In a later issue of the newspaper was a strong statement of expectation for the Saints' use of the book: "We hope and pray that the Saints may be as anxious to keep the commandments, and be governed by the Doctrine and Covenants, contained in said book, as they have been for its publication: if they do observe all the requirements towards perfecting themselves in holiness, that they may serve the Lord acceptably with 'clean hands and pure hearts,' it will be well with them: but if they neglect to walk in all the ordinances of the Covenants and law of the Lord blameless, *they must be chastened*."[38]

The editors of the *Messenger and Advocate* viewed the Doctrine and Covenants as giving a pattern of life that had to be followed in order for salvation to be achieved, for "if the Protestants, can be saved, when they have the Bible only, do you not suppose that a Latter Day Saint can be saved with the Bible, Book of Mormon, and Book of Covenants. Yes verily, the only difficulties are in observing the precepts contained in them, and believing that they are what they purport to be. The Book of Covenants, shows what a man must do, to become a fit subject for baptism; and after he is baptized, it shows him how he is to receive the Holy Ghost, and what he is to do on the Sabbath day, to please his heavenly Father, &c. &c."[39]

John Whitmer felt that the Doctrine and Covenants took its place alongside the Bible and the Book of Mormon as standard scriptures of the Church. A year after its publication, Whitmer explained: "I would do injustice to my own feelings, if I did not here notice, still further the work of the Lord in these last days: the revelations and commandments given to us, are, in my estimation, equally true with the book of Mormon, and equally necessary for salvation, it is necessary to live by every word that proceedeth from the mouth of God; and I know that the Bible, book of Mormon and book of Doctrine and Covenants of the church of Christ of Latter Day Saints, contain the revealed will of heaven."[40]

The missionaries used the Doctrine and Covenants as a teaching tool to introduce the people to Joseph Smith and the role of a prophet. Orson Hyde reported to the readers of the *Messenger and Advocate*: "The servants of God are declaring boldly the counsel of the Most High, as contained in the book of Mormon, the Scriptures and the book of Covenants—Many are repenting and coming to baptism that they may obtain the remission of their sins through faith in the name of Christ."[41] The editors of the newspapers and speakers in meetings began to use the book as soon as it was published. Once accepted by the conference of the Church, the Doctrine and Covenants took its place alongside the Bible and the Book of Mormon as a standard work of the Church.

Further editions of the Doctrine and Covenants have been

published over the years. In 1844, under the direction of Joseph Smith, John Taylor published an edition with 111 sections and the Lectures on Faith. In 1876 a committee chaired by Orson Pratt, under the direction of President Brigham Young, published an edition containing 136 sections plus the Lectures on Faith. It was the first edition to be divided into chapters and verses. The additional twenty-five sections were gathered from the writings and history of Joseph Smith and were approved by the First Presidency to be added to the Doctrine and Covenants. Footnotes were added to this edition in 1879, and in the October 1880 general conference of the Church, the members voted unanimously to accept the revelations recorded in the Doctrine and Covenants as revelations from God.

The next major edition of the book was published in 1921. A committee chaired by Elder George F. Richards added introductions to each section, organized the text in double columns, revised the footnotes, and added an index. It was decided to remove the Lectures on Faith because they were not revelations but rather lectures given to the School of the Elders in Kirtland in 1835.

In 1981 another edition was approved by the general conference of the Church. It contained 138 sections and two Official Declarations. A new footnoting system was used, and new section headings, historical information, and index were incorporated.

The publishing of the Doctrine and Covenants was the result of dedication and faith. It was accomplished not in a climate of peace and tranquillity but rather in an atmosphere of challenge and disruption. The first attempt at publishing, so dramatically disrupted by mob violence, was followed by a determined effort that produced a marvelously simple, powerful book of revelations.

A present-day seeker for truth has testified, "The Doctrine and Covenants legislates for a new religious community, and the way its revelations apply to the details of people's lives seemed right to me. There has to be a connection between testimony, revelation, and ordinary practical life."[42] This connection between revelation and ordinary life was made possible by the publishing of the Doctrine and Covenants. Now ordinary people could have access to the revelations and study them while applying them to daily living. Their knowledge of God and their faith in him have been greatly enhanced by the accessibility of the revelations recorded in the Doctrine and Covenants.

NOTES

1. Pratt, "Explanation of Substituted Names," 228.
2. Kirtland Council Minute Book, 43–44; see Smith, *Teachings,* 70.
3. Benson, *Witness and a Warning,* 30.
4. Smith, *History of the Church,* 1:259.
5. The founding members of the Firm were Joseph Smith, Oliver Cowdery, Sidney Rigdon, John Whitmer, and Martin Harris. At the organization meeting of the Firm, W. W. Phelps was included and shortly thereafter, Jesse Gause was added. Cook, *Joseph Smith and the Law of Consecration,* 44.
6. Cannon and Cook, *Far West Record,* 32.
7. Cannon and Cook, *Far West Record,* 27.
8. Cannon and Cook, *Far West Record,* 29.
9. Cannon and Cook, *Far West Record,* 29.
10. Smith, *History of the Church,* 1:235–36.
11. Kirtland Revelation Book, 16.
12. Smith, *History of the Church,* 1:265.
13. Cannon and Cook, *Far West Record,* 46.
14. Cannon and Cook, *Far West Record,* 46.
15. Smith, *History of the Church,* 1:271.
16. Cannon and Cook, *Far West Record,* 50.
17. Joseph Smith Journal, 1 December 1832, 1, in Woodford, "Historical Development of the Doctrine and Covenants," 1:28.
18. Smith, *History of the Church,* 1:362.
19. *The Evening and the Morning Star,* May 1833, 89.
20. Smith, *History of the Church,* 1:369.
21. Smith, *History of the Church,* 1:373.
22. Smith, *History of the Church,* 1:390–92.
23. William W. Phelps to "Dear Brethren," 29 July 1833; see also Smith, *History of the Church,* 6:448.
24. Smith, *History of the Church,* 1:418.

25. Diary of Joseph Smith, 6 December 1833, as quoted in Cook, *Joseph Smith and the Law of Consecration*, 47–48.
26. See Howard, *Restoration Scriptures*, 201. Also Crawley, "A Bibliography," 474–77.
27. Letter in Joseph Smith Collection, Church Archives, as quoted in Cook, *Joseph Smith and the Law of Consecration*, 54.
28. Smith, *History of the Church*, 2:165.
29. *The Evening and the Morning Star*, September 1834, 192.
30. Kirtland Council Minute Book, 98; see Backman, *Ohio*.
31. Kirtland Council Minute Book, 103; see Backman, *Ohio*, 97–98.
32. Kirtland Council Minute Book, 104; see Backman, *Ohio*, 97–98.
33. Kirtland Council Minute Book, 106; see Backman, *Ohio*, 97–98.
34. Joseph Smith and the others of the First Presidency were visiting in Michigan at the time of this conference.
35. See Woodford, "Historical Development of the Doctrine and Covenants," 1:41.
36. See Crawley, "A Bibliography," 485.
37. *Messenger and Advocate*, 1 May 1835, 122.
38. *Messenger and Advocate*, August 1835, 170; italics in original.
39. *Messenger and Advocate*, 2 January 1836, 249.
40. *Messenger and Advocate*, March 1836, 287.
41. *Messenger and Advocate*, 2 April 1836, 296.
42. King, "A Man Who Speaks to Our Time," 16.

1

BACKGROUND

During the summer of 1830, within a few months of the organization of the Church on 6 April, the Prophet Joseph Smith and others began to compile the revelations of the Lord that had been received up to that time and also to edit these revelations in preparation for future publication. In the spring of 1831 the Saints moved to the area around Kirtland, Ohio (see D&C 37–38), and on 12 September the Prophet and his family moved from Kirtland to the home of John Johnson in Hiram, Ohio, for the purpose of working on Joseph's translation of the Bible.

During the year that the Smiths lived with the Johnsons, Hiram, Ohio (about thirty miles south of Kirtland), became virtually the headquarters of the Church.[1] By 1 November 1831 the revelations of the Lord to Joseph Smith were collected and ready for publication. On that date the Prophet called a special conference of elders in Hiram for the purpose of discussing the project and working out the details.

The need for publication was clearly great because the revelations were the word of God to the Church, and yet most members had no ready access to the actual texts. On the other hand, some of the elders present at the Hiram conference felt it unwise to publish these revelations for the entire world to see, because they had been directed to the Church or to specific individuals. These elders believed the revelations were therefore meant to be private or at least to be restricted in their circulation. After much discussion, the conference decided to publish the revelations received up to that time in a volume to be titled the Book of Commandments. It was further decided that ten thousand copies should be printed, but this number was reduced to three thousand in April 1832.[2]

Several of the elders attending the conference were assigned to write a preface for the soon-to-be-published revelations, but between the morning and afternoon sessions of the conference, the Prophet Joseph Smith received an additional revelation, which the Lord directed should serve as the preface to the Book of Commandments. This inspired preface, our present section 1, or the Lord's Preface, as it has since been called, was first printed in *The Evening and the Morning Star* in March 1833 and was subsequently placed at the beginning of the 1833 Book of Commandments as chapter 1.

Oliver Cowdery and John Whitmer were then directed at the Hiram conference to take a copy of the edited revelations with them to Independence, Missouri, where William W. Phelps, a member and printer by vocation, would do the actual printing. The press had been purchased by the Church in Cincinnati, Ohio, and shipped to Independence for this purpose. Actual publication of the Book of Commandments, containing sixty-five chapters, did not finally take place until July of 1833, but unfortunately on the 20th of that month, an anti-Mormon mob destroyed the printing press and most of the unbound copies of the book. Only a few copies survived. The fact that chapter 65 of the Book of Commandments was incomplete as printed in the surviving unbound copies suggests the possibility that more material may have been intended for publication as part of the book when the work was interrupted by the mob.

COMMENTARY

1. The islands of the sea. In the idiom of scripture, the islands or isles of the sea can mean any place to which one journeys by water (see Isaiah 20:6; 60:9; 2 Nephi 10:20–21), and so this phrase includes what we call continents as well as true islands. Thus both the Church specifically and the larger world generally, whether near or far, are commanded by the Lord in this verse to hear and to obey the voice of the Lord represented in the revelations. As Elder Ezra Taft Benson observed: "Our message is a world message. It is intended for all of our Father's children. When God the Father and his Son Jesus Christ saw fit to come here to earth and appear to a boy prophet, surely such a visitation was intended to bless all of our Father's children."[3]

2. Unto all men. Sooner or later, whether in this life or the next, all human beings must acknowledge the divinity of Christ and the truth of his word (see Philippians 2:10–11). The gospel will be taught to every person, and every person will be judged by its laws.

4. The voice of warning. The Lord will use the same method to spread his message in the last days as he did anciently—by the preaching and teaching of faithful servants. To these he will give his power and authority, the priesthood, and nothing will prevent them from eventually accomplishing their mission.

6. Mine authority . . . and my preface. The preface to the Doctrine and Covenants (D&C 1) "was not written by Joseph Smith, but was dictated by Jesus Christ, and contains his and his Father's word to the Church and to all the world. . . . This preface stamped the revelations with divine endorsement and therefore the revelations went forth with greater power than otherwise would have been the case."[4] The Lord is God, the great Jehovah, and he does not explain or excuse himself (see v. 38). His command itself is always sufficient authority to warrant obedience.

7. Fear and tremble. Though it is unpopular to say so, those human beings who will not accept the gospel and the mercy it offers ought to fear the consequences of their choice. They ought to be terrified at the thought of the coming of the Lord, for there will be an accounting then for all their sins, and if they will not accept his mercy offered now through the gospel covenant, then they must receive his strict justice when every wrong is punished and the wicked are destroyed (see vv. 9–10).

8. To seal. This expression means "to bind" or "to secure." The properly authorized servants of God have the power to seal the unbelieving and rebellious to judgment and punishment (compare D&C 88:84; 133:71–72). This negative "sealing" can be a literal action or it can be figurative, as when missionaries remove the excuse of ignorance from those who reject the gospel—and thus leave them exposed to the law of justice. It should be noted, however, that such a negative "sealing" does not override the law of agency, nor is such a sealing the cause in itself of condemnation. In one sense, the sealing is a token or indication that all that ought to be done for an individual, a village, or a people has been done, and they may now be fairly subjected to the Lord's judgments. Yet even among those who have been sealed up to judgment, any who will repent of their sins and come to Christ will still be forgiven.

8. The unbelieving. These are those who hear the Lord's message and have full opportunity to accept its truth, but who refuse to do so. Unbelief is thus a condition of choice. Those who have not yet heard the gospel do not qualify as "unbelieving" in the sense used here.

8. The rebellious. These are those who know the message is true but who will not live according to what they know, insisting rather upon their own way and their own lifestyle. Both the unbelieving and the rebellious ought to fear and tremble in view of what is coming to them and about which they have been duly warned.

10. Unto every man. The Doctrine and Covenants, like the other standard works of the Church, often uses the terms *man* or *mankind* generically to designate *all* human beings, both male and female. This was an accepted convention of nineteenth- and twentieth-century English usage.

10. According to his work. Justice demands parity. That is, God must render back to humans in judgment appropriately for what they have done to others while in the flesh. This standard is an inverse application of the Golden Rule (see Matthew 6:14–15; 7:12)—it is done unto us in the Judgment as we have done unto others in life.

13. His sword is bathed in heaven. The sword is a symbol of destruction. This imagery indicates that God's sword has been unsheathed and raised aloft at arm's length, exposed and ready to fall upon the inhabitants of the earth. Until now the Lord has allowed good and evil to exist together in the world, but at the last day—the day of his coming in glory—anything or anyone that cannot tolerate his glorious presence will be cut off and removed by the sword, which is about to fall.

13. The earth. The terms *earth* and *world* do not usually describe the same things in scripture. The earth is the physical planet we live upon; the world is Satan's kingdom, unredeemed human society, made in the image of our carnal selves and our lowest natures. Thus, while the physical *earth* will continue, the day of Christ's coming will be the *world's* last day, for the world and all its wickedness will abruptly end.[5]

15. Strayed. The word *stray* here, meaning "to digress" or "to wander," implies that apostasy has not always involved an abrupt departure from the truth, but can be and has been a gradual process as well. This verse refers to the collective apostasy of the world on many past occasions and extending right up to the present time. God has revealed truth to humanity over and over again, but always it has eventually been rejected or distorted.

15. Ordinances. An ordinance can be understood either as a decree or as a set procedure, ritual, or ceremony. Laws passed by municipalities are often referred to as city ordinances. Thus, in a broad sense, the term *ordinances* includes the rules and commandments as well as the rituals of the gospel.

15. Mine everlasting covenant. This covenant is entered into by accepting the fulness of the gospel of Jesus Christ, which has been revealed and lost in past dispensations and which has been restored in the latter days. The fulness of the gospel includes all the blessings, principles, and ordinances necessary to inherit the celestial kingdom of God, particularly faith in the Lord Jesus Christ, repentance, baptism by immersion for the remission of sins, and receiving the laying on of hands for the gift of the Holy Ghost.[6]

16. Idol. Idolatry is to love the creation more than the Creator (see Romans 1:25). When human beings define God according to their own ideas of what they think he should be like, they create a spiritual idol made up of their own preferences and desires, and they commit idolatry by then worshiping as God their own mental creation rather than the God of heaven who really exists and who reveals himself to human beings.

16. Babylon the great. The wicked world—Satan's system of things upon the earth (see D&C 133:14). Babylon is the world of "me first," of "money buys anything," or of hostility to the true Church and to righteousness. Babylon is the world of things as our carnal selves might wish them to be rather than of things "as they really are" (Jacob 4:13). In order to truly find God, we must be willing to give up our own demands and expectations of what God must be like. We must remove the limits we place on what God can and cannot say or do and change our thinking to accept God as he chooses to reveal himself to us. Everyone worships something—places ultimate value upon something. Some worship God. Others worship their own gods, whether they be wealth, fame, pleasure, professional advancement, intellectual attainment, or social success. These latter are all false gods of Babylon.[7]

Ancient Babylon was viewed by God and the people of Judah as the epitome of wickedness and godlessness and therefore the archenemy of Zion. Thus the prophets of old issued the frequent cry to come out of Babylon and to leave her practices and values behind. This admonition was renewed in the latter day. On 3 November 1831, at the close of the special conference in Hiram, Ohio—and two days after receiving Doctrine and Covenants 1—Joseph Smith received another revelation, now numbered in the Doctrine and Covenants as section 133. In this revelation the Lord commanded the Saints to "go ye out of Babylon" (D&C 133:7; see also v. 5) and "go ye out from among the nations, even from Babylon, from the midst of wickedness, which is spiritual Babylon" (D&C 133:14), thus adopting the imagery of the ancient prophets and applying it to the Church in the latter days.

17. The calamity. Consists of all the unpleasant events associated with Christ's second coming and the end of the world. The gospel has been restored in the latter days to protect those who will receive it from the coming calamity.

17. Commandments. All the revelations are commonly referred to as commandments, even though many of them are not commandments of the "thou shalt" or "thou shalt not" type.

19. Arm of flesh. Refers to human flesh or, in other words, to merely human resources and capacities.

23. The fulness of my gospel. In scripture this phrase always refers to those principles necessary for entrance into the celestial kingdom of God—faith in the Lord Jesus Christ, repentance, baptism by immersion for the remission of sins, and the laying on of hands for the gift of the Holy Ghost (see Articles of Faith 1:4). In the present Church, however, the phrase "the *fulness* of the gospel" is often used to mean "all that the Lord has ever revealed"—including the ordinances of the temple—although this usage differs from the usage of the term in LDS scripture. For example, the scriptures state over and over again that the fulness of the gospel is found in the Book of Mormon (see D&C 20:9; 27:5; 42:12; 135:3; JS–H 1:34), yet the temple ordinances are not found there. Also, the Doctrine and Covenants speaks repeatedly of the early Saints as already having the fulness of the gospel, even before the ordinances of the temple were revealed to them, beginning around 1842 (see D&C 35:12, 17; 39:11; 66:2; 118:4). In the same way, the gospel is defined as faith, repentance, baptism, and receiving the gift of the Holy Ghost (see D&C 33:10–12; 39:6; 3 Nephi 27:13–22).

Non-LDS Christians who have received a conviction that Jesus Christ is the Son of God and the Savior of the world through the witness of the Bible or through the preaching of their ministers, have, in so doing, also received a portion of the gospel of Jesus Christ. Many non-Christian peoples in the world have received a portion of the gospel through the Protestant and Catholic missionaries who first evangelized them. If these individuals have faith in Christ and have also repented of their sins as the Bible directs, they have received an even greater portion of the gospel. But to receive the *fulness* of the gospel is to accept baptism by immersion for the remission of sins through the power of the priesthood and also to be given the gift of the Holy Ghost by the laying on of hands by those in authority to do so, as taught in the Bible and even more clearly in the Book of Mormon.

With the translation of the Book of Mormon, the restoration of the priesthood, and the organization of the Church in 1830, the fulness of the gospel—all those things necessary for salvation in the celestial kingdom of God—had been restored to the earth. Since that time the Lord has also revealed further blessings, such as an understanding of exaltation and its associated principles and ordinances, to those who had already received the fulness of the gospel.[8] There will continue to be opportunities for progress for those who prove faithful to the knowledge they have previously received.

24. I am God. In this, as in all the revelations found in the Doctrine and Covenants, the divine speaker is Jesus Christ.

24. Given unto my servants in their weakness. We need not assume that either Joseph Smith or the prophets before or after him have been perfect individuals, for God called and worked through them all "in their weakness." It reflects the great love of God for us that he works with us in our imperfections in order to make us more like him. But this also means that the revelations given to his servants in their present form are not always perfect in some absolute, unchanging and eternal sense. Rather, they are adapted by God to our human weaknesses and limitations, including our imperfect language and culture, and they are adapted to a specific historical context. The "inspired" quality of revelation does not guarantee perfect spelling, punctuation, or syntax in a text, or perfect vocabulary or skills of expression or composition in a revelator, or perfect interpretation and application skills by later readers.

29. The record of the Nephites. The gold plates delivered to Joseph Smith by Moroni and eventually published in part as the Book of Mormon were part of the record of the Nephites. The book of Ether, a record of the Jaredites, was included in the plates and was also published in the Book of Mormon.

30. The only true and living church. The gospel is not just the particular religious system used by Latter-day Saints to enter God's kingdom—it is the only way *anyone* enters God's kingdom. Although there is truth in other churches and many adherents of those churches are good people, only one church possesses "the fulness of the gospel" and its priesthood keys, and that is The Church of Jesus Christ of Latter-day Saints. Worthy people of other faiths will have to experience a conversion at some point, whether in this life or the next, to the doctrines and principles of Christ as taught by the LDS prophets before they can enter into the celestial kingdom. There is no other way.

Just as a living plant is connected to its roots, so the Church is a "living" church because it is connected to God, the source of life and light, by continuing revelation and by the direct bestowal of priesthood authority. Latter-day Saints have direct and living links with the divine in the chain of priesthood authority from Jesus Christ to Peter to Joseph Smith, and eventually to each priesthood holder, and in the direct revelation granted to themselves and to their leaders. When the communication of direct revelation is cut off, the church dies, just as a girdled tree dies when cut off from its roots. A Christmas tree, for example, may appear to be alive, but it is dead or dying if it is no longer in touch with its roots. In the same way, a church may appear healthy but is dead or dying if contact with the divine, through priesthood authority and continuing direct revelation, does not exist. A living church is one still connected to God, its source, through living apostles and prophets who both hold the keys of priesthood power and receive direct divine guidance.

31. Least degree of allowance. No unrepented sin will be allowed in the celestial kingdom. Sins can be repented of and will be forgiven (see v. 32); however, if we refuse to repent, God cannot allow us entrance. There will be no exceptions. This is not a requirement of perfect performance, as some erroneously believe, but a requirement of complete repentance.

33. From him shall be taken. No one can put the Lord on hold, neither can anyone declare a spiritual "time-out." This verse implies that we deceive ourselves if we think we can reach a comfortable degree of spirituality in our lives and then just relax and maintain that same level indefinitely without attempting to grow any further. Spiritually, when we stop growing, we begin shrinking. To sin willfully and refuse to repent accelerates the loss of our light.

33. Strive. To strive is to "wrestle" or "struggle." The Spirit strives with all of us, both members and nonmembers, at some level of intensity. He wrestles against our carnal selves to tug and pull and prod us in the right direction. There is, however, a degree of rejection of this influence, of this striving with us, that will cause the Spirit to cease its work of coaxing us toward the light and to leave us completely to ourselves (see 2 Nephi 26:11). "God's spirit continues with the honest in heart to strengthen, to help, and to save, but invariably the Spirit of God ceases to strive with the man who 'excuses' himself in his wrong doing."[9]

34. All flesh. The word *flesh* is usually used in scripture to refer to human beings specifically (compare v. 19),[10] although it occasionally refers to the flesh of animals. Here it is used, as usual, to mean all human beings.

35. Respecter of persons. Someone who values one person above another, one who recognizes "special" friends and gives them special treatment not available to others, is a "respecter" of persons. The requirements for salvation are the same for all persons, and the blessings God gives to one, he would give to all on the same terms. With God there are no special persons or special arrangements. It is true that the obedient get closer to God than the wicked and enjoy a better relationship with him, but those who are now wicked might have the same relationship on the same terms if only they would repent (see 1 Nephi 17:35, Alma 13:4).

35. Peace shall be taken. As we move closer to the end of the world, social conditions will deteriorate dramatically. People will not be able to get along with each other, and neither will nations. Thus, there will be wars among nations and violence and civil chaos within society. Ultimately there will be a complete polarization between the realm of Satan (Babylon) and the realm of Christ (Zion). It is pointless to speculate on when these events shall take place. The only chronological certainty is that the end-time is closer now than it was in 1831 (see D&C 45).

36. According to Presidents Harold B. Lee and Ezra Taft Benson, the Lord "shall have power over his saints, and shall reign in their midst" through his appointed servants in his true Church.[11]

36. Idumea. This is the New Testament term for the Old Testament nation of Edom, an implacable enemy of Israel and Judah (see Psalm 137:7). In Jesus' day Idumea had produced King Herod, the evil usurper who tried to murder the infant Jesus and succeeded in killing the babies in Bethlehem. The term *Idumea,* like the term *Babylon,* is used in scripture as a symbol for Satan's realm, the unredeemed world of carnal humanity.

38. It is the same. When apostles and prophets speak as authorized in the name of the Lord, it is as though God himself has spoken. The commandments, promises, and blessings of God are just as valid and binding upon us when voiced by his authorized servants as when voiced by God himself.

NOTES

1. See Brown, Cannon, and Jackson, eds., *Historical Atlas,* 20.
2. See Cannon and Cook, eds., *Far West Record,* 27.
3. In Conference Report, Apr. 1961, 114.
4. Smith, *Church History and Modern Revelation,* 1:252.
5. See the commentary on D&C 19:3.
6. See the commentary on D&C 1:23; 66:2.
7. See Kimball, "False Gods We Worship," 3–6.
8. See the commentary on D&C 14:10; 20:9; 22:1; 42:12; 66:2.
9. Kimball, *Integrity,* 2.
10. Compare the commentary on D&C 77:12 with Moses 3:7.
11. See "Way to Eternal Life," 12; "'Strengthen Thy Stakes,'" 4.

DOCTRINE AND COVENANTS

2

BACKGROUND

In the spring of 1820, young Joseph Smith, then but fourteen years of age, had received the divine manifestation now known to the Church as the First Vision. On that occasion Joseph had gone to a wooded area near his home in Manchester, New York, to pray for divine guidance in knowing which church to join. In answer to Joseph's prayer, the Father and his Son appeared to him and instructed him not to join any church, for the true church of Jesus Christ was not then upon the earth but was shortly to be restored (see JS–H 1:18–20).[1]

For three and a half years after this first vision, Joseph, according to his own account, "continued to pursue . . . common vocations in life until the twenty-first of September" in 1823 (JS–H 1:27). Then a young man of seventeen, Joseph was living with his family on their farm in Manchester. On that night after he had retired, Joseph "betook [himself] to prayer and supplication to Almighty God" (JS–H 1:29), desiring to be forgiven of his youthful sins and indiscretions and also to receive some further assurance of divine concern. As he thus called upon God, an angel appeared who identified himself as Moroni and who told Joseph that the Lord had a great work for him to do. Moroni then informed the young prophet of certain gold plates, records of an ancient American people, which also [contained] the fulness of the gospel. These plates were buried in a hill not far from the Smith home, together with the Urim and Thummim, by which the plates could be translated.

Moroni further instructed Joseph by quoting to him certain passages of biblical scripture, among them Malachi 4:5–6, though some of these passages were quoted differently from what is found in the King James Version. In all, Moroni appeared to Joseph three different times on the night of 21 September and once again the next day. He repeated exactly the same message, adding details each time. Our Doctrine and Covenants 2 consists of Malachi 4:5–6 as Moroni quoted it to Joseph Smith on these occasions.

The prophet Malachi had been the last of the Old Testament prophets, writing around 430 B.C. to a nation that was already declining into apostasy (see Malachi 1–2). He reproved his people for their sins, and then in closing his prophecy and, as it turned out, the entire Old Testament, he foretold the comings of John the Baptist (see Malachi 3:1) and of the prophet Elijah (see Malachi 4:5–6) to prepare the way for the Savior. These prophecies have been fulfilled relative to both the mortal ministry (see Matthew 11:10–11; Luke 9:30–31) and the second coming of Christ (see D&C 13:1; 110:13–16). It is the mission of both Elijah and John to prepare the way for the coming of the Savior—both his first and his second comings. John, who held the keys of the Aaronic Priesthood, had a role in preparing for the mortal ministry of Christ. Elijah, who held the keys of the sealing power of the Melchizedek Priesthood, has had a role in preparing for the Second Coming. Because Joseph Smith was to be instrumental in the latter-day work of Elijah, it was fitting that Moroni should quote this passage to the young prophet as an example of those things that were about to be fulfilled.

It should perhaps be noted that Moroni's version of Malachi 4:5–6 (in D&C 2) is also found in Joseph Smith—History 1:38–39 in the Pearl of Great Price, where Joseph describes Moroni's visit. Doctrine and Covenants 110:14–15; 128:17–18; 3 Nephi 25:5–6; Joseph Smith Translation Malachi 4:5–6, however, all agree with the wording of the King James Version (KJV) rather than with section 2 or with Joseph Smith–History 1:38–39. This clearly indicates that we are dealing here not with "correct" and "incorrect" versions of the biblical passage but rather with different shades or levels of meaning reflected in the different versions. Thus, a different reading in the KJV than is found in the Book of Mormon or in the Joseph Smith Translation does *not* always indicate that one or the other is "incorrect."

Doctrine and Covenants 2 was first published in the 15 April 1842 *Times and Seasons,* and although it is chronologically the oldest of the revelations in the Doctrine and Covenants, it was not added to that book of scripture until 1876 by Orson Pratt under the direction of President Brigham Young.

COMMENTARY

1. Reveal unto you. This change in the King James Version wording pointed out to Joseph Smith his future role in the latter-day work of Elijah.

1. Priesthood. Priesthood is the authority to act as God's agent in conducting God's business. Such agents cannot be self-appointed, no matter how sincerely they may desire to manage God's affairs. In this verse, "priesthood" (referring to the *fulness* of the priesthood) includes the keys of the sealing power, which Joseph would receive in the Kirtland Temple twelve years later on 3 April 1836 (see D&C 110:13–16). Joseph, however, actually received the Aaronic and Melchizedek Priesthoods, though not all the keys pertaining to them, at the hands of other messengers *before* the 1836 appearance of Elijah (see D&C 13:1; 27:12–13).

1. By the hand of Elijah. Presumably, by the literal laying on of Elijah's hands. Elijah the Tishbite was the last prophet of the Old Testament to hold all the keys of the sealing power of the Melchizedek Priesthood (c. 900 B.C.; see 1 Kings 17–2 Kings 2) and the one designated to restore those keys to later dispensations.[2] This is the same Elijah who appeared to Peter, James, and

John on the Mount of Transfiguration to give them keys and who later appeared to Joseph Smith and Oliver Cowdery in the Kirtland Temple for the same purpose (see D&C 110:13–16). The pattern in ordaining and giving keys today is done by the laying on of hands, which pattern was established by Joseph Smith through the administration of angels.

1. The great and dreadful day of the Lord. This day is the day of the Lord's coming in glory. It is often called the "last" day and will be "great" or "dreadful" depending on who we are—the righteous or the wicked. For the righteous it will be great. They shall be delivered from all their enemies, be united with Christ, and live on a millennial earth that will have been raised to a paradisiacal glory (see Articles of Faith 1:10). On the other hand, that day will be dreadful for the wicked, for they shall be consumed by fire and delivered into the power of Satan in that spirit prison where their debts will be paid to the uttermost farthing.

2. The fathers. Refers specifically to the patriarchs, the first fathers of the house of Israel: Abraham, Isaac, and Jacob (see D&C 27:10).

2. The promises made to the fathers. These are the collective promises of the Abrahamic covenant, the new and everlasting covenant of the gospel, that God made anciently to the patriarchs of the house of Israel: Abraham, Isaac, and Jacob. Abraham 2:8–10 specifies these promises to include the gospel, the priesthood, and eternal life.

2. The children. These are the posterity of Abraham, Isaac, and Jacob, either by lineage or by adoption, who, through the restoration of the new and everlasting covenant, receive from God the same promises that the patriarchs did. This then turns their hearts, their concern, to *their* fathers—their own immediate ancestors—in the hope of sharing these great blessings with them through vicarious work for the dead and the sealing power of the priesthood.[3]

3. Wasted. In other words, "made waste" or "destroyed." This version from the angel Moroni to Joseph Smith specifies that the "curse" mentioned in the King James Version is the wasting or destruction of the earth. Elijah assists in preparing the world for the second coming of Christ, for without the preparations now being made in sealing both the living and the dead in the fulness of the gospel covenant, the Second Coming would be "dreadful" for the entire human family rather than just for the wicked.

NOTES

1. See also Backman, *Joseph Smith's First Vision,* 169.
2. See also Smith, *Teachings,* 172.
3. See Smith, *Doctrines of Salvation,* 2:102–28, for a description of Elijah's latter-day effect on the hearts of the children.

3

BACKGROUND

On 22 September 1827, twenty-one-year-old Joseph Smith received the gold plates and the Urim and Thummim from the angel Moroni and soon thereafter began the process of translating the Book of Mormon. Unfortunately, increased persecution at his home in Manchester, New York, made it necessary for Joseph and his wife, Emma, to move from that town before the end of 1827 to Harmony, Pennsylvania, where Joseph had worked the year before and where Emma's family lived. Joseph was followed to Harmony in the spring of 1828 by his friend Martin Harris, a prosperous farmer from Palmyra, New York, who had already gained some conviction of the Prophet's divine calling. Sometime between December 1827 and February 1828, Martin Harris had received a vision affirming the divinity of Joseph's calling.[1] In February 1828, Harris had taken a transcript of some characters from the Book of Mormon plates together with their translation to New York to be evaluated by Professor Charles Anthon of Columbia College. According to Harris, Anthon had declared the translation to be correct, and shortly thereafter Harris went to Harmony to assist the Prophet Joseph.

Martin Harris assisted the Prophet Joseph as Joseph translated the Book of Mormon between 12 April and 14 June 1828. Martin's wife, Lucy, was not happy with Martin's involvement in the project and began to pressure him for evidence that his new pursuits were truly of God. Consequently, Martin asked the Prophet if he might borrow the 116 pages of the Book of Mormon translation that had been completed up to that point—the only copy there was—in order to show them to his wife and family, and thus satisfy them of the validity of the work.

When Joseph inquired of the Lord, he was told through the Urim and Thummim that it was not wise for Martin to take the manuscript. A second request received the same response. At Martin's strong insistence, Joseph inquired yet again, and this third time "permission was granted him to have the writings on certain conditions; which were, that he show them only to his brother, Preserved Harris, his own wife, his father and his mother, and a Mrs. Cobb, a sister to his wife. In accordance with this last answer, I required of him that he should bind himself in a covenant to me in a most solemn manner that he would not do otherwise than had been directed."[2] Still, because he had wearied the Lord with his pleading and had not accepted the Lord's first answer, the plates and the Urim and Thummim were taken away from Joseph for a while at this time.[3]

Martin did not keep his covenant concerning the manuscript pages: "He did show them to others, and by stratagem they got them away from him, and they never have been recovered unto this day."[4] The loss of 116 pages of the Book of Mormon manuscript, the product of two months' work, caused great anguish for the young prophet. When Joseph learned of what had happened while visiting his parents in Manchester, he cried out:

"'Oh, my God! . . . All is lost! all is lost! What shall I do? I have sinned—it is I who tempted the wrath of God. I should have been satisfied with the first answer which I received from the Lord; for he told me that it was not safe to let the writing go out of my possession.' . . .

" . . . 'And how shall I appear before the Lord? Of what rebuke am I not worthy from the angel of the Most High?'"[5]

Greatly adding to Joseph's grief at this time was the death of his first child, an infant son who died on 15 June, and the near death of Emma from complications of the birth.[6]

When Joseph returned to Harmony, the angel Moroni appeared to him and briefly returned the Urim and Thummim, allowing Joseph to receive section 3. This was in July of 1828. Then the Urim and Thummim were taken from him again, together with the gold plates, for a period of about two months. According to Mother Smith, they were returned to him on 22 September 1828.[7]

The reader should be aware that after section 3 the next revelation received by Joseph Smith was section 10. Reading the revelations in the order in which they were received—Doctrine and Covenants 3, 10, and then 4—gives the reader an understanding of the historical events surrounding the receiving of these revelations.[8]

COMMENTARY

1. The purposes of God. After the loss of the 116 pages, Joseph needed instruction from the Lord. Among other things, Doctrine and Covenants 3 is the Lord's evaluation of Joseph's situation and the situation of the Lord's ongoing work.

2. Crooked paths. God is righteous and unvarying. He does not wobble and dodge one way and then another, trying to avoid unforeseen obstacles or problems. Rather, his course is the one fixed constant in eternity, and he has already anticipated all the angles. God is never taken by surprise, and he never has to adjust his plans to meet new circumstances. He knows everything all at once.

2. One eternal round. This phrase is found twice in the Doctrine and Covenants (see also D&C 35:1) and three times in the Book of Mormon (see 1 Nephi 10:19; Alma 7:20; 37:12). God's course is absolutely straight, but oddly enough it ends where it began. It is, therefore, a circle, or a round. For example, Christ is the Alpha and Omega, both the beginning *and* the end of God's plan. But if the end is the same as the beginning, then the course is, in one sense at least, circular. Christ is the Creator in the beginning—our source. Through the Atonement we become what he is—our goal. When the source is the same as the goal, then we have a cycle, or a round, and this cycle starts in Christ and ends in Christ.

Similarly, humanity starts in a celestial world, descends through a terrestrial Eden to a fallen, telestial earth, there to be redeemed and restored—first to a paradisiacal or terrestrial glory during the Millennium and thence back to a celestial glory once again. Thus, God's is an undeviating course that brings us back around to where we started though *we* may be different when we finish the course than we were when we started. The cycle begins and ends with the same eternal constants.

In another sense, God's course is an eternal round since, from a human perspective, he and his works are without beginning or end, like a ring or a circle.

3. Remember, remember. Note the repetition for emphasis.

5. You have been entrusted. Though it was Martin Harris who lost the manuscript, it was ultimately Joseph's responsibility to protect it, and thus it was ultimately Joseph's fault when it was lost.

5. These things. The plates, the Urim and Thummim, and the manuscript.

6. How oft you have transgressed. Joseph was human, and he made mistakes and committed human transgressions. We must remember that on the absolute scale of God's perfect righteousness, all of us are guilty of these same charges; so this is not to be taken as evidence for any particular wickedness on Joseph's part. As Joseph himself stated in Joseph Smith–History 1:28, "No one need suppose me guilty of any great or malignant sins. A disposition to commit such was never in my nature."

7–8. Although men set at naught . . . yet you should have been faithful. Joseph, with his experiences and his knowledge, is held to a higher standard than other men. "For of him unto whom much is given much is required" (D&C 82:3). Perhaps the source of Joseph's fear was that he believed Martin Harris was indispensable not only as a scribe but also in providing the financial means for publishing the finished book to the world. Also, Martin was older and was well respected in the community, while Joseph was relatively young and inexperienced. It was natural that Joseph might fear losing the support of such an important man as Martin Harris, and that fear may have led him to make a wrong decision in the affair of the 116 pages.

8. Fiery darts. This phrase is figurative. A dart is any kind of missile used as a weapon: an arrow, a javelin, and such. *Fiery* means burning and could indicate a poison that has penetrated a person's soul.

8. The adversary. "Adversary" is one meaning of the word *devil* (*diabolos*) in Greek (see D&C 76:26–28).[9] Had Joseph more fully exercised his faith, the Lord would have protected him against anything Satan could have thrown against him.

9. Joseph. There is a connection between the Prophet's name and his divine calling.[10] The Prophet was foreordained, and both his name and his calling were foretold (see 2 Nephi 3:6, 15).

9. Wast chosen. Joseph was chosen not just in his mortal lifetime but in the premortal council in heaven as well (see D&C 138:53–56).

11. Gift. Specifically, the gift of translation (compare D&C 5:4), but because Joseph would "become as other men" if he lost this gift, perhaps the term should also be understood to include his divine calling.

12. Wicked man. This is Martin Harris, who had broken his strict covenant with the Lord and lost the sacred manuscript. Martin was not merely deceived or cajoled; he broke his sacred oath. He preferred his own judgment to God's, and he boasted in his own wisdom (see v. 13).

14. Privileges. These included possession of the plates and the Urim and Thummim and the right and power to translate the sacred scriptures.

15. Thy director. This term likely refers to the Lord and perhaps also to Moroni, the angel who appeared to Joseph at least twenty-two times in his career and instructed him along the way. Hyrum M. Smith and Janne M. Sjodahl suggest that "thy director" is the Urim and Thummim,[11] but elsewhere in scripture (see D&C 17:1; Mosiah 1:16; Alma 37:38, 45) and in early LDS usage, "director" or "directors" always referred to the Liahona rather than the Urim and Thummim. Because there is no evidence that Joseph had possession of the Liahona "from the beginning" of his work, this reference is more likely to the One who ultimately directed Joseph, who is Jesus Christ, or to Moroni, the Lord's messenger.[12]

16. Testimony of the Jews. The Bible.

17–20. In the Book of Mormon the term *Nephites* eventually includes, besides the descendants of Nephi, also the descendants of Sam, Jacob, Joseph, Zoram, and Mulek, while the term *Lamanites* includes the descendants of Laman, Lemuel and Ishmael. Note the difference in accountability between the Lamanites whose condition was largely due to "the iniquity of their fathers," and the Nephites, whose destruction was due to "their [own] iniquities and their abominations" (v. 18).

Later on in the Book of Mormon, in the Zion society described in 4 Nephi, all these various lineages merged into one people (see 4 Nephi 1:17), and when the people later separated into parties they did so along religious and political lines rather than genealogical lines (see 4 Nephi 1:20, 37–38). Therefore, modern "Lamanites" are just as likely to be descended from Nephi, Jacob, and Sam as they are from Laman and Lemuel. As used in Doctrine and Covenants 3:20, the term *Lamanites* includes all the children of Lehi (see D&C 10:48). "No descendants of Lehi need ever be ashamed nor embarrassed to call themselves 'Lamanites.' . . . We look upon the name as proper and dignified and fully acceptable. The Lord consistently called His people 'the Lamanites.'"[13]

19–20. Promises. One specific purpose of the Book of Mormon is to bring the descendants of Lehi to a knowledge of their fathers and of the religion of their fathers, in fulfillment of God's promises to their fathers.

20. Rely upon the merits of Jesus Christ. This phrase is a reference to "justification through the grace of our Lord and Savior Jesus Christ," which is stated so well in modern revelation. Through the Book of Mormon the descendants of Lehi can come to believe the gospel and learn to rely upon Christ for their justification and thus be saved in the kingdom of God (see D&C 20:30; 2 Nephi 2:8; 31:19; Alma 22:14; 24:10; Helaman 14:13; Moroni 6:4; JST Romans 3:25).

NOTES

1. See Jessee, *Papers of Joseph Smith,* 1:9.
2. Smith, *History of the Church,* 1:21.
3. See Jessee, *Papers of Joseph Smith,* 1:10.
4. Smith, *History of the Church,* 1:21.
5. Smith, *History of Joseph Smith,* 128–29.
6. See Perkins, "'Thou Art Still Chosen,'" 15–19.
7. See Smith, *History of Joseph Smith,* 135.
8. See D&C Chronological Order of Contents.
9. See also the commentary on D&C 76:26, 28.
10. See the commentary on D&C 18:7–8.
11. *Doctrine and Covenants Commentary,* 20.
12. See Peterson, "Moroni," 53–55, 63–65.
13. Kimball, *Lamanites,* 3.

4

BACKGROUND

The Urim and Thummim and the gold plates had been taken away from Joseph Smith in July of 1828. According to Lucy Mack Smith's account, the sacred items were returned to Joseph two months later, on 22 September, exactly one year from the time they had originally been entrusted to his care.[1] But Joseph did not proceed again with the translation at that time. After the loss of the 116 pages, he was not permitted to rely on Martin Harris, and he had no other scribe but Emma, who had almost died in childbirth that summer.

On 25 August Joseph had purchased thirteen acres of land from his father-in-law, Isaac Hale, and began to farm it, since he needed to support his family and did not know at that time how long the Lord might withhold his prophetic privileges. When the plates were returned, Joseph, having no regular scribe and no other means of support, continued to work his little farm. By then his wife's family had rejected him and Emma, and there was not much support available to them. Joseph Knight Sr. described the Smith family's situation during the winter of 1828–29: "Now, he could not translate but little, being poor and [having] nobody to write for him but his wife, and she could not do much and take care of her house, and he being poor and [having] no means to live but work. . . . I let him have some little provisions and . . . a pair of shoes and three dollars in money to help him a little."[2]

In February of 1829, some of Joseph's family, including his father Joseph Smith Sr. traveled from Manchester to Harmony to visit with Joseph and Emma. During this visit, the Prophet received Doctrine and Covenants 4 on behalf of his father.[3]

Many passages of scripture, such as Ruth's entreaty of Naomi (see Ruth 1:16–17) or Psalm 23, so precisely fit their occasion and so aptly express the moment that they become classic formulations for all those who later find themselves in similar circumstances. Such an expression is section 4. This revelation for Joseph Smith Sr. so simply and movingly calls him to the Lord's work and so carefully states the virtues necessary for those who would perform His work successfully that it has become the classic and archetypical call to service in this dispensation.

Although this section is often used in the context of missionary work, it was given through Joseph to his father, who was not being called on a mission. It can therefore be applied to anyone who serves in the kingdom of God and not just to full-time missionaries.

COMMENTARY

1. A marvelous work. This phrase refers to the revelation of the fulness of the gospel, the restoration of the priesthood, the organization of the true Church, the gathering of Israel, and the establishment of Zion and the millennial kingdom. This revelation was a prophecy at the time it was given, and today we are seeing much of it fulfilled. The Church continues to grow in a marvelous way throughout the world as the gospel goes forth to cover the earth.

2. See that you serve him. In this verse, the Lord indicates his expectations for us who serve in his kingdom. We are to serve him with *all* our heart, might, mind, and strength.

Each of these words denotes an important part of our being.

The heart indicates the emotions and feelings we have. Might represents abilities and gifts given to us. Mind represents our mental capacities. Strength deals with physical and spiritual abilities. In other words, if we are to serve God, we are to serve him with *all* of our capacities (D&C 64:34). Only then can we give an accounting to our Father in Heaven that would allow us to stand blameless before him.

3. If ye have desires . . . ye are called. "Called" is used here in its less technical sense—in fact, the Church hadn't even been organized yet. We do not need to wait for a vision or other authorization to engage in God's work. Although some service in the kingdom requires special callings, keys, or ordinations, much Christian service simply needs a willing heart and nothing more. Every member who desires to serve the Lord can be a missionary. Every member who feels Christ's love can share it with those who need it. All those who feel a desire to be witnesses for Christ, whether in word or deed, are invited or "called" and encouraged to do so.

4. The field is white. Wheat is green as it grows but loses its color as it matures. The paler the stalks, the closer they are to harvesting.

4. Already. The word *already* here means "now." The world is now ready to have the gospel preached to it, and people are prepared to receive it. The harvest is now ready.

5. Charity and love. The *and* here indicates that charity is not used merely as a synonym for love as in the King James Version. The 1828 edition of Webster's dictionary defines *charity* specifically as a "brotherly predisposition," whereas the New Testament generally uses *charity* to mean "love" in a more general sense (see 1 Corinthians 13:1–13; Moroni 7:47).

5. Faith, hope, and charity. Note the order of faith, then hope, and then charity. It indicates that we must first have faith in Jesus Christ and his atonement. Then we will develop a hope or an assurance that the Atonement applies to us personally and that we can receive the blessings of exaltation. Hope then leads to the marvelous gift of charity, the pure love of Christ that the Savior offers to each of us. His pure love expressed through the Atonement can be enjoyed by each individual. With this gift, we can develop to the point where our eye is single to God's glory. Our focus then will be to serve the children of our Father in Heaven. With this gift, we can be qualified for the work.

5. An eye single to. When our eyes are focused upon a single point, we see clearly, but when we try to focus on more than one object at one time, our vision is distorted. Jesus Christ taught this idea when he warned that "no man can serve two masters" (Matthew 6:24; 3 Nephi 13:24).

6. Remember faith. See 2 Peter 1:5–8; Doctrine and Covenants 107:30–31.

NOTES

1. Smith, *History of Joseph Smith,* 134–35.
2. In Jessee, "Joseph Knight's Recollection," 35; spelling, punctuation, and capitalization standardized.
3. See Jessee, "Joseph Knight's Recollection," 29–39.

DOCTRINE AND COVENANTS

5

BACKGROUND

By winter's end of 1829, it had been eight months since Martin Harris had lost the 116 pages of translation. Martin knew full well the magnitude of his error and that he had lost his privilege to serve as scribe, but apparently he also still felt an obligation to the work and to assist financially with the printing of the Book of Mormon. Therefore, in March 1829, a somewhat humbled Martin Harris traveled to Harmony from his home in Palmyra to determine whether Joseph Smith still had the plates and the power to translate them (see v. 1). To settle the question to his satisfaction, he wanted to see the plates, and in response to his request Joseph Smith received Doctrine and Covenants 5.

Verses 18–19 read differently in the present Doctrine and Covenants from the way they read in the 1833 Book of Commandments. The changes were made by the Prophet Joseph himself in the 1835 edition, perhaps because of the inflammatory effect the original words had on the enemies of the Church. The 1833 wording, though not now officially the scripture of the Church, is provided in the endnotes.[1]

COMMENTARY

1. Has desired a witness. Martin seemed always to be looking for proof. On this occasion he wanted to know for sure if

Joseph still had the plates. Though Martin had already had a remarkable witness of the divinity of the work, he did not yet have sufficient faith that it is true. It was Martin who had taken the Nephite characters to Professor Charles Anthon in New York,[2] though history shows Anthon probably couldn't have read them anyway. In 1821–22 Jean-Francois Champollion had begun a series of studies on the Rosetta Stone, which culminated many years later in his Egyptian grammar and dictionary.[3] By 1829 a few of Champollion's studies from the Rosetta Stone had been published in Europe, but no Egyptian dictionary or grammar was yet available anywhere in the world. Surely Professor Anthon could not have read a *reformed* Egyptian text with any degree of confidence in 1829, nor could he credibly have pronounced someone else's translation either correct or incorrect.

1. That you . . . have got the plates. Martin wanted to actually see the plates and the Urim and Thummim, since in his mind this would be the surest way to satisfy himself that Joseph still had them. But Joseph did not have control over these sacred items; rather, the Lord did, and the Lord forbade Joseph to show them to Martin or anyone else except at the Lord's specific command. Not even Joseph's immediate family was allowed to view the plates.

2. You should stand as a witness. Joseph's calling was not to display the sacred objects to others, but only to testify of them. Only God could authorize them to be shown, and after the episode of the lost 116 pages, Joseph was not about to disobey the Lord on this point. Still, we probably don't fully appreciate the emotional burden put on Joseph by his not being allowed to show the plates to others, not even to his wife and family.[4]

4. Gift. Joseph did not yet hold the priesthood, but he had been given the gift of translation to which other spiritual gifts would be added in time.

10. This generation. In one sense this designates Joseph's own generation (1805–44), for future generations of Saints will receive additional revelation through their own prophets. But in a larger sense, "Joseph's generation" is the whole present dispensation of the gospel, which enjoys the fulness of the gospel only through the work of the Prophet Joseph Smith.

11. Testimony of three. This refers to the Three Witnesses to the Book of Mormon—Oliver Cowdery, David Whitmer, and Martin Harris. In accordance with the ancient law of witnesses (see Deuteronomy 19:15; 2 Corinthians 13:1), the Lord would call these Three Witnesses besides Joseph to testify to the divine origin of the Book of Mormon. These witnesses would know as surely as Joseph did that the book is the word of God, and their testimony would be sent forth with the Book of Mormon when it goes to all the world.[5]

12. Know of a surety. These three will not merely have faith, they will *know* because they will "behold and view" (v. 13) the sacred objects, will see and converse with the angel Moroni, and will hear the voice of God bear witness from heaven.

14. None else. Even though the Eight Witnesses would be shown the gold plates by Joseph, they would not have the same glorious manifestation shared by the Three Witnesses. For example, they would not see the angel nor hear the voice of God.

14. The coming forth of my church out of the wilderness. See the commentary on Doctrine and Covenants 33:5.

14. Clear as the moon. This is a citation from Song of Solomon 6:10 (see also D&C 105:31; 109:73).

16. Manifestation of my Spirit. A spiritual witness of the Spirit may be received by all human beings in answer to their honest prayers. Still, this does not mean they have received the gift of the Holy Ghost, which comes only by the laying on of hands as one enters the gospel covenant (see Acts 8:17–19).

16. Born of me. That is, born of Christ. When we are born again in the gospel covenant, we are born spiritually as the sons and daughters of the Christ who gives us life through his suffering and his atonement (see Mosiah 5:7; 27:25; Ether 3:14; Moroni 7:19).

16. Of water and of the Spirit. This passage refers to the ordinances of baptism and receiving the gift of the Holy Ghost by the laying on of hands. It also refers to spiritual rebirth.

17. Ordained. Joseph did not yet hold the priesthood necessary to perform the ordinances alluded to in verse 16. Approximately two months later, on 15 May 1829, Joseph and Oliver received the Aaronic Priesthood from the resurrected John the Baptist (see D&C 13; JS–H 1:68–72).

19. Desolating scourge. *Scourge* means literally "a whipping" or "a flogging" and refers here figuratively to the punishment that is about to be poured out upon the nations. Attempts to identify this scourge with any particular disease or disaster are all too narrow in their scope for, as described in Doctrine and Covenants 87, this scourge or punishment is to come in many forms—war, famine, plague, earthquake, and so on—"until the consumption decreed hath made a full end of all nations" (D&C 87:6). It is a "desolating" scourge because it will ultimately leave the world empty or desolate of inhabitants. As it was in the days of Noah, even so in our own dispensation, as the Second Coming approaches, all who will not repent will be erased. It is either repentance or destruction—in giving us this choice the Lord is treating our dispensation no differently from how he treated the ancient inhabitants of Jerusalem, or the Nephites, or the inhabitants of Sodom and Gomorrah. The world in our dispensation will find his ultimatum just as unavoidable as it was anciently (see v. 20).

In agreement with Doctrine and Covenants 87, the earlier wording of this revelation as found in the 1833 Book of Commandments implies that the great scourging will begin with the Civil War: "The sword of justice hangeth over their heads."[6] Brigham Young clearly believed this: "The war now raging in our nation [the Civil War] is in the providence of God, and was told us years and years ago by the Prophet Joseph; and what we are now coming to was foreseen by him, and no power can hinder."[7]

19. Consumed . . . by the brightness. What provides the energy that will consume the wicked on the last day? It will be the very glory of the resurrected Christ himself as he appears to the unshielded eyes of mortals. As he transforms the earth by the glory of his divine presence, that glory will burn away all things that cannot abide at least a terrestrial law. Thus, the earth will "be renewed and receive its paradisiacal glory" (Articles of Faith 1:10).[8]

20. Destruction of Jerusalem. Jerusalem was destroyed in 587 B.C. by the Babylonians and again in A.D. 70 by the Romans. In the former case the people were warned by Jeremiah and Lehi among others (see 1 Nephi 1:18). In the latter case they were warned by the Savior himself (Joseph Smith–Matthew 1:4–20).

21. Repent and walk more uprightly. The gospel is the same for everybody. Everyone, even prophets like Joseph, must repent when they make mistakes.

22. Even if you should be slain. Even this early in his ministry, the Lord foreshadows the eventual death of the Prophet.

23. The man that desires the witness. This indirect description of Martin Harris may show that the Lord is not entirely pleased with him.

24. A view. The Lord will give Martin another chance. Martin will actually see the sacred items as he desires, if he is prayerful and humble as the Lord commands. Note that this firm promise to Martin Harris (and later to the other two witnesses; see D&C 17) *before* he ever saw anything is strong evidence that Joseph did, indeed, have the plates. If Joseph had been acting fraudulently and had no plates, it is unlikely that this promise, which surely excited Martin's expectations, would have been made. Yet all three witnesses were convinced that this promise was fulfilled and that they really saw the gold plates. It is truly remarkable that Joseph specified what the witnesses would see before they saw it and before he had even met two of them (see v. 11, 15, 18) and that they later confirmed that they *did* indeed see it.

25. Know of a surety. Martin would see and hear with his own physical senses. He would know as Joseph knew, with no further need of faith in Joseph's testimony (see Ether 3:19). He would know of himself with no need of any other witness.

26. By the power of God. As a result of seeing the angel and hearing the voice of God, Martin would know that his witness did not come in any way from Joseph Smith or by any other human means. But Martin had to learn prudence, especially not to speak of sacred things without permission. When it was appropriate, he had to say what he was commanded to say and no more, or else he would break his covenant with God and stand condemned (see v. 27).

27. The covenant. This covenant is specified in verses 2–3.

28–29. Martin was wealthy and impetuous, and despite the witnesses he had received, was not yet sufficiently humble, even after losing the manuscript. This was Martin's last chance. If he would not repent and humble himself, the Lord did not want to be troubled again concerning him. In this respect, Doctrine and Covenants 5:28–29 might be called Martin Harris's "wake-up call."

30. Stop for a season. Fortunately, Martin did repent and humbled himself, and eventually he was allowed to see the plates. Joseph did *not* have to stop the work of translation, though it progressed slowly without a full-time scribe until the arrival of Oliver Cowdery a few weeks later.

32. Receive a witness. Sometimes the Lord answers our prayers in small ways and we *know* we have been answered—but we still want an answer that is bigger, flashier, or more concrete. We want a louder, more impressive answer. This is a sin; it is rejection of the Lord's Spirit simply because our carnal nature wants more reliable proof than God's whispered word! If Martin would not accept a witness of the Spirit but continued to demand more proof before he would believe, then he would fall.

35. Lifted up. A synonym for *exalted*. It refers in the short run to being lifted up from the earth at the second coming of Christ when all wickedness is left behind and burned (see D&C 88:96; 1 Thessalonians 4:17). In the long run, it refers to receiving all the blessings and privileges of the highest degree within the celestial kingdom.

35. The last day. Refers to the last day of Babylon, or the world, which is the present telestial earth. It will also be the day of Jesus' return in power with his Saints.

NOTES

1. Following are the additions to verses 18–19 according to the 1833 Book of Commandments, where they were numbered as verses 5–6:

   "And thus, if the people of this generation harden not their hearts, I will work a reformation among them, and I will put down all lyings, and deceivings, and priestcrafts, and envyings, and strifes, and idolatries, and sorceries, and all manner of iniquities, and I will establish my church, like unto the church which was taught by my disciples in the days of old.

   "And now if this generation do harden their hearts against my word, behold I will deliver them up unto satan, for he reigneth and hath much power at this time, for he hath got great hold upon the hearts of the people of this generation: and not far from the iniquities of Sodom and Gomorrah, do they come at this time: and behold the sword of justice hangeth over their heads, and if they persist in the hardness of their hearts, the time cometh that it must fall upon them."

2. See Smith, *History of the Church,* 1:19-20.
3. 1836–41 and 1841–43, respectively.
4. See the commentary on D&C 17:8.
5. See the Testimony of Three Witnesses.
6. Text in endnote 1.
7. Young, *Journal of Discourses,* 10:294.
8. See also 2 Thessalonians 2:8, in which, in the Greek text, the word translated *brightness* is actually *appearance*—"with the appearance of his coming."

6

BACKGROUND

It was common practice in early nineteenth-century New York for schoolteachers to board in the homes of their students. Thus it happened that twenty-two-year-old Oliver Cowdery, a schoolteacher in Manchester, New York, came during the winter of 1828–29 to board at the home of Joseph Smith Sr., for Oliver taught the Prophet's younger brothers and sisters in school. In the Smith home, Oliver soon learned of Joseph Jr. and of the gold plates, and received an initial witness that the story was true. As he put it, "The subject . . . seems working in my very bones, and I cannot, for a moment, get it out of my mind."[1] According to an 1832 history of Joseph Smith, Oliver eventually saw the Lord and the plates in vision even before seeking out the Prophet: "After much humility and affliction of soul [Joseph Smith] obtained them again when [the] Lord appeared unto a young man by the name of Oliver Cowdry and shewed unto him the plates in a vision and also the truth of the work."[2] To pursue the matter further, Oliver decided to travel the 125 miles to Harmony with Samuel Smith to determine for himself what his part in this great work might be.

Meanwhile, in the two or three weeks since Martin Harris had left Harmony and returned to Palmyra, Joseph had made some effort to continue translating the Book of Mormon with the help of his wife, Emma. According to Lucy Mack Smith, however, the demands already placed upon Emma as a wife and the necessity laid upon Joseph to provide for his family's temporal needs made for very little progress in the work of translating. Finally on 2 April 1829, Joseph asked the Lord to send him a scribe, and the Lord indicated to him that help would soon arrive. Three days later Oliver Cowdery arrived at Harmony with the Prophet's brother Samuel. Of course Joseph knew immediately why Oliver had come.[3]

The Prophet Joseph said: "Two days after the arrival of Mr. Cowdery (being the 7th of April) I commenced to translate the Book of Mormon, and he began to write for me, which having continued for some time, I inquired of the Lord through the Urim and Thummim, and obtained the following"—Doctrine and Covenants 6.[4]

COMMENTARY

1–9. With very slight variations, the text of Doctrine and Covenants 6:1–9 is the same as 11:1–9, a revelation given later to Hyrum Smith, Joseph's brother. Also, Doctrine and Covenants 6:1–6 is the same as 12:1–6, a revelation to Joseph Knight, and 6:1–5 is the same as 14:1–5, a revelation to David Whitmer. Further, Doctrine and Covenants 6:6 is also very similar in substance to 14:6, and section 4 is very similar in substance to the opening verses of all these subsequent revelations—sections 6, 11–12, and 14.

This repetition should not be understood as a divine "form letter" implying less than personal or individual concern for the recipients. Rather, it emphasizes the importance of the calling made to these servants and to all who have followed them in the Lord's service. The sacred ordinances of the gospel, while creating an individual, personal bond with each person, often employ the same words for all who receive them. That the Sermon on the Mount was repeated on more than one occasion, for example (see

Matthew 5–7; Luke 6; 3 Nephi 12–14), emphasizes the tremendous importance of the sermon.

2. Sharper than a two-edged sword. This refers not to a one-handed foil or a saber, but to a heavy, two-handed broadsword that is sharpened on both its edges. Thus, the same weapon may defend and save the repentant and the contrite or punish the wicked and rebellious (compare D&C 136:33; Helaman 3:29; Hebrews 12:4). It "cuts both ways," so to speak (compare D&C 33:1).

2. Quick. This term is used in its older sense to mean "alive" or "living."

6. As you have asked. Doctrine and Covenants 4, 6, 11–12, 14 were all given in response to requests from individuals that Joseph inquire of the Lord in their behalf.

6. Seek to bring forth and establish Zion. The Church had not yet been organized.

6. Zion. Zion is the kingdom of God upon the earth, a society that governs itself by celestial principles. Spiritual Zion now consists of the faithful membership of The Church of Jesus Christ of Latter-day Saints. The land of Zion will be established at some future time and will consist of the consecrated gathering-places of the Saints prior to the second coming of the Savior.

7. The mysteries of God. "A mystery is a truth that cannot be known except through divine revelation—a sacred secret. . . . In our day such great truths as those pertaining to the restoration of the Priesthood, the work for the dead, and the re-establishment of the Church are 'mysteries,' because they could not have been discovered except by revelation."[5]

9. Say nothing but repentance unto this generation. According to President Joseph Fielding Smith, "When the Lord calls upon his servants to cry nothing but repentance, he does not mean that they may not cry baptism, and call upon the people to obey the commandments of the Lord, but he wishes that all that they say and do be in the spirit of bringing the people to repentance."[6]

10. Gift. The gift here mentioned is Oliver's *calling* to be the scribe of Joseph, to assist in the translation of the Book of Mormon, and to establish Zion. This gift, together with its attendant blessings of revelation, was lost by Martin Harris through his carelessness and lack of faith.

11. Know mysteries. Anything that is known to God and not known to man is a mystery to man.[7] One of the promises made to Oliver and others in this dispensation is that if they seek, they can know mysteries. At the time of this revelation, the content of the Book of Mormon was a mystery, and much of what we take for granted today as basic principles of the restored gospel was still a mystery to Oliver and Joseph in 1829.

12. Make not thy gift known. Oliver's gift, his calling and its attendant blessings, was sacred and not to be cast indiscriminately before the world.

13. Gift of salvation. Though some would try to take credit for "working out their own salvation," the scripture here reminds us that salvation is ultimately a gift of God—not a purchase, not a contractual obligation, not a just reward or a wage. Salvation is a *gift,* through the mercy of God and the atonement of Christ.

14–15. Thou hast inquired. Oliver, like Nephi, for example, and unlike Laman, asked God to know if these things were true (see 1 Nephi 2:16, 19). In response to his requests, both prior to and upon this occasion, the Spirit answered him with varying degrees of confirmation, including the direct witness mentioned here. Usually such enlightenment is rather subtle: "While this spiritual communication comes into the *mind,* it comes more as a feeling, an impression, than simply as a thought. Unless you have experienced it, it is very difficult to describe that delicate process."[8]

16. None else save God that knowest thy thoughts. At times there are discussions as to whether Satan can know our thoughts. Elder James E. Faust has clearly taught, "He cannot know our thoughts unless we speak them."[9] Other prominent commentators have also understood this verse to mean that the devil cannot know our unspoken thoughts.[10]

19. Faults. Even prophets have faults. Joseph and Oliver had been called to admonish and encourage each other.

20. Thou art Oliver. Note the parallel address to Joseph in Doctrine and Covenants 3:9.

22. Cried unto me in your heart. Joseph Smith later related what Oliver had told him after Doctrine and Covenants 6 was received: "After we had received this revelation, Oliver Cowdery stated to me that after he had gone to my father's to board, and after the family had communicated to him concerning my having obtained the plates, that one night after he had retired to bed he called upon the Lord to know if these things were so, and the Lord manifested to him that they were true, but he had kept the circumstance entirely secret, and had mentioned it to no one; so that after this revelation was given, he knew that the work was true, because no being living knew of the thing alluded to in the revelation, but God and himself."[11] Oliver had also informed his close friend David Whitmer of the remarkable witness he had received. According to Whitmer, Oliver "wrote me that Joseph had told him his [Oliver's] secret thoughts, and all he had meditated about going to see him, which no man on earth knew, as he supposed, but himself, and so he stopped [at Harmony] to write for Joseph."[12]

26. Records . . . kept back. Portions of the Book of Mormon itself have been kept back. Other such records would also include parts of Joseph Smith's translation of the Bible (see D&C 35:20), the book of Moses (revealed June 1830–February 1831), and also the book of Abraham. Undoubtedly, there are other records still waiting to be brought forward.

28. Two witnesses. Oliver was to be a second witness of the Restoration, Joseph Smith being the first witness. Oliver was involved with every major Restoration event—the translation of the Book of Mormon, the restoration of the Aaronic Priesthood, the restoration of the Melchizedek Priesthood, and the restoration of priesthood keys in the Kirtland Temple. It would be Oliver's duty and right to bear witness of these events. Joseph would no longer stand alone.

29–30. Perhaps these verses foreshadow the 1844 martyrdom, as does Doctrine and Covenants 5:22. If so, it might have been Oliver rather than Hyrum Smith who died with the Prophet at Carthage had Oliver not left the Church by that time.[13]

32–34. Where two or three are gathered. Remember that at this time, in all the world there *were* just a handful of disciples who knew the truth of the work. It was indeed a little flock!

37. Behold the wounds. Verse 36 may suggest that this is just figurative language enjoining Oliver simply to "consider," or "think about" the sacrifice of the Savior as described in scripture. Oliver's vision sometime in 1828–29,[14] however, may suggest that a more literal reminiscence could be involved.

NOTES

1. Smith, *History of Joseph Smith,* 139.
2. Jessee, *Personal Writings of Joseph Smith,* 8.
3. See Smith, *History of Joseph Smith,* 141.
4. Smith, *History of the Church,* 1:32–33.
5. Smith and Sjodahl, *Doctrine and Covenants Commentary,* 141; see also the commentary on D&C 8:11.
6. Smith, *Church History and Modern Revelation,* 1:57.
7. See the commentary on D&C 6:7.
8. Boyd K. Packer, in *Ensign,* Nov. 1991, 21.
9. Conference Report, Oct. 1987, 43.
10. See McConkie, *Mormon Doctrine,* 777; Gibbons, in *Ensign,* Nov. 1991, 78–79.
11. Smith, *History of the Church,* 1:35.
12. Jenson, "Three Witnesses," 208.
13. See Smith, *Doctrines of Salvation,* 1:219.
14. See background to D&C 6.

DOCTRINE AND COVENANTS

7

BACKGROUND

Four revelations recorded in the Doctrine and Covenants (sections 6–9) were received at Joseph's small farm in Harmony, Pennsylvania, during April of 1829, the first month of Oliver Cowdery's service as Joseph's scribe. Concerning Doctrine and Covenants 7, Joseph recorded that "during the month of April I continued to translate, and he to write, with little cessation, during which time we received several revelations. A difference of opinion arising between us about the account of John the Apostle, mentioned in the New Testament [John 21:22] as to whether he died or continued to live, we mutually agreed to settle it by the Urim and Thummim and the following is the word which we received."[1]

Through the Urim and Thummim, Joseph translated a parchment document that had been written anciently by the Apostle John himself and which gave a more full account of the episode recorded in John 21:21–23 than is now found in the New Testament. This parchment may have been an original manuscript of John's Gospel, or it may have been another account written by John concerning the same incident.

As in John 21, the historical setting for the conversation recorded in Doctrine and Covenants 7 is the appearance of the resurrected Jesus to his disciples at the Sea of Tiberias, or Galilee.

According to the New Testament, on this occasion the Savior ate fish with the disciples and instructed Peter to feed his sheep (see John 21:9–17). Peter then asked the Savior what the Apostle John would do and received an ambiguous answer—at least as it is now recorded in John's gospel (see John 21:20–23). Joseph and Oliver had read the New Testament account and, wondering whether John's life had been prolonged or not, they consulted the Lord by the Urim and Thummim, through which Joseph translated John's ancient account.

A shorter version of section 7 was first published in the 1833 Book of Commandments with a heading that stated it was "translated from parchment, written and hid up" by John the Revelator. Verses 6–7 were added to the text of section 7 in the 1835 edition of the Doctrine and Covenants under the supervision of the Prophet Joseph Smith, and the wording of other verses was revised at that time by the Prophet. Because Joseph worked on the Joseph Smith Translation after section 7 was received, it may be that he obtained additional insights on John 21:20–23 from that labor, which he then added to this revelation in the 1835 edition.

COMMENTARY

1. Doctrine and Covenants 7 explains that in the episode recorded in John 21, Jesus had asked his apostles what they desired of him in much the same way that he later asked his American disciples (see 3 Nephi 28:1–12). While Peter asked to come speedily to Christ in his kingdom, John wanted to keep working on the earth to bring more souls to Christ. John was therefore allowed to remain upon the earth until the Second Coming to minister to those who would be heirs of salvation.

1. John, my beloved. The Bible nowhere explicitly identifies the "beloved disciple" as the Apostle John, though that has been the traditional understanding of the term for centuries. Only here and in 3 Nephi 28:6 is that identification made explicit in the scriptures.

2. Power over death. This refers to immunity from death in the usual sense. John's spirit and body would not become separated in the normal fashion; instead he would remain a "translated" being until the second coming of Christ. According to Joseph Smith, "Translated bodies are designed for future missions,"[2] and John's status is that of a translated being, for whom the change of death is indefinitely postponed, and whose body is raised from a telestial to a terrestrial condition. After his mission, however, John's body will finally undergo the change we call death but will make the transition from a translated body to a resurrected body in the twinkling of an eye, and will thus avoid all the unpleasantness usually associated with dying (see 3 Nephi 28:6–10).[3]

3. Shalt prophesy before nations. According to Revelation 10:11, John received a commission to "prophesy again before many peoples, and nations, and tongues, and kings." When this commission was given, John was already an old man, far beyond threescore and ten years. According to Joseph Smith, John's mission was to prepare the ten tribes of Israel for the final gathering (see D&C 77:14). At a conference of the Church held in June 1831, Joseph Smith said that John the Revelator was then among the ten tribes of Israel who had been led away by Shalmaneser, king of Assyria, to prepare them for their return from their long dispersion.[4] It is not necessary to assume, however, that the ten tribes know who they are or that they know John by his biblical identity; it is only certain that wherever they are and whatever they know, he is among them and is working to prepare them to receive the fulness of the gospel and to witness the second coming of the Savior.

4. Come unto me in my kingdom. Peter's desire was to pass through both death and the spirit world to become a resurrected, celestial being in the kingdom of God. It was in this glorious condition that Peter later appeared to Joseph and Oliver (see D&C 27:12).

5. Good desire. Sometimes people read jealous motives into Peter's question about John's future, when it is perhaps more likely that Peter was afraid he had asked for the wrong thing. The Lord reassured Peter that his request was a good one, but that John desired to do a greater work upon the earth before he came to Christ in his kingdom.

5. A greater work. John's desire to do "a greater work" does not necessarily mean a greater work than Peter's in some competitive sense. It may simply mean a greater work than John himself had done so far, without any implied comparison to Peter's performance.

6. Who dwell on the earth. John's extended ministry will be to those who live on this earth, including the lost tribes of Israel (see D&C 77:11, 14). This should dampen any speculation that the lost tribes may not be upon the earth (see also D&C 110:11).

7. I will make thee. The Lord is still speaking to Peter, who will minister for James and John in some unspecified manner. The three of them together will hold the keys of the priesthood until the Second Coming. When one who holds the keys bestows them upon another, the former does not cease to hold them. Rather, he lengthens the chain of authority by another link. Christ presently holds all the keys, but so do Peter, James, and John, on whom Christ bestowed them, and so also does the Prophet Joseph Smith, on whom these three bestowed the same keys.

7. The keys of this ministry. The keys given to Peter, James, and John constitute the authority of the Presidency of the Church.[5] These keys were given to Peter, James, and John by the Savior, Elijah, and Moses on the Mount of Transfiguration. Peter, James, and John in turn bestowed the keys on Joseph Smith and Oliver Cowdery (see D&C 27:12; 128:20).

NOTES

1. Smith, *History of the Church,* 1:35–36.
2. Smith, *Teachings,* 191.
3. Smith, *Teachings,* 170–71.
4. See Smith, *History of the Church,* 1:176; Smith, *Church History and Modern Revelation,* 1:48.
5. See Smith, *History of the Church,* 3:387–89.

DOCTRINE AND COVENANTS

8

BACKGROUND

Shortly before this revelation was received, Oliver Cowdery had been promised the gift of translating the Book of Mormon plates if he so desired (see D&C 6:25). Soon thereafter, Oliver informed Joseph that he did desire it and that he was now ready to make the attempt. Consequently, Joseph inquired of the Lord through the Urim and Thummim about how they should proceed and received this revelation in Oliver's behalf sometime in the latter half of April 1829.[1]

COMMENTARY

1. Engravings of old records. The Book of Mormon plates are engravings, and, possibly, so are other records. Oliver would be able to translate them if he so desired and if he had the necessary faith.

2. Mind and . . . heart. The Lord works with both systems—the mind—our intellect—and the heart, our feelings. The translation process would involve both Oliver's intellect and his feelings. Revelation is neither emotion devoid of sense nor intellect without feeling, but a combination of both faculties working together in harmony. Because the Holy Ghost is a revelator, his presence will enlighten the mind; no truly spiritual exercise can ever be "mindless." The Holy Ghost, however, dwells not in our mind, but in our *heart*—we will feel his influence rather than deduce it. While the Holy Ghost speaks *to* our minds, he speaks *from* our hearts, and those who will not trust their hearts are at a disadvantage in following the Spirit.

As Joseph Smith later said: "A person may profit by noticing the first intimation of the spirit of revelation; for instance, when you feel pure intelligence flowing into you, it may give you sudden strokes of ideas, so that by noticing it, you may find it fulfilled the same day or soon; (i.e.) those things that were presented unto your minds by the Spirit of God, will come to pass; and thus by learning the Spirit of God and understanding it, you may grow into the principle of revelation, until you become perfect in Christ Jesus."[2]

3. The spirit of revelation. The Holy Ghost. This is the same spirit by which Moses received his revelations at the Red Sea, and by which revelation comes to both the prophets and the followers of Christ.

4. This is thy gift. The gift is the spirit of revelation (see v. 2). To *have* such a gift, however, is not the same as knowing how to use it. In order to successfully exercise his gift, Oliver would have to himself supply an added ingredient: effort (see D&C 9:7–8). When Oliver learned to "apply unto," or inquire of, the gift of revelation the Lord had given him, it would deliver him in times of need.

6. Another gift. Oliver's first gift was the gift of revelation (see v. 4). His second gift was the "gift of Aaron."

6–8. The gift of Aaron. Aaron was the older brother of Moses who was appointed by God to act as Moses' spokesman. God had instructed that Moses' rod[3] was to be the instrument by which he and Aaron would perform signs and wonders. This rod was then carried by Aaron, and was sometimes called the rod of God (see Exodus 4:20; 17:9) and sometimes the rod of Moses (see Exodus 9:23; 10:13; 17:5), but usually it was called the rod of Aaron (see Exodus 7:10, 12, 19; 8:5, 16; Numbers 17:6–10). It was a tangible symbol of Aaron's authority and stewardship, of his relationship to Moses and to God, and an instrument by which he accomplished what God commanded him through the mouth of Moses.

In verse 6, the 1833 Book of Commandments read "the gift of working with the rod" instead of "the gift of Aaron." In verse 8 it read "rod of nature." Thus, it would appear that the "gift of Aaron" mentioned here is associated with the rod of Aaron and that the changes to the 1835 wording by the Prophet Joseph were meant to make clear that Oliver's gift was to stand in the office of Aaron possessing a rod like Aaron's. Of course, the references to a rod in the 1833 edition might be figurative or metaphorical, but there is some evidence that Oliver Cowdery may have possessed an actual rod, a rod of Aaron, appropriate to his office as spokesman and scribe for the Prophet.[4] Such a literal understanding would seem to be supported by the wording of Doctrine and Covenants 8:8, which tells Oliver "you shall hold it in your hands."

What is clear, however, is that Joseph and Oliver occupied the role in the modern Church once held by Moses and Aaron anciently. They were a modern Moses and Aaron (see D&C 28:2–3). Later in 1833, Sidney Rigdon was given a commission similar to Oliver's—that of spokesman (see D&C 100:9–11).

9–11. Ask. Verses 1, 9–11 all emphasize the necessity of asking God for what we want. Apparently, this message got across to Oliver loud and clear. He asked. He did not, however, then work for what he had asked.[5] Faith is the moving force of all things,[6] and whenever we approach God it must be done in faith if it is to be successful. Also, we should not ask for that which is not in our realm to receive. Oliver was to use his gift to aid in the translation and eventually to receive mysteries that would be revealed to the Church through him and Joseph.

11. Mysteries of God. It is appropriate, now that Oliver had been given the gift of revelation (see v. 3), that he also be encouraged to ask questions of the Lord and exercise his gift in receiving answers. The term *mystery* is used two ways in the modern

Church. Used positively, it means necessary or useful information that can be obtained only by revelation from God, such as Oliver's new gift. In this sense, Oliver was encouraged to seek "the mysteries of God," as in this verse (see also Alma 12:9–11). The scriptures always use "mysteries" in this positive sense.

On the other hand, the term *mysteries* is used more commonly in the contemporary Church in a negative sense to mean information unnecessary for our salvation or for our personal progress, information which the Lord has chosen, for whatever reason, to withhold from us. A preoccupation with such things can distract us from the really important truth that *has* been revealed and often leads to a loss of spiritual balance, then to contention, doubt, and apostasy.

NOTES

1. See Smith, *History of the Church,* 1:36. For the dating of section 8, see Anderson, "Mature Joseph Smith and Treasure Searching," 555, n. 119; Smith, *History of Joseph Smith.* 832, 853.
2. Smith, *History of the Church,* 3:381.
3. Originally his shepherd's staff; see Exodus 4:2–4.
4. See Anderson, "Mature Joseph Smith and Treasure Searching," 527–32.
5. See the commentary on D&C 9:7–9.
6. See Smith, *Lectures on Faith,* 1.

9

BACKGROUND

During April of 1829, the work of translating the Book of Mormon continued on Joseph's farm in Harmony, Pennsylvania. The Lord had granted permission for Oliver Cowdery to translate the plates if he so desired (see D&C 6:25). Oliver had responded by affirming his desire and had been given instructions on how to proceed with the translation (see D&C 8). But when Oliver actually made an attempt to translate from the plates, though he began well enough, he was not able to continue with the same success. Doctrine and Covenants 9 was given to Oliver through the Prophet Joseph after Oliver's largely unsuccessful attempt to translate.

COMMENTARY

1. After his attempt at translation, Oliver was instructed not to worry further about translating but to act as scribe for the Prophet until the Book of Mormon was completed. Most of the Book of Mormon manuscript was written in the hand of Oliver Cowdery, a measure of his obedience to this command.

2. Other records. This may refer to the book of Abraham, which was later translated by Joseph with the assistance of Oliver. Had Oliver not left the Church in 1838, he might have had other opportunities to translate. Oliver did act as scribe for Joseph for parts of the Joseph Smith Translation and for the book of Abraham.[1]

4. It is sometimes hard to realize that our calling may be to assist rather than to preside, or to record rather than to translate. Oliver's calling was to assist Joseph, like Aaron assisted Moses, and not to become equal to him.

5. You did not continue. Oliver did begin to translate. Apparently he wore the breastplate, he saw the plates and the characters, and he looked into the Urim and Thummim. He commenced well, but when the task was more difficult than he had anticipated, he feared and lost his opportunity to continue.

6. Do not murmur. Although Oliver may have thought of his unsuccessful attempt as a "failure," there was some reason why the Lord allowed this to happen. His "failure" somehow served God's purpose. No doubt it was a learning experience for Oliver. Perhaps it was important for him to understand the gift of translation so he could function more effectively as a scribe or serve as a more informed witness to the translation process.

7–9. It is important to understand that the contrast described here between a burning of the bosom and a stupor of thought applied *specifically* to the process of translation. The Lord had previously instructed Oliver in other ways that the Spirit is manifested (see D&C 6, 8). These other descriptions do not mention any "stupor of thought." Therefore, it would be unwise to insist that these verses be understood as defining how the Holy Ghost must *always* work in every person's life.

Many faithful Saints have pondered mutually exclusive alternatives without receiving a stupor of thought or by forgetting either alternative. Many have received unsolicited from the Lord distinct impressions, and even audible instructions or angelic visitations, rather than a "burning in the bosom." Moreover, the kind of revelation that Joseph received in the grove or by the appearance of Moroni would not fit into the model explained here.

It does seem, however, that the confirmation of the Spirit as a feeling in one's bosom can be more usually expected by those who seek the Lord's guidance. "If I am to receive revelation from the Lord, . . . his word will come into my mind through my thoughts, accompanied by a feeling in the region of my bosom. It is a feeling which cannot be described, but the nearest word we have is 'burn' or 'burning.' Accompanying this always is a feeling of peace, a further witness that what one heard is right."[2]

Most often revelation is an active rather than a passive process. The receiver must think, must work to understand, must come up with a plan, a proposal, a theory—in short must do as much of the work as possible to bridge the gap between the known and the unknown. Our mental and spiritual efforts to perceive the Lord's will can then be blessed with understanding and confirmation.

10. It is not expedient. Completing the work of the Lord is more important than satisfying the individual wishes and preferences of those called to do it.

11. Fear. Fear is the enemy of faith, and without faith one cannot please God or do his work (compare D&C 8:10).

12–14. Note that the Lord did not condemn Oliver for his inability to translate, and neither should we. As with Peter, who because of fear walked on water for only a moment, that moment was a great deal more than most others can manage. The Lord does not reject Oliver for doing with difficulty what most others could not do at all. This was not the right time, however, to make further attempts; the work is more important than the private wishes of the workers. Oliver was, after all, called to be a scribe, not a translator. The Lord kindly indulged his private desire to translate, but now wanted him to resume his intended role of assisting the Prophet that the work might move forward rapidly.

NOTES

1. See Smith, *History of the Church,* 2:236, 286.
2. S. Dilworth Young, in *Ensign,* May 1976, 23.

10

BACKGROUND

There has been some confusion in the past over the date when Doctrine and Covenants 10 was received. In all editions of the Doctrine and Covenants prior to 1921, the date of section 10 was given as May 1829. Thus it was placed in order between section 9, given April 1829, and section 11, given May 1829. Yet the Prophet Joseph himself had indicated that section 10 was received immediately after Doctrine and Covenants 3, and was the first revelation he received after the plates were returned to him on 22 September 1828.[1]

In 1921, B. H. Roberts and the committee responsible for publication of the 1921 edition of the Doctrine and Covenants recognized that section 10 had been misdated in previous editions, and reckoned the actual date to have been sometime in the summer of 1828, a conclusion based on *History of the Church*.[2] The numerical order of the revelations in the Doctrine and Covenants, however, was not changed at that time. Thus, section 10 is presently out of its proper chronological order, which would place it immediately after section 3. The reader is encouraged for the sake of continuity and perspective to read the sections in that order: 3, 10, 4.

The Urim and Thummim had been taken from Joseph before section 3 was given. It was returned to him for the purpose of receiving section 3, and then both the Urim and Thummim and the gold plates were taken away.[3] When the angel Moroni finally returned the gold plates and the Urim and Thummim to Joseph Smith after the loss of the 116 pages, the Prophet inquired again of the Lord by the Urim and Thummim and received section 10 in answer to his request for guidance.[4]

A few months later, in his preface to the first edition of the Book of Mormon, Joseph Smith included some of the language from section 10 (see vv. 10–11, 14, 41–43).[5]

COMMENTARY

1. Urim and Thummim. This is a Hebrew term meaning, literally, "lights and perfections." The Urim and Thummim are mentioned in the Old Testament as a device by which priesthood leaders determined the will of the Lord (see Exodus 28:30; Leviticus 8:8; 1 Samuel 28:6; Ezra 2:63; JS–H 1:35). There is likely more than one Urim and Thummim. The one used by the Prophet Joseph was not the same one mentioned in the Bible but had been in the possession of the brother of Jared anciently (see Ether 3:22–28). It consisted of two stones that could be set in metal frames connected by a rod to a breastplate. This arrangement allowed the Prophet conveniently to look into or through the Urim and Thummim as he translated the plates. According to Joseph Smith, possession of the Urim and Thummim, also called seer-stones, was what constituted a "seer" in ancient times (see JS–H 1:35). Abraham also received knowledge anciently by use of a Urim and Thummim (see Abraham 3:1–4).

1. Wicked man. The reference is to Martin Harris, who had "set at naught the counsels of God, and has broken the most sacred promises which were made before God, and has depended upon his own judgment and boasted in his own wisdom" (D&C 3:13).

4. Do not run faster . . . than you have strength. You can go only as fast as you can go; you can do only as much as you can do. This is excellent advice for those compulsive over-achievers in the Church who insist on becoming perfect all at once—on sprinting until they burn out. Even the Prophet Joseph had limited resources, and the Lord expected him and us to be wise stewards in using them. For wise stewards, pacing is important (see Mosiah 4:27). In Joseph Smith's *History of the Church*,[6] he informs us that upon receiving the advice in section 10, even though the work of translating was important, and though the plates had been returned to him, he put off translating for a time and began to work his farm in order to provide for his family. Even prophets can go only as fast as they have the resources to go.

5. Pray always. This is one of the most frequently delivered commandments found in the Doctrine and Covenants.[7] Joseph had to understand that he could not perform his task independently of God's help. The secret to overcoming the obstacles and threats of darkness is to be constantly touching base through prayer with the power and protection of the light. Some of this constant prayer can be vocal, but it is more often an attitude of communion with the divine—a constant awareness and acknowledgment of God's hand in our life.

6–7. Even the man. Apparently Martin's guilt and complicity in the affair of the lost 116 pages extended beyond just foolishly losing the manuscript, but it is impossible to know at this time exactly how far beyond. Martin may not have known or agreed with the whole conspiracy, but apparently he was not simply negligent. He was culpable in some degree beyond passive foolishness (see v. 6). He had broken the covenant he had made with God (see D&C 3:12–13). Still, Martin's subsequent repentance and faithful service to the end of his life should also be mentioned here.

8. The Lord held Joseph accountable for the fate of the manuscript: "Wicked men have taken them from *you*."[8] Though the plot was hatched and carried out by others, Joseph may not blame the loss of the 116 pages on them; *he* put the manuscript into their hands, and he did it against the Lord's advice.

10–11. The Lord here warns Joseph of a conspiracy on the part of those who had stolen the 116 pages of the book of Lehi. It was their intent to discredit Joseph as a prophet and the Book of Mormon as scripture by forging parts of the manuscript so that they read differently from the original. Their plan was to wait until Joseph had retranslated the 116 pages; then they would bring forth the altered copy with the claim that Joseph could not translate the plates the same way twice and must therefore be a fraud. But the warning and instructions given him in Doctrine and Covenants 10 enabled Joseph to avoid this trap.

Note that Satan was the source of the idea to alter the words of the manuscript. He can put ideas into the hearts of the wicked, whether they realize the ultimate source of those ideas or not. Satan is also the master counterfeiter. Artificial values, false arguments, lying testimony, and bogus documents are his stock in trade.

15. Tempt the Lord. To "tempt" means to "put to the test." To tempt the Lord is to try to make him jump through our hoops so that we may pass judgment upon him. It is to make God perform for us. After all, it is not Joseph who is really being put to the test here, but the Lord, to see if he can give Joseph the same translation twice.

For us to tempt or test the Lord in ways of our own devising—expecting him to submit to our tests and to our judgment—is a presumptuous sin. It is one form of "seeking a sign." On the other hand, the Lord invites us to prove him by keeping his commandments and then receiving the promised blessings, for example by reading and praying about the Book of Mormon (see Moroni 10:4) or by paying tithing (see Malachi 3:10).

20–33. These verses dramatically reveal how Satan works in human affairs and with our human weaknesses to discredit the truth and destroy the unwary.

21. They will not ask of me. The proper way to find out if the Book of Mormon or the work of the Prophet Joseph Smith are true is to ask God. The wicked, like Laman and Lemuel (see 1 Nephi 15:8–11), will not ask. They prefer subjecting God to their own little tests, thus tempting God. But God will not comply with such demands. He, not we, makes the rules and sets the terms. Knowledge of the truth of the restored gospel comes only one way: by asking God in faith if it is true.

23. I will require this at their hands. They will have to pay for stealing the manuscript and preparing their trap for Joseph.

24. Anger. The carnal self loves to be angry. It is a self-indulgence that Satan plays upon to keep us distracted from finding the truth.

25. Flattereth. It is flattery because Satan tells them that what is ugly and base about them is actually admirable and a virtue, and they believe it and feel good about themselves.

26. He causeth them to catch themselves in their own snare. They end up trapped and in Satan's power by their adoption of his methods. When we adopt Satan's methods, we also enter his world and accept his lordship over us.

28. Such are not exempt. The end does *not* justify the means. To use the tactics of wickedness to fight against wickedness is still *wickedness,* and it will be punished by God. This verse seems to indicate that we belong to the one whose methods we adopt and use.

32. Harden the hearts. Choosing to believe bad publicity and indulging a lust for anger and for condemnation makes the human heart less sensitive to the whisperings of the Spirit. To harden our hearts is to make them less sensitive to the subtle vibrations of the Spirit of God.

33–34. Satan's plan for discrediting Joseph by altering the manuscript was based on the assumption that Joseph would retranslate the lost 116 pages a second time. God, in his infinite knowledge, destroyed Satan's plans by providing an alternate set of plates and instructing Joseph Smith not to retranslate the lost 116 pages.

34–37. Show it not. The Prophet was commanded not to

divulge his plans or show the work of the future translation to anyone until it was completed. This was because Joseph would not always be able to tell friend from foe, or the wicked from the righteous, as he learned from his "friend" Martin Harris. Therefore, it would be safer for him to keep the project under wraps until totally completed. Contrary to what many people might expect, God does not always warn Church leaders or members of impostors and false friends.

38. The plates of Nephi. This refers to the small plates of Nephi. Joseph Smith was to avoid the trap laid for him by translating the second time from a different set of plates—from Nephi's own small plates rather than from Mormon's abridgment of Nephi's large plates. Nephi's small plates covered the same period of time as the others but also contained more doctrinal material. "In the episode involving the lost manuscript from the Book of Mormon, we see the interplay of the foreknowledge of God and the agency of man (with our freedom to fail) and the perfect foresight of a loving Lord who 1,500 years before the 'emergency' was ready with an alternative."[9] It is interesting to note that when Nephi wrote his account on the small plates, he indicated he did not know why the Lord had commanded him to prepare it except that it was "for a wise purpose in him, which purpose I know not. But the Lord knoweth all things from the beginning; wherefore, he prepareth a way to accomplish all his works among the children of men; for behold, he hath all power unto the fulfilling of all his words" (1 Nephi 9:5–6).

39. Remember it was said. Note that Joseph and Martin were already aware of multiple accounts of the same material among the Book of Mormon plates. Only now does the Lord explain their purpose to Joseph Smith.

41. The reign of king Benjamin. As Joseph began again to translate, the material covering Lehi to Omni (1 Nephi 1:1–Omni 1:29) was to be taken this time from the small plates rather than from the plates of Mormon as before (the 116 pages).

42. The record of Nephi. The original 116 pages have been called the "book of Lehi," which remains lost to us at the present. But it seems that it was the record of Nephi that the Lord intended all along to be part of our Book of Mormon. In a remarkable demonstration of God's foreknowledge, inclusion of the less doctrinal book of Lehi among the plates was to accommodate the agency of Joseph, Martin, and the conspirators in making wrong choices about the 116 manuscript pages, yet without marring the finished project once those pages were lost. This episode also teaches us that Satan can never stop the work of God, for God will always have anticipated his every move and stratagem.

46–49. The ancient Nephite prophets and apostolic disciples on the American continent prayed that the gospel would eventually come to the Lamanites. They also prayed that the gospel would come to whatever nation might inhabit the American continent in the future. God answered both those ancient prayers by bringing forth the Book of Mormon in the latter days.

50. A blessing upon this land. The Nephite prophets also left a blessing upon future generations, that those who lived here might believe the gospel and have eternal life. God has honored those prayers and that blessing by giving us in the latter days political freedom, the fulness of the gospel, and the true Church (see Enos 1:15–18; Mormon 8:25).

52. That which they have received. The fulness of the gospel does not take away from what people may already know of God; rather it expands and builds upon what they already have to bring them to a fulness of understanding. The restored gospel is not hostile to the truth found in other churches or in other religions. It is not intended to take away people's light, but rather to add to it.

53. Will establish. Remember this is still 1828; the Church has not yet been organized, but God will shortly keep his promises to the ancient Nephites to bring this about.

55. Whosoever belongeth . . . shall inherit. This refers not to the theoretical membership of merely having one's name on the records, but to the actual membership of full activity in the

Church. Those who have made and who are keeping the gospel covenant are truly members of his Church (see v. 67).

56. Fear me. The term is used here and elsewhere not in the sense of terror, but in the sense of awe, reverence, and respect. The "fear of God" is one of the most misunderstood phrases in scripture, a misunderstanding caused by unfortunate shifts in meaning for some English words since 1611. See, for example, the phrase "fear and trembling," which comes originally from Psalm 2:11 where "fear" is also reverence and "trembling" is not shaking with fear but with joy.

56. To get gain. That is, priestcraft. Religion for money or religion as a commodity to be bought and sold is an abomination that characterizes the kingdom of the devil. The true Church is not about money or preoccupation with money; true religion cannot be bought or sold for money.

57. Jesus Christ. The reader will note that it is Jesus Christ, God the Son, who speaks to us in the Doctrine and Covenants, as in almost all the scriptures.

57. Mine own. This refers to the Jews of the first century A.D., who were the chosen seed of Abraham, but who largely rejected the Savior and his gospel.

58. I am the light. Compare John 1:5.

59. Who said—Other sheep have I. Jesus told his disciples in Jerusalem about the Nephites (see John 10:16), whom he would visit and who would receive a dispensation of the gospel, though some of his disciples did not understand (see 3 Nephi 15:16–24). Publication of the Book of Mormon will (1) tell the story of these "other sheep" and show what the Lord did for them, (2) reveal their marvelous works, (3) teach the true doctrine of Christ that they possessed, (4) settle religious questions for the faithful, and (5) correct the errors of those who distort what the Bible says.

63. Contention. Those who become angry or inflamed on points of doctrine, or who enjoy "scripture bashing" or contending against a supposed "enemy" are under the influence of Satan, who uses religion to increase hatred and ill-will in the world. This is not a characteristic of those who follow the Holy Spirit. One cannot use the scriptures as a weapon; to do so is to wrest the scriptures, or force them out of their proper role and meaning. Many "scripture bullies" might profit from rereading verse 63. As Jesus Christ is the Prince of Peace, so his doctrine will bring peace. Satan, on the other hand, is the god of strife, war, and contention.

64–65. This great mystery. Anything that can be known only by revelation is a mystery. The Lord reveals his intention of gathering Israel in the latter days, just as he attempted to gather Zion formerly (see Matthew 23:37; 3 Nephi 10:5).[10] This is the first hint of the gathering to Zion that will take place in Kirtland, Missouri, Nauvoo, and in the western United States. Already as early as 1828, the Lord alluded to the literal gathering to come.

66. Waters of life. Symbolic of the love of God (see 1 Nephi 11:25) and the blessings of redemption and exaltation. Thus, the waters of life can also be the sacrament water or wine, the oil of anointing, or other symbols of God's redeeming love (see John 7:38; Alma 5:34; 42:27).

67. Cometh unto me. To become one with Christ in the gospel covenant of faith, repentance, baptism, and receiving the Holy Ghost.

67. My church. The Lord's church—not just equivalent to the names on the membership records. The true Church consists of those who actually come to Christ in the covenant of the restored gospel and who remain faithful to that covenant. Perhaps "of" is implied before "my church," as is stated in verses 68–69.

68. More or less. When anyone strays very far from preaching the pure gospel of faith, repentance, baptism, and receiving the gift of the Holy Ghost, he or she ceases to be representative of the Church and becomes instead a potential obstacle to the faithful. All the standard works reveal the same basic and pure doctrine. To say either more or less than the Lord has said or commanded us to say—either to put words in the Lord's mouth or take them out—both distort the message the Lord wants delivered (see also D&C 93:25; 3 Nephi 11:40; 18:13). We are not justified in preaching as doctrine that which we have added to the Lord's word, neither are we justified in ignoring or failing to preach and practice what the Lord has clearly revealed.

69. Endureth of my church to the end. Because "enduring" is to remain faithful to our covenants, then enduring "of my church" is to remain a faithful member of the Church until death. Those who leave the Church for whatever reason will not be excused. We cannot be faithful to covenants made in and through the Church while leaving the Church or fighting against it. Those who leave the Church also leave the kingdom. Those who endure in the Church are established on the rock of Christ, and the gates of hell shall not prevail against them. This is the same promise given to the Church anciently (see Matthew 16:18).

69. Hell. Here *hell* may mean the spirit world. Although a person may die and pass for a time into that realm, through the power of the resurrection, brought about in Christ, the gates of hell cannot keep such a person locked in and will not ultimately prevail over him.

70. Life and light of the world. Christ is the power who created both the world and its sun, and he sustains them and us minute by minute (see D&C 88:6–13, 41; John 1:3–4; Colossians 1:16–17). Thus, he is quite literally the ultimate source as well as the sustaining power of our lives and of our light.

NOTES

1. See Smith, *History of Joseph Smith,* 135; see Smith, *History of the Church,* 1:23. This would likely make the date of section 10 late September of 1828; see also Cook, *Revelations of the Prophet,* 17–18, 122–23; Parkin, "Preliminary Analysis of the Dating of Section 10," 68–84.
2. See Smith, *History of the Church,* 1:23.
3. See Smith, *History of the Church,* 1:21–22.
4. See Smith, *History of the Church,* 1:23.
5. The full text of that preface, which is no longer printed with the

Book of Mormon, may be found in Cook, *Revelations of the Prophet,* 18–19.

6. See Smith, *History of the Church,* 1:28.
7. Eleven times exactly so; eighteen times in slightly different form.
8. Emphasis added.
9. Maxwell, "Doctrine and Covenants," 6.
10. For a discussion of the phrase "as a hen gathereth," see the commentary on D&C 29:2.

11

BACKGROUND

In May 1829, only a month or so after Oliver had begun to act as scribe for Joseph Smith, Joseph's younger brother Samuel H. Smith came again to Harmony, Pennsylvania, from the family home in Manchester, New York, to visit and observe. Within a short period of time, Joseph and Oliver convinced Samuel to pray concerning the truth of their work, and in answer to his prayers Samuel received a witness that the work was indeed divine. He was baptized by Oliver on 25 May 1829 and returned to his home in Manchester full of enthusiasm for the Restoration.

At this time, Hyrum Smith, elder brother of the Prophet, also traveled from Manchester to Harmony to visit. When Hyrum arrived, the Prophet and Oliver were immersed in translating the Book of Mormon, and Hyrum became deeply interested in their work. Almost immediately he wanted to make copies of what had been translated so far and to begin preaching and teaching from it in the surrounding areas. Using the Urim and Thummim, Joseph inquired of the Lord concerning what part Hyrum should play in the Restoration and received Doctrine and Covenants 11 in answer to his inquiry.

This revelation directs Hyrum to prepare himself for the Lord's service, but to wait until the translation is finished to begin his work rather than to start out only partially prepared. First things first.[1] Hyrum Smith was baptized in June 1829, soon after section 11 was received, and he was subsequently chosen as one of the Eight Witnesses of the Book of Mormon who were privileged to see and handle the gold plates.

Since Hyrum's visit followed the return of his younger brother Samuel to Manchester, New York, section 11 must have been received at least several days after Samuel's baptism in Harmony on the 25th—this estimate allows time for Samuel's return to New York and Hyrum's subsequent journey to Harmony. This revelation to Hyrum should therefore be dated to the last few days in May 1829. It is further apparent that Doctrine and Covenants 13, which describes the restoration of the Aaronic Priesthood on 15 May, should logically precede section 11, since Oliver exercised his Aaronic Priesthood to baptize Samuel Smith on 25 May, several days before section 11 was received.[2]

Chronologically, then, the sequence for the first thirteen revelations in the Doctrine and Covenants would be section 2 on 21 September 1823, section 3 in July 1828, section 10 in September 1828, sections 4–9 from February to April 1829, section 13 on 15 May 1829, sections 11–12 in late May 1829, and section 1 on 1 November 1831.

COMMENTARY

1–9. These verses have slight variations to Doctrine and Covenants 6:1–9, which was given just a few weeks earlier to Oliver Cowdery. But this is not therefore a "used" or "recycled" revelation. These instructions are precisely what the Lord wants to communicate to those who desire to serve him in the Restoration.[3]

10. Thou hast a gift. The gift promised to Hyrum appears to be the gift of the Holy Ghost, which will "enlighten your mind" and "fill your soul with joy" (v. 13).[4] Actually, the gift is promised to Hyrum on certain conditions, which suggests a covenant arrangement. If Hyrum would seek the Lord with faith and an honest heart, he would be able to use his gift in the service of God.

11. It is I that speak. The Lord is speaking here, not Joseph Smith. Evidently, Hyrum needed to learn that the Urim and Thummim revealed the word of God through the mouth of Joseph.

12–13. But how does one with little previous experience recognize the Spirit of God? His Spirit is the Spirit that leadeth (1) to do good, (2) to do justly, (3) to walk humbly, and (4) to judge righteously. When one follows that Spirit which leads to these four ends, then the Spirit will "enlighten your mind" and "fill your soul with joy." No other spirit leads in this manner or has this effect, only the Spirit of God. Any spirit that does not lead us to enlightenment and joy must be judged an impostor.

15. You need not suppose. Hyrum is mistaken in thinking that one can become a minister of the restored gospel by self-appointment. His desire to preach is not so much evil as it is naive and premature, and he has much to learn about priesthood, calling, ordination, stewardship, lines of authority, and accountability. In the Restoration, preachers cannot be *self*-appointed (see Articles of Faith 1:5). It was important for Hyrum and the early members to learn this lesson, for they lived in an environment where itinerant, self-appointed preachers were the norm. The Lord used this occasion to teach the correct practice.

16. Wait a little longer. Hyrum had to wait until he better understood the gospel he wanted so much to preach, and until he was more educated in the order of the Lord's kingdom. Hyrum needed to focus on keeping the commandments and on curbing his tremendous enthusiasm, which put him at risk of setting out prematurely and unprepared. Therefore, he needed to practice *not* speaking—"hold your peace" (v. 22)—and waiting for the direction of the Spirit. Ideally, modern missionaries are under the same obligation to prepare themselves in the months or years before receiving their calls.

19. Cleave. This verb has two almost contradictory meanings:

"to split or separate," as in cleaving firewood, and "to bond or stick to," as in spouses cleaving to one another. The usage here might be understood colloquially as a command to "stick like glue."

19. You may assist. Hyrum stayed in Harmony to help Joseph and Oliver in their work and a few weeks later was privileged to be one of the Eight Witnesses of the Book of Mormon.

19. Be patient. Hyrum had such enthusiasm and desire that he had to be restrained a little. Would that all the Lord's missionaries needed the same advice.

20. Keep my commandments. No one can become a truly successful missionary or magnify a calling who cannot keep the commandments. This exhortation describes, however, an orientation to the commandments rather than to absolute success in keeping all of them all the time. To "keep the commandments" is to strive, desire, and work to do so with all our might, mind, and strength. This effort is to be the focus of our lives. Yet the Lord knows we will fail in some degree, and so he has prepared repentance and the sacrament for us to renew our commitments on a regular basis and thus avoid losing our covenant relationship and its blessings through our human weakness.

21. Declare . . . obtain. You cannot preach what you do not know. Hyrum had to wait to read the Book of Mormon and the revelations of Joseph; then he would be prepared to teach them to others. Only then could he preach by the Spirit and thus have the power to convert the honest in heart (see v. 18). In God's kingdom, one first has to learn the gospel and then be called by authority to preach it.

22. My word which hath gone forth. The Bible.

22. My word which shall come forth. The Book of Mormon, which was then in the process of being translated.

22. All which I shall grant . . . this generation. The Doctrine and Covenants, the Pearl of Great Price, the Joseph Smith Translation, and other revelations to the Prophet Joseph Smith. Hyrum was promised that if he would be diligent in learning what the Lord had already given and what he would yet give, "then shall all things be added thereto." This promise was also given to the Church at large. If we are diligent in learning all that the Lord has revealed publicly, he will then continue to reveal his mysteries to us privately—on the strict condition that they *remain* private (see Alma 12:9).

23. Thou art Hyrum, my son. The name *Hyrum* has several variants but probably comes from the Hebrew word for "free-born" or "noble." "My son": Hyrum was about to be baptized and therefore to be "born again" as a son of Jesus Christ, who speaks here.[5]

24. My rock. The term *rock* is used in scripture with several different meanings. It is true that "the rock" is sometimes revelation, but Christ is also the Rock (see 1 Corinthians 10:4; Helaman 5:12), and so also, in one context, is Peter (or Cephas), whose name both in Greek and in Aramaic means "rock." Peter was the last one to hold all the keys anciently (see D&C 27:12; see also Matthew 16:18–19, where "rock" has more than one meaning).

In this verse, the gospel is the rock, as it is also in Doctrine and Covenants 18:5 and 3 Nephi 11:32–39.

25. Deny not. The spirit of prophecy or revelation here is the Holy Ghost. Taken to its extreme, denying this Spirit can have eternal repercussions (see Matthew 12:31).[6] In lesser degrees, denying the spirit of revelation cuts us off from the heavens and banishes the influence of God and interaction with his Spirit from our daily lives (see D&C 59:21). The Holy Ghost is a revelator. If we deny the spirit of revelation, we cannot at the same time receive the gift of the Holy Ghost, who *is* the spirit of revelation.[7] In the religious environment of Hyrum's day, without the fulness of the gospel, it was common for preachers to deny even the possibility of additional revelation or prophecy, and Hyrum was warned against this common error.

27. I speak unto all. The information and advice given to Hyrum in this revelation was intended not for Hyrum alone, but for all who might subsequently have the same desires Hyrum had to serve God and to build his kingdom.

30. Become the sons of God. Those who come to Christ become his children and are born again in the gospel covenant as sons and daughters of Christ. This status empowers us to follow the path of the Savior, to become what Jesus Christ—our spiritual Father—is, and to inherit what he inherits (see Mosiah 5:7; Romans 8:14–17; D&C 84:38), thus becoming exalted beings like him. This is the same power given to Jesus' disciples anciently (see John 1:12) and is explained in Doctrine and Covenants 25:1; 39:1.

NOTES

1. Compare this to the advice to Joseph in D&C 10:4.
2. See Smith, *History of the Church,* 1:39, 44–45; Smith, *History of Joseph Smith,* 142.
3. See the commentary on D&C 6:1–9.
4. Another interpretation is given by Joseph Fielding Smith: "The great gift which [Hyrum] possessed was that of a tender, sympathetic heart, a merciful spirit" (Smith, *Church History and Modern Revelation,* 1:52.)
5. See the commentary on D&C 25:1; 11:30.
6. See the commentary on D&C 76:35.
7. See Smith, *Teachings,* 328.

12

BACKGROUND

As early as 1826, Joseph Smith had worked near Colesville, New York, a town about twenty miles from Harmony, Pennsylvania, for a farmer and mill owner named Joseph Knight Sr. This old gentleman had subsequently become a close friend of Joseph's and had assisted him on several occasions. Brother Knight lent the Prophet his horse and buggy the day Joseph married Emma Hale, and Joseph borrowed it again for the trip to Cumorah on the morning he first received the plates from Moroni. At about the same time that Hyrum Smith visited Joseph in late May of 1829, Joseph Knight Sr. also came to visit. Brother Knight, "having heard of the manner in which we were occupying our time, very kindly and considerately brought us a quantity of provisions [including some badly needed writing paper], in order that we might not be interrupted in the work of translation by the want of such necessaries of life; and I would just mention here, as in duty bound, that he several times brought us supplies, a distance of at least thirty miles, which enabled us to continue the work when otherwise we must have relinquished it for a season. Being very anxious to know his duty as to this work, I inquired of the Lord for him, and obtained the following: [section 12]."[1]

Later the Prophet described Brother Knight in these terms:

"For fifteen years he has been faithful and true, and even-handed and exemplary, and virtuous and kind, never deviating to the right hand or to the left. Behold he is a righteous man . . . ; and it shall be said of him, by the sons of Zion, while there is one of them remaining, that this man was a faithful man in Israel; therefore his name shall never be forgotten."[2]

In Doctrine and Covenants 23, Joseph Knight was instructed to join the Church, which he did in June of 1830. Brother Knight's family of nine, all of whom joined the Church, formed the real strength of the Colesville Branch. Brother Knight's son Newel is also mentioned in the Doctrine and Covenants (sections 52, 54, 56, 124). Faithful to the end, Joseph Knight Sr. died at Mt. Pisgah, Iowa, during the exodus of the Saints from Nauvoo.

COMMENTARY

1–6. See the commentary on Doctrine and Covenants 6:1–9; 11:1–9.

7. Compare Doctrine and Covenants 11:27.

8. No one can assist. Because many who are not yet perfectly "humble and full of love, having faith, hope, and charity" do in fact assist in the work, this must be qualified somewhat, perhaps in the manner of Doctrine and Covenants 46:9: "him that *seeketh* so to do."[3]

8. Humble. Without a knowledge of our utter dependence upon God, we cannot serve him effectively. It is *his* plan, *his* gospel, *his* Spirit, *his* work, and *his* glory.

8. Love. According to Joseph Smith, "Love is one of the chief characteristics of Deity, and ought to be manifested by those who aspire to be the sons of God. A man filled with the love of God, is not content with blessing his family alone, but ranges through the whole world, anxious to bless the whole human race."[4]

8. Being temperate. This is to exercise moderation or self-control and to resist the carnal urge to indulge in extremes, particularly in personal and physical habits and in physical indulgences. Examples of intemperance would be not getting enough sleep, or getting too much sleep; not eating enough, or eating too much; not exercising enough, or exercising too much. Geographically speaking, the temperate zones are those latitudes that don't suffer the extremes of tropical heat or arctic cold but which maintain a moderate climate. A temperate individual is one in whom extremes are similarly not often manifested, but who maintains a moderate "climate" in his personal life.

9. Compare Doctrine and Covenants 11:28.

NOTES

1. Smith, *History of the Church*, 1:47–48.
2. Smith, *History of the Church*, 5:124–25.
3. Emphasis added.
4. Smith, *History of the Church*, 4:227.

13

BACKGROUND

When Moses led the children of Israel out of Egypt, it was with the intention that they should become a Zion people, enjoying the blessings of the fulness of the gospel and of the ordinances of the Melchizedek Priesthood. When Israel sinned in the wilderness, God took the fulness of the gospel and the Melchizedek Priesthood away from them but left the lesser priesthood, the priesthood of Aaron, in their midst. The law of carnal commandments and performances functioned under this priesthood, and with the law of Moses constituted a training program to prepare immature and rebellious Israel for the fulness of the gospel. The Aaronic Priesthood cannot, however, administer the fulness. As a lesser or preparatory priesthood, it is limited in its authority and prerogatives (see D&C 84:23–28;[1] JST Exodus 34:1–2).

The last man to hold the keys of the Aaronic Priesthood anciently was John the Baptist. Because the major function of the Aaronic Priesthood is to prepare Israel for receiving the Melchizedek Priesthood, it is entirely fitting that John should prepare the way for Christ, who holds the keys of the Melchizedek Priesthood. Thus, John goes before the Savior and prepares the way for him, the preparatory priesthood preceding the higher priesthood. John prepared the way for the Savior in his mortal ministry, in his ministry to the spirits in the postmortal spirit world, and in the restoration of the gospel in the latter days before Jesus' second coming (see Matthew 17:11–13).

About five weeks into their translation of the Book of Mormon, on 15 May 1829, Joseph Smith and Oliver Cowdery retired to the woods on the banks of the Susquehanna River near Joseph's farm in Harmony, Pennsylvania, and inquired of the Lord concerning baptism and the remission of sins, which had been mentioned in the material they were then translating, 3 Nephi 11. As they prayed, John the Baptist appeared and informed them that he had been sent to them under direction of the Apostles Peter, James, and John. The Baptist laid his hands upon the heads of Joseph and Oliver and conferred upon them the Aaronic Priesthood, using the words that now constitute Doctrine and Covenants 13.[2]

John also gave Joseph and Oliver some instruction on the nature of the Aaronic Priesthood, including the fact that it did not have the power of bestowing the gift of the Holy Ghost. He then instructed Joseph and Oliver to baptize one another and to ordain each other to the Aaronic Priesthood.[3]

Following this event, Joseph and Oliver had both the right to function as priests themselves and the keys or power of presidency in the Aaronic Priesthood. These keys gave Joseph and Oliver the right of administration or control, the right to ordain others, and also the right to direct how and when those others would be allowed to use their priesthood.[4]

COMMENTARY

1. My fellow servants. From the greatest to the least in the kingdom of God and from the time of Adam to the present, all those who labor for the gospel are fellow servants of Christ. Across the centuries and around the globe, we are all companions, partners, and friends in the service of God.

1. Messiah. John here uses the anglicized form of the Hebrew title *meshiach*, which is equivalent to the more familiar Greek form *christos*, both of which mean "Anointed One" or "Christ."

1. Priesthood of Aaron. The priesthood given to Joseph and Oliver at this time was the same priesthood given anciently to Aaron and his descendants (see D&C 84:25–27; 107:13–15).

1. Keys. There is a difference between holding the priesthood and possessing its keys. Keys are the right of administration or control. Priesthood leaders hold the keys and thus preside over and direct the work of others who hold the priesthood but who are not authorized to exercise it independently. For example, an elder may have the authority to perform baptisms, but he may not baptize someone without permission from the bishop, mission president, or other leader who has received the keys for that work.

1. Ministering of angels. With the Aaronic Priesthood comes the right to receive the assistance of heavenly messengers, to preach repentance, and to administer baptism by immersion for the remission of sins. This power is referred to elsewhere as the "preparatory gospel" because it prepares an individual to receive the fulness of the gospel (see D&C 84:26–27; 107:20), membership in the Church of Jesus Christ, and the blessings of the higher Melchizedek Priesthood.

1. Sons of Levi. This refers to literal descendants of Levi, one of the twelve sons of Jacob (Israel). The sons of Levi were designated anciently to hold this priesthood and will bear it again in the restoration of all things in the latter days.

1. Until. The wording here does not mean the Aaronic Priesthood will be taken from the earth when the sons of Levi finally resume their rightful roles. It is rather an assurance that the priesthood would remain in place during the entire process of restoring all things. Oliver Cowdery supported this view in his remembrance of John's words: "Upon you my fellow servants, in the name of Messiah I confer this priesthood and this authority, which shall remain upon earth, *that* the sons of Levi *may yet offer* an offering unto the Lord in righteousness"[5] (see also D&C 128:24; JS–H 1:71).

1. The sons of Levi do offer again an offering. Joseph Smith taught elsewhere that "it is generally supposed that sacrifice was entirely done away when the Great Sacrifice [i.e.,] the sacrifice of the Lord Jesus was offered up, and that there will be no necessity for the ordinance of sacrifice in the future; but those who assert this are certainly not acquainted with the duties, privileges and authority of the Priesthood, or with the Prophets. . . .

"These sacrifices, as well as every ordinance belonging to the Priesthood, will, when the Temple of the Lord shall be built, and the sons of Levi be purified, be fully restored and attended to in all their powers, ramifications, and blessings. . . ."[6]

Joseph Smith also taught that Jehovah gave Noah "the offering of sacrifice, which also shall be continued at the last time; for all the ordinances and duties that ever have been required by the Priesthood, under the directions and commandments of the Almighty in any of the dispensations, shall all be had in the last dispensation. . . .

" . . . Those things which existed prior to Moses' day, namely, sacrifice, will be continued."[7]

On the other hand, President Joseph Fielding Smith suggested that this will be only a temporary resumption of animal sacrifice for the purpose of demonstrating the restoration of all things.[8]

NOTES

1. See also the commentary on D&C 84:23–28.
2. For documents and discussion of the events surrounding the restoration of the Aaronic Priesthood, see Cannon, "Priesthood Restoration Documents," 164–66.
3. See Smith, *History of the Church*, 1:39–44.
4. See McConkie, "Keys of the Kingdom," 3.
5. Cowdery, "Dear Brother," *Messenger and Advocate*, 16; emphasis added.
6. Smith, *Teachings*, 172–73.
7. Smith, *History of the Church*, 4:210–12.
8. See Smith, *Doctrines of Salvation*, 3:94.

DOCTRINE AND COVENANTS

14

BACKGROUND

During the school year of 1828–29, while Oliver Cowdery was teaching in Palmyra and living in Manchester with the Smith family, he had become acquainted with a man named David Whitmer who lived in nearby Fayette, New York. Oliver had discussed the claims of the Smith family with the Whitmers and visited them in Fayette on his way to Harmony to become Joseph's scribe early in April 1829. While working as the Prophet's scribe in Harmony, Oliver wrote the Whitmers more than once expressing his testimony of the work.[1]

As Oliver and Joseph continued to translate the Book of Mormon in Harmony, Pennsylvania, they began to encounter persecution. This persecution intensified during the month of May to the point that it became necessary for them to move from the Prophet's home in Harmony. Joseph and Oliver decided to ask Peter Whitmer Sr. if they could finish the translation at the Whitmer home in Fayette, New York. The Prophet recorded the Whitmers' response to this request: "In the beginning of the month of June, his son, David Whitmer, came to the place where we were residing, and brought with him a two-horse wagon, for the purpose of having us accompany him to his father's place, and there remain until we should finish the work."[2]

The Whitmers proved to be a great help to the young prophet

as he translated the Book of Mormon: "Upon our arrival, we found Mr. Whitmer's family very anxious concerning the work, and very friendly toward ourselves. They continued so, boarded and lodged us according to arrangements; and John Whitmer, in particular, assisted us very much in writing during the remainder of the work.

"In the meantime, David, John and Peter Whitmer, Jun., became our zealous friends and assistants in the work; and being anxious to know their respective duties, and having desired with much earnestness that I should inquire of the Lord concerning them, I did so, through the means of the Urim and Thummim, and obtained for them in succession the following revelations"—Doctrine and Covenants 14–16.[3] It took about a month to finish translating the Book of Mormon after Joseph and Oliver moved from Harmony, Pennsylvania, to the Whitmer farm in Fayette, New York.

COMMENTARY

1–6. For a discussion of these verses, see the commentary on Doctrine and Covenants 6:1–9; 11:1–9.

7. Endure to the end. This does not mean to be sinless or perfect, but to remain loyal to Christ and endure faithful to the covenants of his gospel throughout one's life.

7. Eternal life. This means exaltation in the celestial kingdom of God. Immortality—simply living forever—will be granted to everyone, good or bad, through the gift of resurrection, in any of several degrees of glory. But eternal life in the fullest sense is to live as the Eternal One himself lives—exalted not as servants but as sons and daughters in a celestial kingdom.[4] This exaltation, like all other degrees of glory, is available to us only through the resurrection and atonement of Christ and is therefore a gift of his grace—"the greatest of all the gifts of God." No one earns exaltation completely on their own merits, though we do participate in the process to the degree that we are able. Exaltation is ultimately a gift.

8. Stand as a witness. Note the foreshadowing of David Whitmer's role as one of the Three Witnesses. But in order to bear witness, he would need first to receive the Holy Ghost, for it is ultimately the Holy Ghost that bears witness to both the one who testifies and the one who hears the testimony.

9. Living God. That is, Jesus Christ—the one who died and who now lives. The adjective *living* is often applied to God in the scriptures to mean "truly and eternally living" or "resurrected," that is, with a body and spirit united not in a mortal but in an immortal state (see Luke 24:5; 2 Nephi 9:13; D&C 138:43).

10. Fulness of my gospel. In the scriptures this phrase usually refers both to the doctrine that must be learned and to the ordinances that must be received to enter into the celestial kingdom of God, including the authority to perform them. The *fulness* of the gospel is necessary for the *fulness* of salvation, which is not telestial or terrestrial salvation but salvation in the celestial kingdom.[5]

10. The Gentiles. In the meridian of time, under the direction of Peter the apostle, Paul and others were instructed to take the fulness of the gospel to the Jews first and then to the Gentiles. In this last dispensation, the order has been reversed: the gospel will be taken first to the Gentiles—that is, to all the nations of the earth besides the Jews—and then, finally, once again to the Jews. Thus, in our dispensation "the last [the Gentiles] shall be first, and the first [the Jews] shall be last" (1 Nephi 13:42; see also Luke 13:30). We now live in the "times of the Gentiles" when the gospel is being taken to every Gentile nation, kindred, tongue, and people (D&C 45:25–30).[6]

NOTES

1. See Pratt and Smith, "Report of Elders Orson Pratt and Joseph F. Smith," 772.
2. Smith, *History of the Church,* 1:48–49.
3. Smith, *History of the Church,* 1:49.
4. See Smith, *Doctrines of Salvation,* 2:8.
5. See the commentary on D&C 20:9; 42:12.
6. See the commentary on D&C 45:25, 28–30.

15 AND 16

BACKGROUND

Doctrine and Covenants 14–16 were all given at the same time—June 1829—and share the same historical setting. Refer to the chapter on section 14 for the background pertinent to sections 15–16. Sections 15–16 are identical except for the names in verse 1 and the one word *unto,* which was added in Doctrine and Covenants 16:5, apparently through a copying error in the 1844 edition: "which I have given *unto* you." The previous commentary concerning the similarities between sections 6, 11–12, and 14 apply to sections 15–16 as well.

COMMENTARY

2. With sharpness and with power. This is similar to what was said to Oliver Cowdery in Doctrine and Covenants 6:2, where the Lord's words are referred to as both "powerful" and "sharper than a two-edged sword."

2. Mine arm. This refers to God's ability to act or to perform what he intends. One's arm is often symbolic of one's strength, ability, or power.

3–4. Both John Whitmer and Peter Whitmer Jr. asked the Lord repeatedly and privately what he would have them do. Here the Lord reveals to them, as he did to Oliver Cowdery in section 6 and also anciently to Nathanael (see John 1:47–51), that he knows the thoughts of their hearts. In verse 6 they receive their answer.

5–6. John and Peter Whitmer are "blessed" for asking God what he desired of them and for speaking God's word according to the commandments they had already received from the Bible and perhaps from revelations through the Prophet Joseph. Their righteous efforts, even before they had gained a full knowledge of the Restoration, received God's approval and blessing. In the long run, that which will prove to be of "most worth" to them will be to preach the gospel of repentance and to bring souls to Christ. The same is true of all prospective missionaries.

6. Rest. The celestial kingdom is often referred to as a place of rest when the struggles of mortality are over, the contest with Satan and with our own carnal nature is won, and our place in the kingdom is secured.

The term *rest* is also used to refer to the state of being sealed up to exaltation in the celestial kingdom[1] and receiving God's oath that we shall inherit that kingdom, even while we remain in mortality. To see and converse with God while still in the flesh and receive his personal promise of exaltation would also, then, be considered entering "into his rest" (D&C 84:24).[2] Joseph Smith Translation Exodus 34:2 equates entering into God's presence with entering into his rest.

NOTES

1. See the commentary on D&C 68:12.
2. See the commentary on D&C 84:24.

DOCTRINE AND COVENANTS

17

BACKGROUND

As Joseph, Oliver, and their various helpers among the Whitmers and the Smiths approached completion of the translation of the Book of Mormon at the Whitmer farm in Fayette, they discovered through reading the words of Moroni in Ether 5:2–4 that there should be three special witnesses to the Book of Mormon in the latter days (see also 2 Nephi 11:3; 27:12). At that time, also, a repentant and somewhat chastened Martin Harris had come again from Palmyra to Fayette to see how the work was going. Because the Lord had already intimated that Martin Harris (see D&C 5:11–13, 24–28), Oliver Cowdery (see D&C 6:25–28), and David Whitmer (see D&C 14:8) might be witnesses to his work, those three individuals requested that Joseph inquire of the Lord if they might not be the Three Witnesses. Joseph inquired by the Urim and Thummim and received Doctrine and Covenants 17 in answer.[1] For some reason section 17 was not printed in the Book of Commandments in 1833 but was added to the 1835 edition of the Doctrine and Covenants (as were several other sections) from the *Kirtland Revelation Book,* a collection of revelations recorded in Kirtland during 1831–34, the early years there.

COMMENTARY

1. The witnesses were not to see just the Book of Mormon plates but also other artifacts associated with Book of Mormon history and used by the Nephites and Jaredites in Book of Mormon times: the breastplate, the sword of Laban, the Urim and Thummim, and the Liahona. This fact bears particular witness that it is not just the text or the doctrine of the book that is true, but the historical account of events as well. Not only did the witnesses know that the book was of God, they also knew that it was based on real history and real people who really did what the book claims they did, for they saw for themselves the artifacts associated with that history. Thus, the Testimony of Three Witnesses makes untenable any claim that the Book of Mormon may be inspired without being historical.

1. Urim and Thummim. The Urim and Thummim Joseph used to translate the Book of Mormon was the same one given to the brother of Jared (see Ether 3:28).

1. Miraculous directors. The Liahona (see 1 Nephi 16:10, 16; Alma 37:38).

3. You shall testify of them. With the opportunity to see the plates came the responsibility to bear witness of their truthfulness ever after. To partially fulfill this responsibility, the witnesses wrote and signed the statement that has been published with every authorized Book of Mormon since 1830. All three men also bore individual witness to the book and its message for the rest of their lives, though all three left the Church because of personal conflicts.[2] It should be noted, however, that two of these three witnesses (Oliver Cowdery and Martin Harris) eventually returned to full membership in the Church.

4. That my servant Joseph Smith, Jun., may not be destroyed. One purpose of having the Three Witnesses of the Book of Mormon and other miraculous elements was to spread the burden of testifying among several individuals and, thus, protect the Prophet Joseph from being the single focus of the wrath of the world. Whether the world accepts their testimonies or not,

God has always provided two or more witnesses to the truth of his work. In this way, the hearers are left without excuse should they reject the testimony of multiple witnesses (see D&C 42:80; Deuteronomy 17:6; Matthew 18:16).

6. As your Lord and your God liveth it is true. "You will never find another book in the world with that stamp of approval given by the Lord (except one, . . . and that is the Doctrine and Covenants)."[3] This does not mean the text is inerrant, for there might be printer's errors, copyists' errors, or other human errors, as there always are when humans are involved. Note, for example, the last paragraph in "A Brief Explanation about the Book of Mormon":[4] "Some minor errors in the text have been perpetuated in past editions of the Book of Mormon." The book itself, however, both in its historical claims and in its doctrines, remains true.

7. Same power. The Three Witnesses knew for themselves that the restored gospel is true on the same basis of direct empirical knowledge as the Prophet Joseph knew. Having first exercised sufficient faith, they received a witness beyond faith. Now they *knew.*

8. These last commandments. The commandments just delivered to them in Doctrine and Covenants 17:3–6.

8. My grace is sufficient. This is a doctrinal truth sometimes undervalued. Whatever other problems and difficulties we may encounter in life, if we hold on to Christ and to our covenants with him, his grace will prove sufficient to bring us into his kingdom.

8. Lifted up at the last day. This may refer either to the living, who will be caught up to meet the Lord on his return to this earth; to the "dead in Christ," who will be resurrected and raised up at that time (see 1 Thessalonians 4:15–17); or to the Lord's faithful Saints, who are to be exalted (a synonym for "lifted up") at the final judgment.

It might be well to append here accounts of the fulfillment of the Lord's promise to Oliver, David, and Martin (see vv. 1–2), which came at the end of June 1829. Joseph Smith and the Three

Witnesses had retired to a secluded spot in a pasture between two roads on the Whitmer farm.[6] After a period of prayer, Martin Harris, feeling unworthy, separated himself from the others.

David Whitmer recounted what then followed: "We not only saw the plates of the Book of Mormon but also the brass plates, the plates of the Book of Ether, the plates containing the records of the wickedness and secret combinations of the people of the world down to the time of their being engraved, and many other plates. . . . There appeared as it were, a table with many records or plates upon it, besides the plates of the Book of Mormon, also the Sword of Laban, the directors—i.e., the ball which Lehi had, and the Interpreters. I saw them just as plain as I see this bed (striking the bed beside him with his hand), and I heard the voice of the Lord, as distinctly as I ever heard anything in my life, declaring that the records of the plates of the Book of Mormon were translated by the gift and power of God." When asked if he saw the angel at that time, Brother Whitmer replied, "Yes; he stood before us, our testimony as recorded in the Book of Mormon is strictly and absolutely true, just as it is there written."[5] Joseph then left Oliver and David and found Martin Harris engaged in prayer, as he had previously been instructed by the Lord (see D&C 5:24). After joining him in prayer, Joseph and Martin had the heavens open and saw the same vision as the first two.[7]

Joseph's relief at not being the only one to carry the burden of knowing and testifying is reflected in the account written by his mother concerning his return to the house after the vision had been granted to the Three Witnesses. He exclaimed: "Father, mother, you do not know how happy I am: the Lord has now caused the plates to be shown to three more besides myself. They have seen an angel, who has testified to them, and they will have to bear witness to the truth of what I have said, for now they know for themselves, that I do not go about to deceive the people, and I feel as if I was relieved of a burden which was almost too heavy for me to bear, and it rejoices my soul, that I am not any longer to be entirely alone in the world."[8]

Shortly after the angel Moroni had shown the plates and the other Book of Mormon artifacts to the Three Witnesses, Joseph was instructed to show the plates to eight others. These men were shown the plates by Joseph and not by the angel, and they did not see the other artifacts, but their testimony is also published to the world at the front of the Book of Mormon and is called the Testimony of Eight Witnesses.

NOTES

1. See Smith, *History of the Church,* 1:52–53.
2. See Backman and Cowan, *Joseph Smith and the Doctrine and Covenants,* 22–24; Kirkham, *New Witness for Christ in America,* 1:247–54.
3. Tuttle, *Spirituality,* 8–9.
4. Found in the introduction to the current edition of the Book of Mormon.
5. Pratt and Smith, "Report of Elders Orson Pratt and Joseph F. Smith," 771–72.
6. See Smith, *History of the Church,* 1:54–55.
7. See Smith, *Church History and Modern Revelation,* 1:72–73.
8. Smith, *History of Joseph Smith,* 152.

18

BACKGROUND

Doctrine and Covenants 18 is closely associated with the restoration of the Melchizedek Priesthood. No actual record of that event has been preserved, however, and the exact date of the visit of Peter, James, and John to Joseph and Oliver is unknown. It is known that Joseph Smith and Oliver Cowdery received the Aaronic Priesthood on 15 May 1829 (see D&C 13) and that they left Harmony and moved to Fayette, New York, to stay with the Whitmer family around 29–30 May. Because the Melchizedek Priesthood was restored to Joseph and Oliver "in the wilderness [woods] between Harmony, Susquehanna county, and Colesville, Broome county, on the Susquehanna river" (D&C 128:20), it is likely that the restoration took place before 30 May, by which time Joseph and Oliver had left the area where it is reported to have occurred.[1] If this is correct, then the Melchizedek Priesthood was restored within about two weeks of the Aaronic Priesthood and before the move to Fayette, on 29–30 May, and the reception of section 18, sometime between 1–14 June. On 14 June 1829, Oliver Cowdery wrote a letter to Hyrum Smith, which indicates from its many parallels to section 18 that this revelation had already been received by that date.[2]

The dating suggested here is further supported by the order of events as listed in Doctrine and Covenants 128:20–21: *first* the visit of Peter, James, and John, *then* the voice of God in Father Whitmer's chamber.[3] Moreover, the Melchizedek Priesthood is necessary for bestowing the gift of the Holy Ghost and all other higher ordinances of the gospel. It was therefore necessary for this priesthood and its keys to be restored to earth before the Church could be organized in April 1830.

The revelation given at the Whitmer home occurred as follows. After arriving at the Whitmer's on 1 June, the Prophet and some of his associates gathered in prayer "when the word of the Lord came unto us in the chamber, commanding us that I should ordain Oliver Cowdery to be an Elder in the Church of Jesus Christ; and that he also should ordain me to the same office; and then to ordain others, as it should be made known unto us from time to time. We were, however, commanded to defer this our ordination until such times as it should be practicable to have our brethren, who had been and who should be baptized, assembled together, when we must have their sanction to our thus proceeding to ordain each other, and have them decide by vote whether they were willing to accept us as spiritual teachers or not; . . . The following commandment will further illustrate the nature of our calling to this Priesthood, as well as that of others who were yet to be sought after."[4]

Though not itself a part of the Doctrine and Covenants, this revelation, received in Father Whitmer's chamber in Fayette, New York, in June of 1829, is the same revelation referred to in Doctrine and Covenants 128:21, apparently having been received *after* the restoration of the Melchizedek Priesthood alluded to in Doctrine and Covenants 128:20. Following this revelation, Joseph received section 18, which directed him and Oliver in how to proceed in ordaining one another and also in ordaining other prospective elders.[5]

COMMENTARY

1. It is apparent from the language of verse 1 that Oliver Cowdery had asked a question to which the Lord was responding with this revelation, known as section 18. Oliver's actual question, however, was not recorded.

2–3. You know. After the many witnesses Oliver Cowdery had received, which are alluded to in Doctrine and Covenants 6:22–23; 13:1; 17:1, he certainly knew that what he had written as Joseph's scribe was true. Now he was commanded to rely upon what had been written. Modern Saints often ask the Lord to reveal directly to them information that is already available in the scriptures.

4–5. My church. This is only June of 1829, so the Church is not yet organized. Joseph, Oliver, and David, among others, were called to bring that organization about and were here given instructions on how to accomplish it.

4–5. My rock. See the commentary on Doctrine and Covenants 11:24.

6. One major purpose for restoring the gospel to the earth is to call the world, both the Gentiles and the house of Israel, to repentance.

7–8. The Lord pointed out to Oliver the unique mission of the Prophet Joseph Smith. In Hebrew, the name *Joseph* means "added." Joseph Smith is truly "Joseph"—the promised seer who would be an added blessing to the world in the latter days (see 2 Nephi 3:1–15), whose mission would add the fulness of the gospel to those who had only part of it, and to whose name glory will be added forever. Throughout the history of Israel, the name *Joseph* has been borne by choice servants of the Lord.

9. Repent. A call to repentance is not just a plea or a request of God. It is an ongoing commandment given to the greatest and to the least, to the righteous and to the wicked, to members of the Church and nonmembers alike.

9. Paul. The Apostle Paul did anciently what Oliver and David were about to do—take the gospel to the Gentiles. Theirs is the same calling as was Paul's in the meridian of time. This verse further reflects the fact that apostolic authority had already been given to Joseph, Oliver, and David at this time, June 1829.

According to Brigham Young, "Joseph Smith, Oliver Cowdery, and David Whitmer were the first Apostles of this dispensation, though in the early days of the Church David Whitmer lost his standing, and another took his place."[6]

10. Christ was willing to suffer an infinite agony to save our souls. If the Savior valued souls so highly, then so also must those who seek to be like him.

11–13. Christ provided the opportunity for repentance for us at an infinite personal cost. No doubt we underestimate the price the Lord paid to make repentance possible, and we similarly underestimate the joy he feels when we take advantage of his sacrifice and do repent. Simply put, God is on our side—he wants us to win. He willingly died so we could win, and we ought to value more than we do the infinitely costly gift of repentance.

11. He suffered the pains of all men. The agony of Jesus Christ in the garden and on the cross was at least as great as the combined suffering of all human beings.[7]

19. Faith, hope, and charity. These three virtues are not listed together or in this order by accident. Hope here does not mean "wishing" but rather "longing with anticipation." True faith in Christ leads us to expect and to long for our own exaltation according to his holy, unbreakable promises. The overwhelming realization of how much Christ has done for us at so great a cost to himself then creates in us a desire to share his great blessings with others. Thus, true faith leads to real hope, which leads to genuine charity, which is love.

According to Moroni 7:47, "Charity is the pure love of Christ." "Of Christ" may be understood either as a subjective or an objective genitive—that is, both as Christ's love for us and as our love for Christ as expressed to all those around us (see Matthew 25:34–40). Those who do not believe the promises of Christ—and thus do not expect to be exalted, or who have not been moved by his infinite love to love others in turn—cannot serve God effectively until they repent of their lack of faith, hope, and love.

20. Contend. To *contend* is to argue, fight, or "bash." We do not spread the gospel effectively by attacking other churches or by scripture bashing with their members, but rather by taking upon us "the name of Christ" and by speaking "the truth in soberness" (v. 21).

20. Church of the devil. No individual denomination should be singled out as *the* church of the devil. This phrase refers to anyone of any denomination—including the LDS Church—who loves darkness more than light.[8] Our enemies are not the Methodists, or the Baptists, or the Catholics, for there are many people among these denominations and all others who love light and seek to serve God as far as their understanding allows them. Our only enemy is wickedness—those who love darkness more than light and who serve the evil one. Those who attack other churches violate the Lord's command, as stated in this verse, and will not enjoy his Spirit. In fact, they run a great risk that by adopting Satan's methodology—in this case, argument and contention—they may themselves become members of the church of the devil.

21. Take upon you the name of Christ. We take Christ's name by being baptized. By taking his name we accept the obligation to represent in ourselves the character of Christ to the best of our ability—to do what he would do and to say what he would say.

22–25. This simple promise of the rewards of repenting, being baptized, and enduring is sometimes overlooked. Those who enter into the gospel covenant by repenting and being baptized are promised that they will be saved in the kingdom of God if they endure to the end. "To endure" in faith is to remain faithful to one's covenants. It does not mean to be sinless or perfect, but to remain loyal and committed. It is a comforting promise. The other side, of course, is that there is no *other* way, none other name, that will bring us to the same end, for the formalities and ordinances of being called, raised up, resurrected, and so forth, at the last day, all invoke the holy name of Jesus Christ. No other name will work.

27. The Twelve. It took six years for the instructions given in section 18 to be fully implemented concerning the organization of the Twelve. The Quorum of the Twelve was organized in February 1835. The Twelve must desire to take upon them the name of Christ "with full purpose of heart" (v. 27), must preach the gospel to "all the world" (vv. 28, 41), and must rely upon the grace of Christ with personal lives beyond reproach (see vv. 31, 43).

37. Search out the Twelve. The Twelve are to be special witnesses to all the world in much the same way that Oliver, David, and Martin Harris, the Three Witnesses to the Book of Mormon, were special witnesses to all the world. Thus, it is fitting that the first three "special witnesses" should search out the other twelve. Only Oliver and David are specified here, since Martin Harris's life was still not in order at this time (see D&C 19:15, 20), but in 1835 Joseph Smith directed that Martin should also assist in choosing the Twelve.

42. Years of accountability. This is the first mention in the Doctrine and Covenants of an age of accountability, which was later clarified by revelation to be eight years of age (see D&C 68:25; JST Genesis 17:11; see also D&C 20:71).

46. Cannot be saved. Those who have been given the greater blessings are also required to carry the greater responsibility. Those who have received the blessings that are "above all things" (v. 45) will surely not find salvation anywhere else if they then rebel against God.

NOTES

1. See Porter, "Dating the Restoration of the Melchizedek Priesthood," 5–10; Porter, "Restoration of the Priesthood," 3–7.
2. See Porter, "Dating the Restoration of the Melchizedek Priesthood," 7; Woodford, "Historical Development," 1:264–67.
3. In June 1829.

4. Smith, *History of the Church,* 1:60–62.
5. For an excellent compilation of documents relating to the restoration of the Melchizedek Priesthood, see Cannon, "Priesthood Restoration Documents," 162–207.
6. Young, *Journal of Discourses,* 6:320.
7. See Marion G. Romney, in Conference Report, Oct. 1969, 57.
8. See Robinson, "Warring against the Saints of God," 34–39.

DOCTRINE AND COVENANTS

19

BACKGROUND

During the summer of 1829, after the translation of the Book of Mormon was completed, Egbert B. Grandin, owner of the *Wayne County Sentinel* in Palmyra, New York, agreed to print five thousand copies of the book for three thousand dollars. On 25 August 1829, Martin Harris, who had repented of his previous sins and had subsequently received a vision of the angel and the plates to become one of the Three Witnesses of the Book of Mormon, put up 240 acres of his Palmyra farm as collateral to guarantee payment of the three thousand dollars. If the books sold, the proceeds would redeem Martin's note, but if they did not sell, portions of Martin's acreage would be sold at public auction until the debt to Grandin was satisfied.

Opposition to the Book of Mormon was intense even before its publication. During the winter of 1830, a man named Abner Cole had somehow gained access to the printer's copy of the manuscript and attempted to publish parts of it as installments in his newspaper, the *Reflector,* under the pseudonym of O. Dogberry; the first installment was printed on 2 January 1830. The *Reflector* was also printed in Palmyra on E. B. Grandin's press. Cole apparently hoped to profit from his literary theft and at the same time preempt sales of the real Book of Mormon when it appeared, but Joseph was able to stop this infringement of copyright by threatening legal action.[1] Then in March 1830, a large number of citizens in the Palmyra area held a mass meeting in opposition to the forthcoming book and mutually agreed to boycott it when released. These same citizens also applied pressure to Grandin, who, fearing the Smiths might not make good their debt if the boycott proved successful, stopped the printing.

When Martin Harris learned of the planned boycott, being aware he would lose his farm if the book didn't sell, he went to Joseph in Manchester, New York, and demanded a revelation from the Lord. Joseph Knight Sr. later gave this account of that meeting:

"He [Martin Harris] Came to us [Joseph Smith Jr. and Joseph Knight Sr.] and . . . says, 'The Books [Book of Mormon] will not sell for no Body wants them.' Joseph says, 'I think they will sell well.' Says he, 'I want a Commandment [a revelation].' 'Why,' says Joseph, 'fulfill what you have got.' 'But,' says he, 'I must have a Commandment.' Joseph put him off. But he insisted three or four times he must have a Commandment. . . .

"In the morning [the next day] he got up and said he must have a Commandment to Joseph and went home. And along in the after part of the Day Joseph and Oliver Received a Commandment which is in Book of Covenants"—Doctrine and Covenants 19.[2]

After receiving Doctrine and Covenants 19, Joseph and Martin, whose home was in Palmyra, visited Grandin in Palmyra and reassured him that their debt would be paid one way or the other. Consequently, the printing of the Book of Mormon resumed and was finished in March 1830. On 5 February 1831, the debt to the printer became due. Obedient to the Lord's command that he had received in section 19 (see vv. 32–35), on 7 April 1831 Martin sold off 151 of the mortgaged acres at twenty dollars per acre to satisfy the three thousand dollar debt owed E. B. Grandin. This amounted to a little over half of Martin's entire farm.[3]

Doctrine and Covenants 19 is one of the most important revelations we have dealing with repentance, the nature of hell, and the atonement of Christ. As one whose own life had recently been marked with sins and failures (see D&C 3:12–13), but who still desired to serve God, Martin Harris needed to understand the relationship between God's eternal judgments, individual repentance, and the atonement of Christ.

Most of the churches in Joseph Smith's day taught that the punishments of God last forever and that sinners will suffer endless burning in fire and brimstone. Martin had previously suffered the pain of losing the Spirit (see v. 20), and now the Lord informed him that his only choices, like ours, were to repent of his sins or to suffer judgment. The Lord clarified the doctrine of hell in section 19, however, by explaining that the condemned do not suffer *forever*, though the scriptures sometimes give that impression for the sake of increased effect (see v. 7).

COMMENTARY

1. Alpha and Omega. Alpha and omega are respectively the first and last letters of the Greek alphabet. We often refer to our own alphabet and say "from A to Z" when we wish to emphasize inclusiveness. Christ is both the beginning (the Creation) and the end (the Judgment) of our temporal existence, and he is the point of everything in between.

1. Redeemer. The word *redeem* comes from the Latin *re(d)-emo,* which means literally "buy back." Christ did not come to save the righteous who have never sinned (see Matthew 9:13; Moroni 8:8); he came to "buy back" with his own blood and suffering those who are entrapped in slavery to sin.

2–3. Jesus Christ subjected himself and his own will in all circumstances to the will of his Father in Heaven in order that he might eventually gain control over all things. Perfect power came to him only through perfect obedience, just as we receive spiritual power and authority only in accordance with our obedience (see D&C 121:34–37). Had Christ's obedience and submission to the will of the Father not been perfect, he could not have received the power and authority necessary to destroy Satan and his works and to judge everyone else according to their works. In eternity, only one without sin or rebellion himself has the moral right to sit in judgment over those who have sinned and will not repent.

3. The end of the world. The Hebrew word for "world" is *'olam,* meaning either, "world," "age," or "eternity." The end of the world is not the end of the physical *earth,* but the end of the telestial *world,* the fallen wicked state in which the earth now exists, or the telestial social *world* men have built *upon* the earth. Joseph Smith taught: "The end of the world is the destruction of the wicked, the harvest and the end of the world have an allusion directly to the human family in the last days, instead of the earth, as many have imagined."[4]

If we understand *'olam* correctly here as "age," then the "end of the world" could mean the end of an age, or era, or the end of one stage in the earth's progress. The period before the Fall was one age, the period after the Fall another, and the thousand years of the Millennium will be yet another "age" (*'olam*) in the overall history of the earth.

The "end of the world" can also refer to the end of a dispensation of the gospel when judgment comes to the wicked and their social "world" comes to an end. Thus, an "end of the world" took place in Noah's time and again in A.D. 70, when the social world of the Jews came to an end as the Roman general Titus destroyed Jerusalem and its temple. Among the Nephites, an "end of the world" came at the death of Christ (see 3 Nephi 8–10) and again about A.D. 421 when the Nephites were destroyed. The end of the world will also come in the future when those of this dispensation have had their chance to believe the gospel and repent and have become ripe for the judgments of God. That "end" will be both the end of our individual dispensation and the end of the telestial period of earth's existence. Yet the physical earth itself will continue on and will, in fact, receive again the glory it had in the Eden state, the paradisiacal world, before the fall of Adam and Eve (see Articles of Faith 1:10).

3. Last great day of judgment. This is an ambiguous phrase, for there is a last day of judgment for the present *telestial* "world" at Christ's second coming—when the wicked who are alive will be burned and when the righteous, both living and dead, will be raised up. The reference here, however, is probably to the *last* last day of judgment at the end of the millennial age, which is also the end of the earth's *terrestrial* existence or "age." This judgment is also known as the judgment from the great white throne (see Revelation 20:5–7, 11–15)—when all who have not previously been resurrected will be raised up and consigned finally either to some degree of glory or to outer darkness, and when the earth shall also receive its celestial glory.

4. Every man must repent or suffer. Justice is an eternal principle and will inevitably be satisfied in one of only two ways. Either we humans will repent and accept the suffering of Christ in our behalf, or we will suffer ourselves for our own sins. Christ "suffered and died for us, yet if we do not repent, all his anguish and pain on our account are futile."[5]

4–5. For I, God, am endless. . . . I revoke not the judgments. If God is without end, then his *final* judgment upon us must logically also be without end. For example, someone who is judged worthy of being resurrected with telestial glory will possess a telestial body and a telestial glory forever—thus the name "the *last* judgment"—just as those judged worthy of terrestrial or celestial glory will possess that type of body and that degree of glory forever. The judgment pronounced upon us at resurrection is endless and eternal in the classic sense. The pain and suffering for sin may stop, but the assignment of a lesser glory lasts forever.

6. Endless torment. This phrase for the suffering of the wicked is found elsewhere only in the Book of Mormon (see 2 Nephi 9:19, 26; 28:23; Jacob 6:10; Mosiah 3:25; 28:3; Moroni 8:21; see also Revelation 20:10). Here the Lord is probably clarifying a term known to Joseph and Martin from that as yet unpublished book rather than from the Bible. It is explained here as being a term not of duration—torment having no end—but a term of quality—the torment of condemnation by an endless God. Also, the verdict upon the wicked that consigns them to a lesser glory will indeed be endless; nevertheless *their pain stops with their resurrection.* Doctrine and Covenants 76:44 uses similar terms—everlasting punishment, endless punishment, eternal punishment—to describe the fate of those in Perdition after their final judgment.

In the Bible, forms of *'olam* in the Old Testament and also of its Greek equivalent *aion* ("age") in the New Testament have usually been translated as "eternal" or "for ever" when they as easily could have been translated "until the age," or "to the end of the age."[6] Modern readers uniformly understand "eternal" to mean forever and ever without end, but the ancient writers often actually wrote "until the end of the age" with a definite end in view. Thus, the wicked in hell do not suffer without an end, but only until the end of their time in the spirit "world" *('olam).* The end of the spirit "world" for the righteous comes with their resurrection at the *beginning* of the Millennium; for the wicked it comes with their resurrection at the *end* of the Millennium—the first and second resurrections, respectively (see 1 Thessalonians 4:15–17; Revelation 20:4–6). Therefore, linguistically as well as theologically speaking, "eternal" punishment is not punishment that never ends, but punishment that lasts to the end of the spirit "world" or the millennial "age" at resurrection.[7]

7. Eternal damnation. This phrase is found elsewhere in scripture only in Mark 3:29 and Doctrine and Covenants 29:44, where it is used concerning those who sin against the Holy Ghost and who will not repent either in this life or the next. Interestingly, *dammed* and *damned* are not two forms of the same word. *Damned* comes from the Latin *damnare,* "to inflict injury or loss," while *dam* comes from Old and Middle German, the hypothetical root being *dammjan,* "to hinder."[8] Damnation does not refer to stopping one's forward progress, as in "damming" a river. Rather, in the Bible it always translates from forms of the Greek *apoleia,* "destruction," or *krisis,* "judgment." Damnation is the "condemnation" received at judgment. Technically, *eternal* damnation, meaning eternal destruction or eternal condemnation, applies only to those who are cast into outer darkness after the Resurrection and who die the "second death." Perhaps the term is intended by its ambiguity to have an effect on the rest of us—it easily catches our attention and affects our hearts (see v. 7).

8, 10. Mystery. As used in scripture, the term *mystery* refers to that which can be known only by revelation.[9] Due to the ambiguity of previous scripture, without the information revealed in Doctrine and Covenants 19 we could never properly understand the phrases "endless punishment," "eternal punishment," or "endless torment."

9. My rest. See the commentary on Doctrine and Covenants 15:6.

10–12. Those who suffer in hell for their own sins in a sense pay an endless and eternal price, for their eventual assignment to telestial glory will never be changed or upgraded to celestial glory. They will never dwell again with their Heavenly parents, nor will they ever have spirit children of their own. Those options will be closed to them forever and ever. This is explicitly stated in Doctrine and Covenants 76:112, where we are told that telestial beings "shall be servants of the Most High; but where God and Christ dwell they cannot come, *worlds without end*"[10]—that is, no matter how many "ages" or "eons" are linked together. Nevertheless, their hell, or their suffering in the spirit world, does come to an end—after they have repented and turned to Christ—when they are resurrected and receive some degree of glory.

13, 15. I command you to repent. Repent, perhaps, of Martin's chronic doubt and apparent need for repeated assurance, which comes so close to asking for a sign.[11] If one refuses to repent in this life, he or she suffers the pains of hell in the spirit world. If one refuses to repent either in this life or in the spirit world, then at resurrection he or she remains "as though there had been no redemption made, except it be the loosing of the bands of death" (Alma 11:41). Those who are resurrected without repentance are "filthy still" (2 Nephi 9:16; D&C 88:35) and are not redeemed from the devil, but become his children (sons of perdition) to be cast out with him into outer darkness (see Alma 40:13; D&C 76:36–38; Revelation 20:15). This is the one and only context where "eternal damnation" is to be interpreted in its harshest sense of condemnation forever and ever. Everyone else is eventually saved in some kingdom of glory (see D&C 76:39, 43–44).

15. Smite you by the rod of my mouth. The rod or stick with which the unrepentant are metaphorically punished will be the guilty verdict pronounced justly upon them on the day of Judgment—whether for unrepentant mortals at the Second Coming, or for unrepentant spirits at the Resurrection—by the Lord's own mouth (compare 2 Nephi 21:4; Isaiah 11:4).

15. How sore you know not. The actual damage caused by our sins and the debt incurred by them is greater than we suspect, and the pains of hell suffered by the unrepentant between death and resurrection to meet that debt will be much worse than anything they ever encountered here in mortality. Though these pains are the natural consequences of our wrong choices while in the flesh, and though they are a fair and just penalty for our sins, the pain and suffering of hell will be so terrible that all but a few obdurate individuals will finally turn to Christ for redemption— cured forever of serving Satan or pursuing his lifestyle. Those who will not be taught or warned in this life must learn for themselves, through their own suffering, the horrible consequences of sin.

16. I, God. Christ is not only the Son of God; he is God the Son.

16–17. If they would repent. Christ has already suffered all the pains of hell to an infinite degree. If we will repent, his suffering will be accepted in our behalf as though it were our own, but unless and until we repent and accept his atonement, his suffering cannot help us.

17. They must suffer even as I. The wicked will not individually duplicate the experience of Christ in Gethsemane, for it would not be possible for them to suffer the infinite agony Christ suffered in the garden and upon the cross. Only the Son of God could suffer "both body and spirit" to an infinite degree (see v. 18). The unrepentant will, however, each suffer *for their own sins* as he suffered *for the sins of the world,* suffering exactly the same kind of anguish, but not to the same degree. Yet even a finite portion of his infinite agony is beyond our comprehension, and will likely be much, much worse than the unrepentant expect it to be.

Elder Dallin H. Oaks explained that "the person who repents does not need to suffer 'even as' the Savior suffered. Sinners who are repenting will experience some suffering, but, because of their repentance and the Atonement, they will not experience the full 'exquisite' extent of eternal torment the Savior suffered."[12]

18. The greatest of all. Jesus is God the Son, the greatest of all the spirit children of our Heavenly Father and the greatest of all human beings who have ever lived upon this earth or any other created through him.

18. Bleed at every pore. Just as grapes or olives are squeezed in a press until they give up their juice or oil, so Christ bore such an infinite weight of sin in Gethsemane that he, like the grapes and olives, was pressed until he bled through his skin at every pore (see Luke 22:44). *Gethsemane* in Aramaic means "the *press* of oil," a fitting name for the garden where Jesus was *pressed* like grapes or olives. The wine and oil that are produced by "pressing" are thus aptly symbolic of Christ's blood shed in Gethsemane through a similar process.

18. Both body and spirit. The wicked will suffer in spirit between death and resurrection, but only God the Son could suffer in *both* body and spirit to an infinite degree. Physical pain of this magnitude would have snuffed the life out of one who was not the literal Son of God with the divine gift to have life in himself (see John 5:26; Mosiah 3:7).

18. And would that I might not drink the bitter cup. *Would* here means "wish" or "desire." The reference is to Jesus' prayer in the garden: "Abba, Father, all things are possible unto thee; take away this cup from me" (Mark 14:36). The bitter cup here symbolizes the sins and evils of the world, Jesus' infinite agony in

Gethsemane, and his death on the cross. As he realized the enormity of what he was about to suffer, even Christ hesitated, saying, "O my Father, if it be possible, let this cup pass from me: nevertheless not as I will, but as thou wilt."

Elder James E. Faust wrote: "It was not physical pain, nor mental anguish alone, that caused Him to suffer such torture as to produce an extrusion of blood from every pore; but a spiritual agony of soul such as only God was capable of experiencing. . . .

"In some manner, actual and terribly real though to man incomprehensible, the Savior took upon Himself the burden of the sins of mankind from Adam to the end of the world."[13]

18. And shrink. This term does not refer to Jesus' size or indicate that Jesus would grow physically smaller if he drank the bitter cup. Rather, faced finally with full realization of the agony awaiting him, even Christ (1) wished to avoid it—"would that I might not drink"—and (2) shrank from it—that is, at first he hesitated or drew back.

19. My preparations. Christ performed his part in the implementation of the plan of salvation, which required his infinite suffering and atoning sacrifice.

20. Even in the least degree. When Martin Harris lost the 116 pages of the Book of Mormon through his own sinful conduct, he experienced the loss of the Spirit and alienation from God, just as the rest of us do when we sin. The darkness, despair, depression, and hopelessness of being cut off from God and left to our sinful selves in this world is just the tiniest fraction of what Jesus suffered in Gethsemane or what we will feel if we are cut off from God and left to ourselves and to the power of Satan in this world and in the spirit world to come.

21. Preach naught but repentance. In the scriptures "repentance" is often used to indicate the whole process of entering the gospel covenant. It should not be assumed that repentance without faith in Christ, baptism, and receiving the gift of the Holy Ghost would be sufficient for salvation. Repentance as used here means to change one's life in accordance with God's will, to stop doing wrong and start doing right. Such a change in one's orientation, if sincere, naturally includes coming to Christ and entering or renewing his covenant.

21. Show not these things. This means do not reveal for now the mysteries just received in Doctrine and Covenants 19 concerning the temporary nature of "endless punishment" and so on. The world around Joseph and Martin, steeped in traditions about hell as an endless furnace, was not yet ready to be taught such things, nor are these the proper principles with which to begin instruction in the gospel to nonmembers.

22. Lest they perish. Notice that the reason for holding back some deeper truths at this time is God's loving concern for those who are not yet ready to receive them. Only a testimony of the basics of the gospel can prepare the hearts of human beings to receive further light. To teach the more profound doctrines or the mysteries of the gospel (see v. 10) to those who are not yet prepared to receive them by a testimony of the basics is to do them an injury. This is a mistake sometimes made by well-meaning friends, relatives, and missionaries, for it distracts from the crucial message of faith, repentance, baptism, and receiving the Holy Ghost.

25. It is unclear whether this commandment was meant in its original context specifically for Martin in his own personal situation, or for the whole Church generally, or both.

26. Covet thine own property. To consecrate our resources to the Lord and then renege on our promise out of desire for the possessions themselves, or even to give them up but to do so grudgingly or with great regret, is coveting what has been consecrated to God—even though it may still legally belong to us. The New Testament provides the example of Ananias and Sapphira, who covenanted to sacrifice everything for the kingdom if necessary, but then, coveting their own property, withheld part of their consecration from the Lord and lied to Peter to hide that fact (see Acts 5:1–11). No one forces us to consecrate ourselves or our property to the Lord, but once we have done so of our own free will, those possessions have in principle become his, and we must not covet them back.

27. Gentile. The familiar phrase, "every nation, kindred, tongue, and people" (see Revelation 14:6) refers to the Gentiles and the heathen nations (see D&C 45:54; 90:10). The Gentiles make up all the nations of the earth *except* Israel. This present dispensation of the gospel includes the "fulness of the Gentiles" (JS–H 1:41; 1 Nephi 15:13) or the "times of the Gentiles" (see D&C 45:28) when, because of Israel's apostasy in past dispensations, the gospel is to be taken to the Gentiles—to every nation, kindred, tongue, and people.

Because so many different groups of Israelites have been scattered to the four corners of the earth over the last three thousand years, it is likely that by now most of the world's people have at least some minute trace of Israelite blood in their veins. These persons are still called Gentiles because they are not Jews and because they are descended *predominantly* from Gentile blood lines. Yet they are also sometimes referred to in the Church as "Israel" because they are descended in part from Abraham and will ultimately be grafted back into that natural olive tree, which is the house of Israel.[14] Just as someone today might be a direct descendent of Julius Caesar without being Italian, so billions of people in today's world are descended from Abraham without being Israelites. As the seed of Abraham, these persons are heirs of the promises given that patriarch—even though they may be culturally, politically, and for the most part, biologically Gentiles.

On the other hand, it is possible, even likely, that some Saints in this dispensation, like the Prophet Joseph Smith for example, might actually have a majority of Israelite ancestors and be of *predominantly* Israelite descent, though scripture still refers to such persons as "Gentiles" (see 3 Nephi 21:6; 26:8).

The restoration of the gospel through Joseph Smith was the beginning of the times of the Gentiles (see D&C 45:28). Most present members of the Church are ethnically and genetically Gentiles even though they may also be descended in some line of their genealogy from Abraham and therefore possess some of the blood of Israel.[15]

The Book of Mormon was, according to its title page, written in part for the Gentiles—for ourselves and those with whom we share the gospel—that they might be taught the gospel from its pages in the latter days, the times of the Gentiles (see D&C 109:60; 1 Nephi 13–15; 3 Nephi 21:6[16]). According to Elder Orson F. Whitney, "The name Gentile is not with us a term of reproach. It comes from Gentilis, meaning of a nation, a family or a people not of Israel."[17]

27. Jew. The term *Jew* in its strictest sense refers to a member of the tribe of Judah. After the fall of the Northern Kingdom of Israel to the Assyrians in 722–23 B.C., however, *Jew* was also used to mean Israelites of other tribes. For example, all Jewish priests were of the tribe of Levi, and Paul and others were of Benjamin, yet they are all called Jews in the Bible. The Book of Mormon, written after 722–23 B.C., likewise uses the term *Jew* to mean any member of the house of Israel (see 1 Nephi 15:20).

Also, since the Mulekites were specifically from the tribe of Judah, and since they actually outnumbered the Nephites in the city of Zarahemla, their combined descendants might rightly be called Jews in the literal, genealogical sense (see Mosiah 25:2; Helaman 6:10; 8:21).

28. Pray vocally. Church members are commanded to pray aloud and in the hearing of others, as well as privately within themselves. Perhaps vocal, public prayer sometimes requires more emotional investment and commitment from the believer than does silent, private prayer.

29. Glad tidings. These tidings are, of course, the good news of the gospel. "Publish" is used here in the archaic sense of "make available" by any medium, not just in print.

30. Reviling not against revilers. Those who attack the attackers of the Church do so in violation of this commandment. Anti-Mormons can be vicious, but adopting their methods and tactics to become *anti*-anti-Mormons is not compatible with gospel principles.[18]

31. Of tenets thou shalt not talk. *Tenets* are the fine points of theology, and discussing them or arguing about them is fruitless in missionary situations. One may learn more intellectually about the faith of others in this manner, but Martin was to share his *testimony,* not his information or his intellect. He was to be a missionary, not a theologian. Conversion to the gospel seldom comes as a result of discussing the fine points of theology.

32. The last commandment. Martin Harris had demanded a commandment, or revelation, on this matter, and here he gets it— the last revelation that will be addressed directly and exclusively to him in the Doctrine and Covenants. Martin is commanded to restrict himself for the rest of his life to declaring the basic message of the Restoration and to leave theology alone. As Joseph Smith taught, "After all that has been said, the greatest and most important duty is to preach the Gospel."[19] As a special witness to the Book of Mormon, Martin's duty to bear witness of the Restoration was even greater than that of some others. If he ignored the Lord's counsel in these matters, he would both lose his property and suffer misery.

In the matter of Martin's immediate concern, the possible loss of his property, the Lord commanded him to sell what he did not need for the support of his family and to pay the debt to the printer. This was a great sacrifice to ask of him, considering it was not Martin's understanding at the beginning of the project that the publishing costs would come out of his pocket. Originally, payment of the printing costs was supposed to come from the proceeds of book sales, and Martin's property merely guaranteed payment should the book not sell as expected. Eventually, the book did "sell well," as Joseph Smith is quoted as saying in the account of Joseph Knight Sr. but not in time to save Martin's farm. It should be noted that Martin later claimed he got all his money back and more.[20] It is a tribute to Martin that he did as the

Lord commanded him and settled the entire debt out of his own pocket.

35. Release thyself from bondage. Whether with sin or with money, debt is bondage, and to pay our debts is to find freedom. To the extent that we are able, we should owe no one but the Lord. Martin's debt, though incurred for the Lord, is nevertheless his; he had to sacrifice his property and pay his debt in order to be free of it.

36–37. Martin was called on a mission to preach the gospel.

37. Hosanna, blessed be the name of the Lord. *Hosanna* is a compound Hebrew word, a *hiphil* imperative, meaning "save now." It is often associated with the arrival of the Lord at his temple, whether Jesus' triumphal entry into Jerusalem to visit the temple there, or the arrival of the divine presence at a temple dedication in the modern Church. We might also shout "hosanna" whenever the word, Spirit, or presence of God is manifested among us.

"The name of the Lord," or "the name of the Most High God," is Jesus Christ (see also 3 Nephi 11:17). This name is blessed because this is the name by which all things are done for our salvation and exaltation. It is the power of Jesus' name that makes all prayers, ordinances, and performances valid, and anything that is to reach or last beyond this telestial world must be done, asked, or sealed in the name of Jesus Christ, the Son of God.[21]

40. Those who will not repent (see v. 15), make sacrifices for the kingdom (see vv. 34–35), pray (see vv. 28, 38), humble themselves and be wise and meek (see v. 41), or follow counsel (see v. 33) are, like Martin Harris was before his repentance, blind guides unable to find their own way or to lead others correctly in spiritual things.

NOTES

1. See Smith, *History of Joseph Smith,* 164–66.
2. Jessee, "Joseph Knight's Recollection," 37.

3. See Bushman, *Joseph Smith and the Beginnings of Mormonism,* 107–8; Gunnell, "Martin Harris—Witness and Benefactor," 97–100.
4. Smith, *History of the Church,* 2:271.
5. Kimball, *Miracle of Forgiveness,* 145.
6. See Commentary on D&C 19:3.
7. See Robinson, "Eternities That Come and Go," 1, 4.
8. See *New American Standard Dictionary,* s.v. *dam* and *damn.*
9. See the commentary on D&C 8:11.
10. Emphasis added.
11. See Background.
12. Oaks, "Sin and Suffering," 149.
13. Talmage, *Jesus the Christ,* 613.
14. See the commentary on D&C 64:36.
15. "Blood of Israel" is not a scriptural term and should be used with caution.
16. Here the resurrected Christ described members of the latter-day Church as Gentiles.
17. In Conference Report, Apr. 1928, 59.
18. See the commentary on D&C 18:20.
19. Smith, *Teachings,* 113.
20. See Gunnell, "Martin Harris—Witness and Benefactor," 40.
21. See the commentary on D&C 20:37.

20

BACKGROUND

Concerning the period following the restoration of the priesthood in 1829 and the organization of the Church in 1830, the Prophet Joseph Smith wrote: "In this manner did the Lord continue to give us instructions from time to time, concerning the duties which now devolved upon us; and among many other things of the kind, we obtained of Him the following [section 20], by the spirit of prophecy and revelation; which not only gave us much information, but also pointed out to us the precise day upon which, according to His will and commandment, we should proceed to organize His Church once more here upon the earth."[1]

In the months prior to 6 April 1830, and probably as early as late 1829, Joseph and Oliver had been writing down their various instructions from the Lord concerning the duties of Church members. An early draft of Doctrine and Covenants 20 was written in late 1829 by Oliver Cowdery and ends with the notation, "Written in the year of our Lord & Saviour 1829—A True Copy of the articles of the Church of Christ. O.C."[2]

Public sale of the Book of Mormon began on 26 March 1830. Eleven days later on Tuesday, 6 April 1830, following express instructions of the Lord received in the section 20 material, Joseph Smith and Oliver Cowdery, together with Hyrum Smith, David

Whitmer, Samuel Smith, and Peter Whitmer Jr., organized the Church of Christ according to the laws of the state of New York. The restored Church was officially called The Church of Christ at its incorporation in 1830. In 1834 the name of the Church was changed to The Church of the Latter Day Saints,[3] and finally, on 26 April 1838, the name of the Church was changed by revelation to The Church of Jesus Christ of Latter-day Saints (see D&C 115:4). Since the presidency of Harold B. Lee, the initial letter *T* is always capitalized: *The* Church of Jesus Christ of Latter-day Saints.

According to Joseph Smith, the initial organization of the Church took place in Fayette, New York, at the Whitmer home where Joseph and Oliver were then staying.[4] "Whilst the Book of Mormon was in the hands of the printer, we still continued to bear testimony and give information, as far as we had opportunity; and also made known to our brethren that we had received a commandment to organize the Church; and accordingly we met together for that purpose, at the house of Mr. Peter Whitmer, Sen., (being six in number,) on Tuesday, the sixth day of April, A.D., one thousand eight hundred and thirty."[5]

Doctrine and Covenants 20, which is made up largely of revelatory material received before the Church was organized, was known to the early Church as the articles and covenants of the Church of Christ. It was the first summary statement of the history, doctrines, policies, and procedures of the Church. The first printed version of sections 20 and 22, in the Painesville *Telegraph* on 19 April 1831, listed section 20 alone as the articles and covenants. Section 22 had a different heading. The first edition of the Doctrine and Covenants, the 1833 Book of Commandments, also excluded section 22 from the articles and covenants by printing section 22 first with its own, separate heading, followed by section 20, which alone was called the articles and covenants. Section 22 was included with section 20 under the heading of articles and covenants of the Church in the June 1832 *The Evening and the Morning Star,* but this evidence must be judged weaker than the combined witness of the Painesville *Telegraph,* the Book of Commandments, and other early witnesses.[6] Robert J. Woodford and Dean C. Jessee also appear to identify section 20 alone as the articles and covenants.[7]

At the first conference of the Church held in Fayette, New York, on 9 June 1830, Doctrine and Covenants 20 was read to the members and unanimously sustained as the articles and covenants of the Church of Christ, thus making it the first revelation of this dispensation to be formally presented to and sustained by the members. Over the next few years section 20 was revised and expanded several times to reflect additional revelation to Joseph Smith about the unfolding structure of the Church. For example, verses 66–67, concerning high priests, were added after the office of high priest was established by revelation in 1831.

As the articles and covenants of the Church of Christ, section 20 has often been referred to as the Constitution of the Restored Church and, together with section 22 and part of section 27, was sometimes referred to as part of the Mormon Creed.[8] Certainly, this section served as the first priesthood manual or handbook for the Church, and it was read verbatim to the members at many early Church conferences. Section 20, the articles and covenants of the Church of Christ, along with sections 21–22, are foundation documents for the organization of the restored Church.

COMMENTARY

1. Being one thousand eight hundred and thirty years. Many have taken this reference to be a literal count of the years from the birth of Jesus to the organization of the Church. On 6 April 1833, the third anniversary of that organization, Joseph Smith himself wrote, "The day was spent in a very agreeable manner, in giving and receiving knowledge which appertained to this last kingdom—it being just 1800 years since the Savior laid down his life that men might have everlasting life, and only three years since the Church had come out of the wilderness, preparatory for the last dispensation."[9]

On the other hand, several writers, including some modern apostles and prophets, have urged caution in interpreting Doctrine and Covenants 20:1 as an exact count of years. Among these are Hyrum M. Smith, J. Reuben Clark Jr., and Bruce R. McConkie.[10]

It is possible that the "one thousand eight hundred and thirty years" is just an elaborate way of referring to the year 1830 without being intended as an actual count of years.[11] Elder McConkie's summation is helpful, "We do not believe it is possible with the present state of our knowledge—including that which is known both in and out of the Church—to state with finality when [i.e., in which year] the natal day of the Lord Jesus actually occurred."[12]

1. Agreeable to the laws. This likely refers in particular to an 1813 New York statute entitled "an act to provide for the incorporation of Religious Societies," which stated that between three and nine individuals must be listed as members and responsible parties in the foundation documents of any religious organization.[13] In this verse, and again in Doctrine and Covenants 44:4–5 and 58:22, the Lord explicitly instructs the Church to observe the laws of the land.

1. Sixth day of . . . April. At least two Presidents of the Church, Harold B. Lee and Spencer W. Kimball, have affirmed that 6 April is the actual birthday of the Savior as well as the anniversary of the organization of the Church.[14] Apparently, the actual day of Christ's birth is more certain than the actual year.

2. Ordained an apostle. The wording here, particularly the use of the past tense, clearly implies that Joseph and Oliver had received both the Melchizedek Priesthood and the apostolic keys *before* the organization of the Church. Even in 1829, Oliver Cowdery had by commandment written down a revelation foreshadowing Doctrine and Covenants 20, in which he declared himself "an Apostle of Jesus Christ."[15] Moreover, the language of John the Baptist as recorded in Joseph Smith–History, and which is clearly reflected in Doctrine and Covenants 20:2–3, seems to imply that Joseph and Oliver would be ordained to the Melchizedek Priesthood, and that only then would Joseph "be called the first Elder of the Church, and he (Oliver Cowdery) the second" (JS–H 1:72). We know positively that Joseph and Oliver already had the Melchizedek Priesthood by September 1830 from Doctrine and Covenants 27:12: "And also with Peter, and James, and John, whom I have sent unto you, by whom I have ordained you and confirmed you to be apostles."[16]

2. First Elder. This is a Church administrative designation and does not refer to a special office in the priesthood. Joseph and Oliver were already Apostles and thereby also elders (see v. 38). In exercising their authority as Apostles and elders, Joseph was to have administrative precedence over Oliver. Their designation as first and second elders had nothing to do with the sequence of their ordination, but rather with their authority. In the infancy of the Church there was no First Presidency, only a first and second elder who held the keys of the apostleship.

5. Truly manifested. This happened during Joseph's first vision (see JS–H 1:28–30 for expanded explanation).

5. Entangled again in the vanities. In other words, Joseph was a normal teenager. After his vision, he made the same kinds of "foolish errors" teenagers often make, though he said, "no one need suppose me guilty of any great or malignant sins" (JS–H 1:28).

6. By an holy angel. The angel Moroni.

7. Gave unto him commandments. Read the longer account in Joseph Smith–History 1:33–42.

8. The means which were before prepared. The Urim and Thummim.

9. Fulness of the gospel. "The fulness of the gospel" was a much narrower and more limited phrase in the early Church and in its scriptures than it has become in contemporary LDS usage. The correct meaning of the phrase varies according to the knowledge of those who use it. In scripture the Lord defines his gospel, strictly speaking, as faith in the Lord Jesus Christ, repentance, baptism by immersion for the remission of sins, and the laying on of hands for the gift of the Holy Ghost (see Articles of

Faith 1:4; D&C 33:10–13; 39:6; 3 Nephi 27:19–21). The Book of Mormon is a mighty witness of these principles, containing more information on them—including how the ordinances are to be performed—than even the Bible has. Thus, the Book of Mormon contains the fulness of the gospel. "That does not mean it contains every teaching, every doctrine ever revealed. Rather, it means that in the Book of Mormon we will find the fulness of those doctrines required for our salvation."[17]

Though it is common for contemporary Saints to use the phrase "fulness of the gospel" to mean *all* that the Lord has revealed to us in the latter days up to the present time, the Book of Mormon and the Doctrine and Covenants use the term to refer only to the first principles, to the basic "good news" of Christ—consisting of faith, repentance, baptism by immersion, and receiving the gift of the Holy Ghost. For example, while the Doctrine and Covenants solidly affirms here and again at Doctrine and Covenants 27:5 that the Book of Mormon already contains the fulness of the gospel, it is self-evident that the Book of Mormon does *not* contain the many wonderful things revealed to the Saints after 1830, including a knowledge of the degrees of glory, celestial marriage, and vicarious work for the dead. In October of 1831, William E. McLellin was blessed "for receiving mine everlasting covenant, even the fulness of my gospel" (D&C 66:2). Yet section 66 was received in 1831, long before many of the higher principles and ordinances, such as the ordinances of the temple, for example, had been revealed to the Saints.

As *gospel* means "good news," so the *fulness* of the gospel refers to the full message of redemption in Jesus Christ—redemption from the fall of Adam and its effects through the atonement of Christ. Those doctrines, principles, and ordinances necessary to remedy the effects of the Fall and restore us to the celestial kingdom of God constitute the fulness of the gospel in the technical, scriptural sense. After the publication of the Book of Mormon, however, there continued to be great and important revelations to the Saints about the nature of God's kingdom. They learned about degrees of glory (see D&C 76), salvation for the dead (see D&C 128), exaltation in the celestial kingdom, and celestial marriage (see D&C 131–32). They also received those higher ordinances that would take them beyond mere redemption from the Fall and would lead them to become as their heavenly parents are.

Because it has, understandably, become common practice in the modern Church to use the phrase "fulness of the gospel" to mean all that God has revealed,[18] students and teachers of the Doctrine and Covenants should be aware of the distinctions between the scriptural and the contemporary usage and the possible ambiguities involved.[19]

9. To the Gentiles. In this dispensation, which includes the times of the Gentiles, the Book of Mormon and the gospel are to go to the Gentiles first and then to the Jews. This order of things fulfills the ancient declaration that "the last [the Gentiles] shall be first, and the first [the Jews] shall be last" (1 Nephi 13:42; Luke 13:30).

10. Confirmed to others. To the Three Witnesses and the Eight Witnesses of the Book of Mormon.

11. Proving . . . the holy scriptures are true. Often members of the Church will use portions of the Bible, Isaiah for example, in an attempt to interpret the Book of Mormon, or to prove its truth. This is backwards, however; the Lord's intent is just the opposite. It is the Book of Mormon that proves the Bible is true and that provides the keys by which the Bible should be interpreted. For example, though some biblical scholars deny that Jesus himself could have composed or taught the Sermon on the Mount,[20] the Book of Mormon shows that Jesus did (see 3 Nephi 12–14). Though scholars theorize that much of the book of Isaiah was not written by Isaiah but by other writers after the Babylonian conquest in 588–87 B.C.,[21] the Book of Mormon shows this theory to be false. Because Lehi left with the brass plates before the fall of Jerusalem, and because the brass plates at that time already contained a nearly complete copy of Isaiah, if the Book of

Mormon is true, then Isaiah cannot have been written after 600 B.C.

The way in which the Book of Mormon "proves" the Bible true is not scientifically or empirically but with the logic of the Spirit, for if a person learns by the Spirit's witness that the Book of Mormon is true, then he or she also knows that the Bible, of which the Book of Mormon testifies, is true.

Also, the very existence of the Book of Mormon testifies to the world that the heavens are still open and that the Lord of Heaven who spoke to prophets and apostles anciently continues to do so today. He is still the same—yesterday, today, and forever. If humanity is not receiving revelation from God, it isn't because God has changed his mode of operation. Alone among contemporary denominations, the LDS Church, with its belief in modern revelation to apostles and prophets, is consistent with the Old and New Testaments in this respect.

13. So great witnesses. These witnesses are Joseph Smith, the Three and the Eight Witnesses, the Bible, and the testimony of the Book of Mormon itself.

14. Receive it in faith, and work righteousness. Note the importance of both faith and works to those who accept the gospel—faith to enter and begin, and work to remain and grow in the covenant.

14. Crown of eternal life. This implies exaltation in the celestial kingdom. Servants do not wear crowns; only rulers do.

16. The elders of the church. Joseph Smith and Oliver Cowdery, the first and second elders.

17–36. These verses contain a brief statement of the plan of salvation to the extent that it had been revealed to Joseph and Oliver by 1830, along with a short discussion of the basics of the gospel: faith, repentance, baptism, and receiving the Holy Ghost. They also affirm the essential doctrines of justification, sanctification, and grace. The statement proceeds very much like a sort of creed dealing with the same issues and sometimes even in the same language as non-LDS creeds of the day.[22]

17. By these things. By the Book of Mormon and the many witnesses to its truthfulness enumerated in verses 8–16.

17. Infinite . . . unchangeable. Because Latter-day Saints believe in a God with a physical body (see D&C 130:22), we are often accused of believing in a "finite" God, but this statement in the Articles and Covenants of the Church is unequivocal—God is infinite, eternal, and unchangeable. In fact, it is the God of traditional Christianity, who no longer reveals his will to apostles or prophets, who seems rather to have changed from the biblical pattern.

18. Note that Eve as much as Adam is created in the image of God; therefore the use of *God* has a slightly different significance in connection with the Creation than it does in most other contexts. The First Presidency, in 1925, declared, "All men and women are in the similitude of the universal Father and Mother, and are literally sons and daughters of Deity."[23] This may be one of several reasons for the plural noun form *Elohim* in the Hebrew word for God.

19. And gave unto them. The fulness of the gospel was given to Adam and Eve, who taught it to their children (see Moses 5).

19. The only living and true God. If death is the separation of spirit and body, then a truly *living* God is a God, like the Father or like Jesus Christ, who has been resurrected. In this vein, some early Christian literature reserves the phrase "the living Jesus" for the resurrected Christ.[24]

20. It should be noted that man became devilish by transgression, and that we possessed a different nature prior to that transgression that was *not* carnal, sensual, and devilish. Our fallen self with its carnal nature is a temporary, sin-caused aberration. The atonement of Christ restores us to our true and original nature.

22. He suffered temptations. Jesus suffered all the temptations associated with mortality; every temptation we encounter, he encountered. The great difference between us is that when he suffered temptations, Jesus "gave no heed," that is, paid no attention to them (see Hebrews 2:17–18; 4:15; Alma 7:11–12). He was perfectly righteous because of his moral strength in overcoming temptation—not because he never experienced genuine temptation.

25. Be baptized . . . and endure. All who enter the gospel covenant through faith, repentance, baptism, and receiving the Holy Ghost, and who then remain committed and faithful, are assured of salvation in the celestial kingdom of God.

26. The meridian of time. Not necessarily the chronological middle of the earth's temporal existence, but rather the spiritual middle. It is the point that everything before looks ahead to, and that everything after looks back at—the high point in the earth's temporal existence. Just as everything before noon is ante meridian, or A.M., and everything after noon is post meridian, or P.M., so the atonement of Christ is the reference point in time, like noon, that determines the before and after of all things.

26–27. The atonement of Christ was infinite in its scope and nature and blessed not just those who lived after his ascension, but all who have accepted or who will accept the gospel from Adam's time on down to the end of the earth's millennial existence.

28. One God. The term *God* is used here and in many other scriptures in the sense of Godhead, meaning the Father, Son, and Holy Ghost together. In this sense, how many Gods are there? Only one. It is true we believe there is more than one divine being, but they are united. If the Son and the Holy Ghost were not obedient to the Father, or if they deviated from being one with him in mind, thought, and purpose, they would cease to be divine (see Alma 42:13, 22, 25). Even those mortals who are to be exalted and become "as gods" will do so only in a subordinate sense to the degree that they become obedient to and one with the Father, Son, and Holy Ghost. Thus, Latter-day Saints believe in one God(head) consisting of three divine beings, two of whom depend on their perfect oneness with the Father for their divine status (see D&C 93:3).[25]

29. Worship the Father in His name. See the commentary on Doctrine and Covenants 93:19 for a discussion of true and correct worship.

30. Justification. *Justification* is a judicial or legal term, and it means being acquitted or being declared innocent of all charges. Though all of us make mistakes in this life, we may, with repentance and baptism, and thereafter as long as we stay in the gospel covenant, still be declared innocent of all sin, not because of our own perfect performance—which no one has!—but because of Christ's perfect performance and his willingness to share it with us. We are justified or declared innocent before God by the sacrifice of Christ (see Romans 5:9), and our acquittal or victory at the bar of justice is received only through reliance upon the merits of Christ (see D&C 3:20; 76:53, 60–61; 2 Nephi 31:19; Alma 22:14).[26]

It would be an error to define the specific agents of justification or sanctification too narrowly. The scriptures describe us variously as being justified by Christ,[27] by faith,[28] by grace,[29] by works,[30] by Christ's blood,[31] and by the Spirit.[32]

Likewise, scripture describes us variously as being *sanctified* by Christ,[33] by the grace of God,[34] by the truth,[35] by the word of God,[36] by God the Father,[37] by law,[38] by water,[39] by the Holy Spirit,[40] and by blood.[41] Thus, while it is clear that justification and sanctification are true and essential principles, we should not try to define too narrowly the means by which they are gained.

Here in Doctrine and Covenants 20:30, the Lord himself affirms that the worthiness we seek in order to enter the kingdom comes to us only through Christ and because of his merits, mercy, and grace (compare 2 Nephi 2:5–8). This is both a just and a true principle. It is *just* because Christ satisfied the demands of justice that someone pay for our sins, and it is also true (see Ephesians 2:5, 8; 2 Nephi 10:24; Ether 12:27; Moses 7:59).

31. Sanctification. To be made holy, to become Saints. When we have been rendered innocent by being justified through the grace of Christ by baptism, we are then worthy to receive the actual companionship of God in the person of the Holy Ghost. Receiving the Holy Ghost does not just make us clean; it also makes us *holy*—that is sanctified (see 3 Nephi 27:20). For this reason all who have received the gift of the Holy Ghost are referred to collectively as "the Saints," meaning "the holy ones." Through faith in Christ, repentance, baptism, and receiving the gift of the Holy Ghost we are first rendered innocent (justified) and then we are made holy (sanctified), and may be called Saints, "the holy ones." Because we have received this blessing in the latter days, we are called *Latter-day* Saints, a collective term for those in our dispensation who have been justified and sanctified by the grace of Christ and who now work to endure faithfully to the end.

31. To all those who love and serve. Sanctification does not, however, come to everyone who is confirmed simply as an automatic result of the ordinance being performed. Only those who truly love and serve the Lord, who have received the ordinance with sincere intent, will actually be sanctified by the Spirit and truly become Saints (see v. 34).

32. Fall from grace. As wonderful as the gifts of being justified and sanctified are, we may fall from grace after receiving them if we "depart from the living God." For once justified and sanctified by the gift of God, we are then obligated to serve him "with all [our] mights, minds, and strength" (v. 31). Getting into the covenant by grace is easy, but staying in it takes commitment, willingness, and effort. We enter the covenant by faith in Christ and by his grace, but we endure to the end by continuing to serve and obey him. If we refuse to serve God, withhold our loyalty, or renege on our covenants, we can "fall" from the grace by which we were justified and sanctified when we first came to Christ.

Christians who follow the teachings of John Calvin deny the possibility of "falling from grace," insisting instead on the "perseverance of the Saints" (once saved always saved). This is a major difference between Latter-day Saints and Calvinist Christians. We as members of the Church sometimes get confused and insist that coming into the covenant requires works, which, if we perform well, God will then reward with grace. But this is backwards. Entering the covenant requires faith and grace; *staying* in it, enduring to the end and not falling from grace already received, requires work as well.

34. Even . . . those who are sanctified. Exactly who among the total membership of the Church have actually been sanctified is clarified in verse 31. Not every member loves and serves the Lord, but even those who do—the truly sanctified—must pray always, lest they fall into temptation.

Some people believe that in this verse "sanctification" refers to those who have been sealed up to eternal life,[42] or who have received the Second Comforter, but this revelation was received too early in the history of the Church—April 1830—for that phenomenon to be found among the Saints, or to be widely known (see D&C 105:35–36; Alma 13:10–14).[43]

35. Neither adding to, nor diminishing from. The revelations received through the Prophet Joseph Smith and other latter-day prophets reflect all the truths that have been revealed by God since the time of Adam, neither adding to it nor diminishing from it. In nothing does the restored gospel contradict, add to, or diminish from the fulness of the gospel (in the narrow and scriptural sense explained above in v. 9) as revealed to other prophets, including John, the last prophet of the former dispensation (see Revelation 22:18–19).

37. The manner of baptism. The Lord commands the Church to administer baptism: (1) when candidates are humble before God—no bargaining and nothing held back, but willing to do whatever God requires; (2) when candidates really want to be baptized; (3) when they have a broken heart and a contrite spirit; (4) when they can testify to the Church that they have repented— that is, that they have begun the repentance process; (5) when they are willing to take upon themselves the name of Christ; and (6) when they have a determination to serve Christ for the rest of their lives and bear the fruits of membership in his Church.

37. Broken hearts and contrite spirits. A broken heart

suggests an overwhelming sense of grief and loss; in this case not for a lost sweetheart, but for lost worthiness and a lost relationship with God. In our fallen state we have lost these things, but when we enter the gospel covenant we can receive them again, and our broken hearts will be healed. Contrition is the desire to repent and make things right. A contrite heart yearns to do whatever it may take to get right with God and to make amends for sin.

37. Take upon them the name of Jesus Christ. The name of Christ is symbolic for Christ himself and for his power. It is the name of Jesus Christ that makes everything we do work: repentance, prayers, ordinances, justification, sanctification, the Church, and so on. We have faith in the power of his name, repent in his name, are baptized in his name, receive the Holy Ghost in his name, and have access to the Father only in his name. We can use Jesus' name properly, however, only if we are *his;* so to take his name upon us is to accept the power of his name in our own behalf and also to accept the obligation to represent his name to others and to the world. We accept his ownership—his name is "written" upon us—and we accept that we represent his name as we serve him. Finally, bearing his name means assuming his identity and therefore gradually becoming what he is.[44]

37. The Spirit of Christ. Usually, the phrase "Spirit of Christ" refers to the Holy Ghost, just as in the sacrament prayers the priest petitions "that they may always have *his* Spirit to be with them," referring specifically to the Holy Ghost (vv. 77, 79; emphasis added). Here in verse 37, however, it appears that the Spirit of Christ refers to the light or influence of Christ (see D&C 84:45–46; Moroni 7:18) that works on individuals before they enter the covenant and which, when followed, increases in intensity until it brings them to the gospel.

38–59. "The Lord could not reveal to the Church in the beginning all the knowledge and organization which would be essential to the full and complete organization of the Church. Had this been done, it would have been like an overwhelming flood that would have brought destruction. The truth had to come piecemeal—line upon line, precept upon precept, just like knowledge comes to all of us. However, all that was revealed in this section was expedient for the government of the Church at the time of its organization. What the Lord revealed at this time is just as expedient and necessary today. We have had nothing, for instance, given since that day to add to or improve on the instruction concerning the duties of teachers."[45]

Overall, the duties of the priesthood center on looking after the Church and assisting the members in living the principles of the gospel. The key functions of the priesthood are service and blessing. Priesthood should not necessarily be thought of as bestowing special rights, but rather as bestowing special responsibilities.

38. An apostle is an elder. The difference between an elder and an Apostle is not a difference of priesthood. Both hold the Melchizedek Priesthood, but an Apostle holds, with his quorum, the keys of the kingdom and has an additional, special calling to be a personal witness for Christ. High priests and seventies are also elders; that is, they hold the Melchizedek Priesthood, but they also are elders who at times hold specific keys and callings. "*Elder* is the title given all holders of the Melchizedek Priesthood."[46]

44. Take the lead. This means to preside. If an Apostle is present, it is his meeting. He may ask an elder to conduct for him (see v. 45). He may not wish to speak or otherwise participate, but he still presides, and all things in that meeting are done with the permission and authority of the one who presides.

60. Office in the priesthood cannot come by self-appointment. A man must be ordained in proper order by one who already holds the priesthood. The effective power in ordination is the power of the Holy Ghost.

61–62, 81. Conferences. In the early history of the Church, the conferences held were mainly priesthood conferences, but as the Church expanded, the need developed for stake and ward conferences as well as general conferences. In time, conferences have been expanded to include regional and area conferences. The commandment for elders to "meet in conference once in three months" is met today by a combination of general and stake conference priesthood meetings. Note that attendance at these meetings, in person or by telecast, is a commandment of the Lord and an obligation of holding the priesthood (see v. 61).

63–64, 82–84. In the early days of the Church, the method employed to certify the membership, priesthood, and good standing of individuals was to give them certificates of ordination and membership. A person carried this certificate with him from his old branch and presented it to the presiding elder of the new one. Then, by sustaining vote of the new branch, the priesthood holder would be given a license to function in the new branch. Also, membership lists were presented at the various conferences for entrance in the general records of the Church. These usually also included a list of those who had been removed from the Church since the last conference. Today we still issue certificates of membership and ordination, but the function of issuing licenses and maintaining membership records has been assumed by ward, stake, and general clerks using an automated record system. The importance of members keeping their Church records complete and up-to-date is thus underscored by these verses.

65–67. At the time Doctrine and Covenants 20 was received in 1829–30, there were no such offices in the Church as high priest, bishop, or high councilor. As the structure of the Church continued to unfold, section 20 was revised to include the newly revealed offices. Verses 65–67 were added to section 20 at the Prophet's direction in 1835, in order to include and instruct those holding offices that were unknown in 1830. Verse 65 also reflects the need for common consent in the Church (see D&C 26).

68. Expound all things . . . to their understanding. In the early days of the Church, the Lord required that baptized members be taught the basics of the gospel and have an understanding *before* being confirmed and partaking of the sacrament. This obligation now rests with the elders—a major purpose for teaching the missionary discussions—and home teachers and parents, and is generally met before baptism. Baptized members then have a binding obligation to behave according to what they have been taught (see v. 69).

70. While fathers holding the Melchizedek Priesthood can bless their children whenever need arises, they are also commanded in this verse to bless them publicly in church. This commandment is kept, under the direction of a bishop or branch president, by blessing infants and small children in ward or branch fast and testimony meetings. Besides obtaining the obvious blessing of the priesthood for their child, parents who keep this commandment "manifest their faith in the sight of their brethren and sisters, in God's word and in his promises, as well as their thankfulness to him for increasing their posterity and for the safe delivery of his handmaiden. The child is also benefitted by the united faith and responsive prayers of the assembled Saints."[47]

71. Years of accountability. In Doctrine and Covenants 68:25–27 the Lord defined the age of accountability as eight years of age. This age was prefigured in the law of Moses by circumcision of male children at eight days of age (see JST Genesis 17:11) and is perhaps also alluded to in 1 Peter 3:20–21. Children younger than eight do not normally understand the covenant of baptism (see v. 68) nor can they repent, because without knowledge and accountability they cannot sin (see Moroni 8:8–15). "Baptism is for remission of sins. Children have no sins. Jesus blessed them and said, 'Do what you have seen me do.' Children are all made alive in Christ, and those of riper years through faith and repentance."[48]

74. Immerse him or her. The Lord has revealed to the Church that baptism is to be by complete immersion, following the ancient pattern. The consensus of biblical scholars is that Jewish and Christian baptism in the first century was also by immersion. In fact, the verb *baptize* in Greek is normally translated as "to immerse" or "to dip."[49]

75. Bread and wine. Jesus' body is the "bread of life," or the "manna from heaven" (John 6:35; 48–51). His blood is the "living water" (John 4:10–14; 7:37–38) and the "wine" of the Atonement pressed out of him in the press of Gethsemane (see D&C 19:18).[50] As bread is made from crushed wheat and gives life to humans, and as wine is made from the crushed grapes when they are pressed, so bread and wine are ideal symbols for the body and blood of Christ bruised and shed for us that we might live. By partaking of the emblems of the sacrament we symbolically partake of his body and blood. We symbolically take Christ into ourselves and become one with him as he nourishes us and gives us life through his atoning sacrifice (see John 6:53–58).

As Israel under Moses partook of the sacrificial animals that brought cleansing and safety through their deaths, so we partake symbolically of the Lamb of God, sacrificed to bring us cleansing and salvation. Also, when we partake of the bread and wine, or water, in faith and repentance, we receive the same blessings and restore the same covenants as at our baptism. And just as those who are baptized are then given the gift of the Holy Ghost, so those who partake of the sacrament in good faith will then "always have his Spirit to be with them" (D&C 20:77, 79).

Because the bread and wine are symbolic only and are partaken of in remembrance only, and not as a literal transubstantiation, it does not matter what we eat or drink in order to remember his body and blood. Consequently, it is common throughout the Church today to use bread and water for the emblems of the sacrament. This is in accordance with revelation received two months after section 20 was canonized.[51] After Doctrine and Covenants 27 was received, wine and water were used interchangeably for the sacrament until about the turn of the century. Since that time pure water has uniformly been the content of the cup.

76. Shall kneel with the Church. It appears that in the early days the entire Church knelt when the sacrament was blessed, just as in the Book of Mormon (see Moroni 4:1–2). This is largely impractical in modern congregations, though we must still have an attitude of humility and bend the "knees" of our hearts as the priest offers the prayers. It should be noted that all such changes in practice have been inspired, with prophetic authorization.

79. They may witness. *Witness* here means to affirm or to testify. Thus, this portion of the prayer states what those partaking of the sacrament intend to affirm: that they are willing to take his name upon them, that they are willing to remember Christ, and that they are willing to keep his commandments (see v. 37). To the extent that they do these things that they have publicly witnessed before God, they will have his Spirit to be with them.

81–84. See Commentary above on verses 61–62, 63–64.

83. Expelled from the church. The Lord from the very beginning of the Church has allowed for the excommunication of those who violate their covenants and refuse to repent. When an excommunication takes place, the name of the excommunicated person is removed from the records of the Church. By this action they are mercifully released from covenants they will not keep, and they are returned to "the world." Unfortunately, they are also denied certain benefits of the Atonement and can reenter the kingdom only through subsequent repentance and eventual rebaptism.

NOTES

1. Smith, *History of the Church,* 1:64.
2. Woodford, "Historical Development," 1:290; see Cannon, "Priesthood Restoration Documents," 175.
3. See Phelps, "The Saints," 158.
4. See Carmack, "Fayette," 14–19; Peterson, "Book Review of *Inventing Mormonism*," 216–20.
5. Smith, *History of the Church,* 1:74–77.
6. See Anderson, "Organization Revelations," 109–10, 119, note 4.
7. See Woodford, "Historical Development," 1:287, 291; Jessee,

Papers of Joseph Smith, 1:14, n. 1; see also Cook, *Revelations of the Prophet,* 31, 33, 125–26.

8. See "Mormon Creed," *Telegraph,* 3.

9. Smith, *History of the Church,* 1:337.

10. See Smith, *Doctrine and Covenants Commentary,* 138; Clark, *Our Lord of the Gospels,* vi–vii; McConkie, *Mortal Messiah,* 1:349–50.

11. See Lefgren, *April Sixth,* 2; Brown, "Book Review of *April Sixth,*" 375.

12. *Mortal Messiah,* 1:349–50, n. 2.

13. Porter, "Study of the Origins of the Church," 385.

14. See Lee, in *Ensign,* July 1973, 2; Kimball, in *Ensign,* May 1980, 54; see also Roberts, *Outlines of Ecclesiastical History,* 16–17.

15. Woodford, "Historical Development," 1:290.

16. For excerpts from the major documents relating to the restoration of the priesthood and a summary of the issues involved, see Cannon, "Priesthood Restoration Documents," 162–207.

17. Ezra Taft Benson, in *Ensign,* Nov. 1986, 6.

18. See McConkie, *Mormon Doctrine,* 333.

19. See the commentary on D&C 14:10; 42:12.

20. See Funk, *Five Gospels.*

21. See McKenzie, *Anchor Bible: Second Isaiah,* xv–xxiii.

22. See Anderson, "Organization Revelations," 111–13.

23. Clark, *Messages of the First Presidency,* 5:244.

24. See opening line of the Gospel of Thomas in Robinson, *Nag Hammadi Library,* 124.

25. See the commentary on D&C 93:3.

26. See the commentary on D&C 3:20; 76:53, 60–61.

27. See Acts 13:39; Mosiah 14:11.

28. See Acts 26:18; Romans 3:28, 30.

29. See Romans 3:24; D&C 20:30.

30. See James 2:21–25.

31. See Romans 5:9.

32. See Moses 6:60.

33. See 1 Corinthians 1:2; Hebrews 2:11.

34. See Moroni 10:33; D&C 20:31.

35. See John 17:17, 19.

36. See 1 Timothy 4:5.

37. See Jude 1:1.

38. See D&C 88:21, 34.

39. See Ephesians 5:26.

40. See Romans 15:16; 2 Thessalonians 2:13; 1 Peter 1:2; Alma 5:4; 13:12; 3 Nephi 27:20.
41. See Hebrews 9:14; Moses 6:60.
42. See the commentary on D&C 68:12.
43. See McConkie, *New Witness for the Articles of Faith*, 270.
44. See the commentary on D&C 19:37.
45. See Smith, *Church History and Modern Revelation*, 1:95.
46. McConkie, *Mormon Doctrine*, 215.
47. See Taylor, "Blessing of Children," 235.
48. Smith, *History of the Church*, 5:499.
49. See Brown, *Dictionary of New Testament Theology*, 1:144; Ferguson, *Encyclopedia of Early Christianity*, 131.
50. See the commentary on D&C 19:18.
51. See Background to D&C 27.

21

BACKGROUND

When Joseph Smith, Oliver Cowdery, and others met in Fayette, New York, on 6 April 1830, in obedience to the Lord's command to organize the Church (see D&C 20:1), there was a great outpouring of the Spirit of God. Toward the end of that founding meeting, Joseph received and shared with the others present a further revelation, now Doctrine and Covenants 21, which dealt primarily with Joseph's position relative to other members of the fledgling Church.

Joseph explained the reception of section 21 in the following manner: "Whilst the Book of Mormon was in the hands of the printer, we still continued to bear testimony and give information, as far as we had opportunity; and also made known to our brethren that we had received a commandment to organize the Church; and accordingly we met together for that purpose, at the house of Mr. Peter Whitmer, Sen., (being six in number,) on Tuesday, the sixth day of April, A.D., one thousand eight hundred and thirty. Having opened the meeting by solemn prayer to our Heavenly Father, we proceeded, according to previous commandment, to call on our brethren to know whether they accepted us as their teachers in the things of the Kingdom of God, and whether they were satisfied that we should proceed and be organized as a Church according to said commandment which we had received.

To these several propositions they consented by a unanimous vote. I then laid my hands upon Oliver Cowdery, and ordained him an Elder of the 'Church of Jesus Christ of Latter-day Saints;' after which, he ordained me also to the office of an Elder of said Church. We then took bread, blessed it, and brake it with them; also wine, blessed it, and drank it with them. We then laid our hands on each individual member of the Church present, that they might receive the gift of the Holy Ghost, and be confirmed members of the Church of Christ. The Holy Ghost was poured out upon us to a very great degree—some prophesied, whilst we all praised the Lord, and rejoiced exceedingly. Whilst yet together, I received the following commandment"—Doctrine and Covenants 21.[1]

Joseph Knight Sr. also described that meeting in his account of the early Church: "Now in the Spring of 1830, I went with my team and took Joseph out to Manchester to his father. When we were on our way he told me that there must be a Church formed, but did not tell when. . . .

" . . . On the sixth day of April 1830, he began the Church with six members and received the following revelation [section 21]. They all kneeled down and prayed, and Joseph gave them instructions how to build up the Church and exhorted them to be faithful in all things, for this is the work of God."[2]

It should be noted that there were more than six individuals present at this meeting. On 6 April 1830, there were believers in New York state—some of them already baptized but not confirmed—in Manchester/Palmyra, mainly Smiths; Fayette, mainly Whitmers; and Colesville, mainly Knights. Six of these signed the certificate of incorporation as responsible parties on 6 April, to satisfy New York state law. More than twenty individuals were actually present at the organization meeting, however, with some of these others also receiving confirmation into the Church. Thus, the number six does not represent the actual number of members confirmed on 6 April, but rather the number of members who signed the document as legal representatives of the Church to the state of New York.

COMMENTARY

1. There shall be a record kept: From the very first day of the Restoration, the Lord has commanded the Church to keep a record of its meetings, revelations, activities, and daily history. From the time of Adam, the people of the Lord have been a record-keeping people collectively and individually (see Moses 6:5–8).

1. Called a seer, a translator. As head of the Church on earth, Joseph Smith would hold many callings. A *seer* is one who sees—who sees the spiritual as well as the material realities of the world. If reality were compared by analogy to visible light, then a seer perceives the visible spectrum like the rest of us, but he also sees the infra-red and the ultra-violet bands, those spiritual wavelengths that the rest of us cannot see.

A *translator* is primarily one who translates from one language to another, but he is also one who translates obscure or difficult language, or language that might be misleading or easily misunderstood, into a more clear and understandable form, though the "translation" thus produced might be in the same language as the original. The seer does not translate intellectually, as scholars do, but by the divine gift of inspiration. Thus, Joseph Smith not only "translated" the Nephite record from reformed Egyptian to English in the primary sense, but he also "translated" the King James English into clearer, more understandable English in the second sense—the Joseph Smith Translation.

Prophecy is one of the gifts of the Spirit available to all members of the Church, and a *prophet* in the broadest sense is anyone who proceeds with the Spirit of God and with a testimony of Christ in the performance of his or her stewardship. Prophets teach, preach, expound, and exhort by the power of the Spirit. In LDS Church usage, *the* prophet is a title for the one who teaches, preaches, and otherwise operates by the Spirit in directing the affairs of the whole Church—this is his stewardship alone. It is common for people to think of a prophet primarily as one who foretells the future, but this is only part of a prophet's calling. "A prophet is a teacher of known truth; a seer is a perceiver of hidden truth; a revelator is a bearer of new truth. In the widest sense, the one most commonly used, the title *prophet,* includes the other titles and makes of the prophet a teacher, a perceiver, a bearer of truth."[3]

An *Apostle* is a special witness of the Lord Jesus Christ to the whole world. All members of the Quorum of the Twelve Apostles also hold the keys of the priesthood and therefore preside collectively as a quorum over the affairs of the entire Church in all the world. An Apostle is one who holds the Melchizedek Priesthood and has also received special apostolic keys and callings.

The title of *elder* properly designates anyone who holds the Melchizedek Priesthood. Thus, all General Authorities of the Church bear the title of elder, as do also the most recently ordained nineteen-year-old missionaries.

2. Lay the foundation. The imagery used here comes from the New Testament and refers to the symbolic temple—the collective Church. The apostles and prophets are the foundation of this temple, Jesus Christ is the chief cornerstone (see Ephesians 2:20–22), and we individual members are "lively stones"—that is, living bricks—in the holy structure being built (1 Peter 2:5).

Most of the small group gathered on 6 April 1830 could not really have understood the great movement that was beginning on that date. The true Church of Jesus Christ, the stone "cut out of the mountain without hands" (D&C 65:2), which was ultimately to fill the whole earth, was beginning to roll forth (see Daniel 2:34–35, 44).

2. The most holy faith. This refers to all the doctrines and ordinances necessary for exaltation in the celestial kingdom. On 6 April 1830, the foundation was laid. In the fourteen years to follow, the Prophet would receive and convey to the Church the promised fulness, the restoration of all things—the most holy faith. This would include both the fulness of the gospel as contained in the Book of Mormon, and also the ordinances of the temple, including the new and everlasting covenant of marriage, which would be received later.

4. Meaning the church. The Lord now addressed the Church itself and commanded the members to heed the words of Joseph and to keep the commandments as Joseph received and revealed them. Notice the obligation of the Church to heed all the words of the Prophet that he might receive from the Lord.

4. Walking in all holiness. The antecedent of the participle *walking* is likely the Church rather than Joseph. This would mean that the Church, walking in all holiness, is to obey Joseph. It does not mean that the Church is to obey Joseph only when, in their opinion, Joseph is walking in holiness.

5. As if from mine own mouth, in all patience. This is perhaps the most radical verse in this revelation, because it lays out what it truly means to be founded on the principle of living revelation. If Joseph is truly a prophet, holding the keys of the ancient apostleship, if he truly spoke for God, then when Joseph spoke in his prophetic capacity, his voice was God's voice. Such a conviction requires faith in God and in the Restoration, patience at times with the imperfect mortal who wears the prophetic mantle, patience with God who does not always choose to answer our questions either directly or through the Prophet, and patience with ourselves in our flaws and imperfections as we strive to be like Christ.

One might argue that Joseph was a fraud, but if one accepts the restoration of the gospel as divine—or the Book of Mormon, or the doctrine that "Families are Forever," and so forth—then one cannot consistently reject the authority of the Prophet who revealed them. As Elder Ezra Taft Benson stated, "We don't need a prophet—we have one—we need a listening ear."[4]

6. Gates of hell. One of the three promises made to the faithful in this verse is that the gates of hell will not prevail against them. In scripture the word *hell* (Hebrew *sheol* or Greek *hades*) almost always refers to that place in the spirit world where the wicked suffer for their sins. "To prevail" is to win a contest or struggle. The metaphor here is of the righteous wrestling with the powers of hell and trying not to be pulled in through its gates (or "jaws" in D&C 122:7). Through the atonement of Christ, the faithful will "win" their struggle with hell and not be pulled in to suffer inside its gates under Satan's power.

On the other hand, if *hell* here is to be understood as a larger term for the entire spirit world, then the promise is that we will not be captives there permanently. Ultimately, the atonement of Christ will prevail over the gates of the spirit world, and all who are held captive there will be released through redemption in Christ and the power of the Resurrection.

The other two promises made in this verse are that God will disperse the powers of darkness, and that he will cause the heavens to shake for our good.

7. To move the cause of Zion. This means to work to establish a Zion people and a Zion place—like the City of Enoch (see Moses 7:19), or Zarahemla following the appearances of the Lord (see 4 Nephi 1:2–18), or the New Jerusalem (see Moses 7:62). Joseph attempted to establish both a Zion people and a Zion place during his lifetime.

9. The Comforter. This is the Holy Ghost as experienced by baptized and confirmed members of the Church (see John 14:16, 26). The Holy Ghost is called a Comforter for members because his presence in our lives guarantees to us that we are in the gospel covenant. The gift of the Spirit is given to us as "earnest money," or as a down payment, on our future inheritance of all things (see 2 Corinthians 1:22; 5:5; Ephesians 1:14). The companionship of the Holy Ghost assures us that we are right with God, justified before his law, approved of him, and worthy of a celestial reward. Thus, the gift of his companionship is truly a *comfort.*

10. Ordained by you. Both Joseph and Oliver already held the Melchizedek Priesthood and the keys of apostleship. These were bestowed upon them by ordination under the hands of Peter, James, and John. The ordination referred to here is to a specific office *in the Church,* which did not exist before 6 April 1830.

Joseph and Oliver already had the authority to ordain anyone to any office in the Church, but only on this occasion did the Church actually come into existence. Everyone who holds a priesthood office in the Church and kingdom of God must be ordained to that office. Joseph Smith was no exception, and so he was ordained to his *Church* office by Oliver.

11. This being an ordinance unto you. *This* refers to the instructions that follow. The term *ordinance* is used here to mean a rule or commandment, as in a city or county ordinance. Thus, the following instructions are a command of God that Oliver must remember and observe. The ordinance then applies the ordinal "first" here to Joseph Smith and not to Oliver.

11. He being the first. The Lord explained the priesthood line of authority and relative stewardships of Joseph and Oliver in clear and unmistakable terms: Joseph had the priority, and Oliver was his subordinate. This is something Oliver later had trouble with (see D&C 28:3, 5–7).

12. And the first preacher of this church. This "first" refers to Oliver Cowdery, the first person to proclaim the gospel in a public meeting of the Church in this dispensation. On the next Sunday, 11 April 1830, a meeting was held in the home of Peter Whitmer Sr., and Oliver was the principle speaker. Oliver was also the first in this dispensation to preach to the Lamanites ("the Jews," see D&C 28:8; 57:4), and had a special commission from the Lord to preach whenever he felt so inspired (see D&C 24:10, 12; 28:3–4, 16).

NOTES

1. Smith, *History of the Church*, 1:74–78.
2. Jessee, "Joseph Knight's Recollection," 36–37; spelling, punctuation, and capitalization standardized.
3. Thomas J. Fyans, in Conference Report, Korea Area Conference 1975, 17.
4. In Conference Report, Sept.–Oct. 1961, 71; see also J. Reuben Clark Jr., in Conference Report, Oct. 1948, 79–80.

22

BACKGROUND

Sometime between Tuesday, 6 April 1830, when the organization of the Church took place, and the following Sunday, 11 April, Joseph Smith was approached at his family home in Manchester by sincere investigators who believed the Book of Mormon was true and who wanted to be members of the Church. These people felt, however, that since they had already been baptized as Christians, it should not be necessary to repeat that ordinance. Elder Orson Pratt later explained the origin of Doctrine and Covenants 22 in these words: "In the early days of this Church there were certain persons, belonging to the Baptist denomination, very moral and no doubt as good people as you could find anywhere, who came, saying they believed in the Book of Mormon, and that they had been baptized into the Baptist Church, and they wished to come into our Church. The Prophet Joseph had not, at that time, particularly inquired in relation to this matter, but he did inquire, and received a revelation from the Lord. . . . These Baptists had to be re-baptized: there was no other way to get into this Church."[1]

Doctrine and Covenants 22 is often said to be part of the articles and covenants of the Church, since it was included with Doctrine and Covenants 21 under that title on the first page of the first edition of *The Evening and the Morning Star* in June 1832. In an earlier source, however, where sections 20, 22, and 27 appear together, only section 20 was labeled the articles and covenants of the Church of Christ.[2] Moreover, in the 1833 Book of Command-ments—the first official publication of the revelations—section 22 appears *before* section 20 and without the title, section 20 alone being identified as the articles and covenants of the Church of Christ. The majority of other early sources also exclude section 22 as part of the articles and covenants.[3]

William E. McLellin's journal contains a very early copy of Doctrine and Covenants 22 with the following appended: "April 16th 1830 Joseph Smith."[4] This would put the reception of this revelation only ten days after the organization of the Church.

COMMENTARY

1. The new and everlasting covenant of baptism supersedes all previous covenants and obligations. Baptisms performed by minis-ters without the priesthood restored to Joseph Smith and Oliver Cowdery by John the Baptist and by Peter, James, and John are merely dead works—purely human attempts to reach God, and of no avail. The issue is not sincerity, but authority. God must reach out to humans, and has done so in the restoration of the true Church. Baptism by proper priesthood authority is the gateway into the true Church and into the kingdom of God, and all people must obey his command to repent and be so baptized. There are no exceptions, not even for the Savior himself (see Matthew 3:13–15).

1. Old covenants. Many Christians have little or no under-standing of priesthood authority. Accordingly, because little or no importance is placed on priesthood, in their view almost anyone may baptize, and baptisms performed in one church are quite gen-erally accepted in another. This was the hope of those who came to Joseph in April 1830, desiring to unite with the Church by virtue of their previous baptisms. Many sincere persons seek to come to God and even submit to ordinances or make covenants to serve him while they are members of other faiths. These ordinances and covenants, though they may be sincere, and though God may be pleased with the righteous desires of these individuals and bless them accordingly, are still of human origin. They are human attempts to reach God, and all such attempts are superseded by that covenant that has its origin in God and reaches from God to us.

1. A new and an everlasting covenant. Doctrine and Covenants 66:2 defines the new and everlasting covenant as the fulness of the gospel—as known to the Saints in October 1831, when section 66 was received. As one of the ordinances that make up that fulness, however, baptism itself may be described as *a* new and everlasting covenant, just as the ordinance of marriage is later described as *the* new and everlasting covenant in Doctrine and Covenants 131:2. The gospel covenant is "new" because, from our perspective, it has just recently been restored to the earth and is a change from the old "orthodoxies." It is "everlasting" in that it is the same covenant God made with Adam, Enoch, Noah, Abraham, and all those from the beginning to the end to whom he has revealed or will reveal the fulness of the gospel.

2. The strait gate. *Strait* is not the same as *straight.* The former means "narrow" while the latter means "without curves." A strait or narrow gate must be approached deliberately and at just the right angle. It is restrictive. Only what has originated or been sealed on God's side of the gate, that which is eternal, can be carried with us through the gate into God's kingdom. The saying "You can't take it with you" is not true of priesthood blessings, ordinances, and sealings.

2. The law of Moses . . . your dead works. The law of Moses was a law of rules designed to lift Israel from a telestial to a terrestrial level of obedience—from the golden calf to the Ten Commandments, from wickedness to observance of law, and so on, to prepare Israel for the fulness of the gospel. But the effectiveness of the law of Moses depended solely upon the obedience of the individual; because we are all sometimes disobedient, law cannot perfect us and bring us into the celestial kingdom. This requires the gospel of Jesus Christ, its priesthood authority, its mercy, grace, and atonement. Just as the law of Moses, centered upon the works of the individual, cannot save us, neither can religion, even *Christian* religion, that originates with man and not with God—nor can baptisms or other ordinances initiated by man and not by God. Without divine priesthood authorization and power, these religions represent human attempts to find God—that is, human works rather than Christ's saving work done in our behalf. They are called "dead works" (v. 3) because without God's priesthood, they cannot bestow eternal life but are merely human efforts, representing faith in our ability to manipulate God. When we enter the gospel covenant we leave behind the dead works of merely human efforts, of law of Moses righteousness, of sin (see Hebrews 6:1; 9:14), and of faith in ritual rather than faith in Christ (see Moroni 8:23). The Savior similarly rejected the "dead" baptism of the Pharisees (see JST Matthew 9:18–21).

4. The gate. The gate into the Church and kingdom of God is baptism (see 2 Nephi 31:17).

4. Seek not to counsel your God. In some of the more democratic Christian denominations it is acceptable for the membership to instruct the leaders by vote or otherwise. But in the true Church of Christ, with continuing revelation and the priesthood line of authority, and where the words of the prophet are to be received as if from God's own mouth (see D&C 21:5), to counsel our leaders uninvited is to seek to "counsel our God." It is self-contradictory to justify such actions as obedience to a higher good, or to God, when those same actions violate the instructions of the apostles and prophets who speak for God.

NOTES

1. Orson Pratt, *Journal of Discourses,* 16:293–94.
2. See Background to D&C 20 for description of the Painesville *Telegraph,* which printed section 20 as the Articles and Covenants.
3. See Anderson, "Organization Revelations," 109–10.
4. In Shipps and Welch, *Journals of William E. McLellin,* 236.

DOCTRINE AND COVENANTS

23

BACKGROUND

Shortly after the organization of the Church on 6 April, the Prophet Joseph returned to his family's home in Manchester, New York. There five persons, of whom four had just been baptized, sought to know the will of the Lord and their respective duties in the Church. Of this occasion Joseph later recorded: "The following persons being anxious to know of the Lord what might be their respective duties in relation to this work, I enquired of the Lord, and received for them the following [section 23]: *Revelation to Oliver Cowdery, Hyrum Smith, Samuel H. Smith, Joseph Smith, Sen., and Joseph Knight, Sen. Given at Manchester, New York, April, 1830.*"[1]

The 1833 Book of Commandments records these five responses as five separate revelations, but in all subsequent editions of the Doctrine and Covenants, at the direction of the Prophet, they have been combined into one section.

COMMENTARY

1. No condemnation. The Lord's response to four of the five men who sought his direction assured them that they were under no condemnation. They were, after all, just baptized. Joseph Knight Sr., however, was given no such assurance, for he had to

158

this point not yet submitted to baptism and entered the covenant that alone justifies us before God through faith in Christ.

1. Pride. On this subject President Joseph Fielding Smith remarked that pride "was one of Oliver Cowdery's besetting sins. If he could have humbled himself in the troubled days of Kirtland he would not have lost his place and membership in the Church. That which had been bestowed upon him was exceedingly great and had he been willing to humble himself, it was his privilege to stand with the Prophet Joseph Smith through all time and eternity, holding the keys of the Dispensation of the Fulness of Times. However, at this particular time when this word was sought, he was free from condemnation."[2]

3. In Doctrine and Covenants 11 Hyrum Smith had been restrained from preaching the gospel. He was told he was first to obtain and study the word, and only then he could preach (see D&C 11:21–22). Now the time had come to receive his calling and for his tongue to be loosed. The Book of Mormon was now published, the Church was organized, and Hyrum had had an opportunity to learn more concerning the Restoration. His calling was specifically to exhortation—preaching aimed at influencing behavior—and to strengthen the Church, which he did, side by side with his brother the Prophet, for the rest of his life.

3. Thy duty is unto the church . . . because of thy family. This statement "evidently conveys the thought that he [Hyrum] would succeed to the office of Patriarch and that *it should continue in his posterity to the end of time,* for, surely, it would have to continue in this way to last forever in the Church upon the earth among mortal men. Then again, the blessing pronounced upon the head of Hyrum Smith's father, was that this calling was to come upon his head *'and his seed after him, to the uttermost.'* And so, down through the history of the Church, this doctrine has been recognized."[3] "Because of thy family" is apparently equivalent here to "because of thy lineage."

4. Thou are not . . . to preach. Samuel H. Smith, at the age of twenty-two, was not yet called to preach before the world, but rather to assist in strengthening the Church. "Samuel was the third person baptized in this dispensation. He was one of the first to be ordained to the office of elder, and it was not long after this revelation when he was sent forth to teach, which he did with marked success, far beyond his own realization."[4] One of the underappreciated founding members of the Church, Samuel was one of the Eight Witnesses to the Book of Mormon and is generally credited with being the first full-time traveling missionary in this dispensation, serving at least five missions in the succeeding fourteen years. He helped build the Nauvoo Temple, served as an alderman in Nauvoo, bishop of the Nauvoo Ward, member of the Nauvoo Legion, and served in the Presiding Bishopric of the Church. Faithful to the end, Samuel died on 30 July 1844, one month after his brothers were martyred on 27 June.

5. Thy duty from henceforth and forever. See the commentary on Doctrine and Covenants 23:3.

6. Take up your cross. "And now for a man to take up his cross, is to deny himself all ungodliness, and every worldly lust, and keep my commandments" (JST Matthew 16:26). For Joseph Knight and for others with his aversion to praying or speaking in public, the specific commandments meant are to "pray vocally before the world" (v. 6) and to come forward and join the Church (see v. 7).

6. Pray vocally before the world. Evidently, one of the challenges that Joseph Knight Sr. faced was praying in front of other people. Perhaps he was one of those painfully shy individuals for whom humbling themselves and taking up their cross means, despite their fear, to reveal and share their inner feelings and their faith in God by praying, testifying, or declaring his word publicly before the world. There are many in the Church for whom praying or speaking in church is a heavy cross to bear, but who humble themselves and obey the commandment for the kingdom's sake.

7. Unite with the true church. Joseph Knight Sr. had been a Universalist before his acquaintance with Joseph Smith. Though a believer and a staunch supporter of the Restoration, he was fairly liberal in his theology and apparently did not yet grasp the importance of baptism. In obedience to this direct command, he was baptized on 29 June 1830.

NOTES

1. Smith, *History of the Church,* 1:80.
2. Smith, *Church History and Modern Revelation,* 1:120–21.
3. Smith, *Doctrines of Salvation,* 3:164.
4. Smith, *Church History and Modern Revelation,* 1:121.

DOCTRINE AND COVENANTS

24

BACKGROUND

Immediately after the first conference of the Church on 9 June 1830, Joseph returned to his own home in Harmony, Pennsylvania. A short time later, together with his wife, Emma, Oliver Cowdery, John Whitmer, and David Whitmer, he again visited Colesville, New York, about twenty miles north of Harmony, to see the Joseph and Newel Knight families and to arrange for the baptism of a number of believers in the Colesville area. Opposition to Joseph and the Church was increasing rapidly in this area, largely through the efforts of local ministers, and when the brethren erected a dam across a local stream to create a pool for baptisms, a mob tore it apart during the night. Two days later the brethren quietly rebuilt the dam, and thirteen people were baptized.

Enraged at the proceedings, a mob of about fifty people gathered and surrounded the home of Joseph Knight Sr., where the Prophet had a confrontation with them. Shortly afterward Joseph was arrested at the Newel Knight home on the charge of being a disorderly person and causing an uproar in the community by preaching the Book of Mormon. He was tried in Chenango County, but all the evidence turned out to be rumor and hearsay, and he was acquitted. He was, however, immediately rearrested on a similar warrant from Broome County, though he was acquitted again for the same reasons—no one could offer actual eyewitness testimony of any wrongdoing on Joseph's part. After this second acquittal, the infuriated mob attempted to tar and feather Joseph and to ride him on a rail, but they were unsuccessful.[1] During this same general period of time, July 1830, while Joseph was at his farm in Harmony, the Prophet received the "vision of Moses" now found in the Pearl of Great Price (see Moses 1). He also received sections 24–26 of the Doctrine and Covenants.[2]

COMMENTARY

1. Delivered from all thine enemies. This is probably a reference to the mob actions and legal harassment in Colesville as well as to previous opposition encountered ever since the First Vision (see JS–H 1:21–24). To the frustration of his enemies, none of the plots or stratagems against Joseph succeeded in stopping his work.

2. Not excusable in thy transgressions. Notice Joseph's honesty in recording for posterity even those portions of his revelations that reflect badly on him, even though he could easily have edited them out. The Prophet was not perfect, but he was nevertheless eminently worthy to translate the Book of Mormon, receive the keys of the kingdom, restore the gospel, and build up the kingdom of God.

3–7. Joseph was to plant his crops, then go and seek support for his family from the other Saints, who were located mainly in three areas: Colesville, Fayette, and Manchester. Joseph's calling was to build up the kingdom of God as a full-time prophet. The obligation of the Saints was to support him in this, temporally as well as spiritually, with material sacrifice as well as with prayer. If they kept this commandment they would be blessed, if not they would be cursed. This is not a form of divine extortion, for the Lord is asking the Saints to do only what they had already obligated themselves in principle to do—just as in the Church today.

It is sometimes necessary for those who labor full time for the kingdom to be supported by the kingdom. Today there are individuals in the Church who are called to serve full time for an extended period who are treated according to this principle. For example, General Authorities today who require assistance in order to devote full time to the Lord's work are provided for, though usually from the resources of Church-owned businesses rather than from member contributions. Many full-time missionaries are supported by contributions from family, friends, or other faithful members who desire to build the kingdom (see D&C 42:71–73; 43:12–14).

3. Magnify thine office. See the commentary on Doctrine and Covenants 84:33.

3. Sowed thy fields. This revelation was given in July, which is not a good time to plant in Harmony, Pennsylvania, but the Prophet had been too busy planting and nurturing the Church and the Saints to plant his own fields at the appropriate time. The Lord's advice is to go ahead and plant his crops late, and then rely on the Saints for additional help if he should need it.

8. Be patient in afflictions. Righteousness and service do not guarantee freedom from afflictions or trials. Even prophets have troubles and must bear them as faithfully as others. Neither membership nor faithfulness will spare us from the natural consequences of the Fall or from the malice of "Babylon," or the world. In fact, the more good we do, the greater the opposition we may expect from Satan's world.

9. In temporal labors thou shalt not have strength. Joseph's talents did not lie in farming, business, finance, real estate speculation, or other temporal or practical matters. His strength and calling was in building the kingdom; that is what the Lord wanted him to worry about. Church members sometimes assume that Church association implies increased chances of temporal success or at least lessened risk in business or financial matters; this is not true. Members and nonmembers, active and less active, all share the conditions and risks of mortal life.

10–12. Oliver Cowdery was also given encouragement by the Lord. He was to put all his labors into the Lord's work and to preach mightily, as is appropriate for the "first preacher" of the Church (see D&C 21:12).

11. Oliver received a gentle reminder that he was to glory in God and not in himself. This was perhaps another hint of the wedge of pride in Oliver's character that later almost destroyed him and that did cause him to lose many blessings.

13. Require not miracles. Contrary to popular belief, miracles of themselves do not convert people and therefore are not to be used or promoted as a missionary tool. The purpose of miracles is to bless and protect rather than to impress or convert.

13–14. Joseph and Oliver had the apostolic authority to perform miracles as did the Apostles of old, but they were not to use it in this manner unless asked by those who had need of their spiritual power. For example, a request to perform a healing should be granted if those requesting really desire to be healed rather than merely to witness a miracle. It would be appropriate to heal someone with an illness if that person or their loved ones sincerely asked in faith that they be so blessed. It would also be appropriate to cast evil out of an afflicted person if the afflicted or his or her loved ones so requested, but it would not be proper to perform such acts at the request of third parties who simply want to see a supernatural sign. It is equally inappropriate to solicit opportunities to bless those who have not asked for blessings in order to impress them or other onlookers with one's priesthood power. It would also be inappropriate for priesthood holders to visit hospitals uninvited, soliciting opportunities to give blessings.

Note the similarities in verses 12–19 to the apostolic commissions of Mark 16:15–18 and Matthew 10:7–15. Doctrine and Covenants 24 constitutes in part an apostolic commission for the last pruning of the vineyard in the latter days (see v. 19). Apparently, verses 13–19 were addressed to both Joseph and Oliver, for the old English *ye* is the second person plural form of the pronoun *you*.

15. Casting off the dust of your feet. Casting the dust off one's feet is not a "curse" in the usual sense; rather it is a witness or a testimony that people have been warned and that the consequences of their rejection are on their own heads.[3] According to Elder James E. Talmage, "To ceremonially shake the dust from one's feet as a testimony against another was understood by the Jews to symbolize a cessation of fellowship and a renunciation of all responsibility for consequences that might follow. It became an ordinance of accusation and testimony by the Lord's instructions to His apostles. . . . In the current dispensation, the Lord has similarly directed His authorized servants to so testify against those who wilfully and maliciously oppose the truth when authoritatively presented (see D&C 24:15; 60:15; 75:20; 84:92; 99:4). The responsibility of testifying before the Lord by this accusing symbol is so great that the means may be employed *only under unusual and extreme conditions,* as the Spirit of the Lord may direct."[4]

16–17. Violence . . . cursed by the law. God assured that whatever men did to Joseph and Oliver would be done also to them. If they were violent, God would smite them in return, in his own due time. If they used the law and the courts to attack the apostles and prophets, they would suffer themselves by the law and the courts. "Whoso diggeth a pit shall fall therein" (Proverbs 26:27).

18. Purse nor scrip. A *purse* is a coin-pouch, and a *scrip* is a knapsack or a pack for one's gear (Greek *pera*). Therefore, the Lord was instructing the elders to travel without money or luggage. They were to depend upon the Lord, the Church, and the good people they contacted and taught for their temporal support.

19. Prune my vineyard . . . for the last time. The dispensation of the fulness of times is the last time the gospel is to be preached to the world. The Lord refers to this as a pruning, meaning there will be a separation of good, fruit-bearing vines from those that have gone bad and bear no fruit. What bears fruit will be nurtured and strengthened; what will not bear fruit will be cut off. This work of pruning the Lord's vineyard is still underway. It is a mighty pruning to prepare the vineyard, the earth, for the second coming of the Lord, the owner and master of the vineyard.

NOTES

1. See Joseph Smith's full account of the mob action in this period in Smith, *History of the Church,* 1:86–101.
2. See Smith, *History of the Church,* 1:98–104.
3. See Lane, *Gospel According to Mark,* 208–9.
4. Talmage, *Jesus the Christ,* 345; emphasis added.

25

BACKGROUND

Emma Hale Smith, the daughter of Isaac and Elizabeth Hale of Harmony, Pennsylvania, was a year and a half older than her husband Joseph, whom she met while Joseph was working for Josiah Stowell in the Harmony area. Joseph and Emma were married on 18 January 1827. Eight months later, Emma had accompanied Joseph to Cumorah and waited with the team and wagon on the morning Joseph received the gold plates from the angel Moroni. She then served as his scribe in translating the Book of Mormon for a short period, though this was difficult for her because of her other domestic responsibilities.

Emma was baptized a member of the Church by Oliver Cowdery on 28 June 1830, and was confirmed by her husband, Joseph, in early August of that year. She was with Joseph and Oliver during the mob action and Joseph's two arrests and trials in the Colesville area. She herself was also at risk of physical injury during that time, and, like Joseph and Oliver, she suffered considerable harassment and vilification from the mobs. As a result of her New York experiences, Emma Smith was as much in need of encouragement from the Lord as were her husband and Oliver Cowdery (see D&C 24), having endured persecution with them ever since her wedding three and a half years earlier. Sometime during the month following her baptism, in July 1830, after returning home from New York to their farm in Harmony, Pennsylvania, Emma received Doctrine and Covenants 25 through her husband, Joseph.[1]

COMMENTARY

1. My daughter. This is not Heavenly Father referring to Emma as his spirit-daughter. Rather, this is Jesus Christ referring to her as a spiritually begotten daughter, born again as his child through her baptism and his atonement (see Mosiah 5:7; 4 Nephi 1:17; Mormon 9:26; Ether 3:14; Ephesians 1:5). Through his suffering and death, Jesus Christ "begets" all who are born of the Spirit and inherit the celestial kingdom. As our Heavenly Father is the father of our spirits and our mortal fathers are the fathers of our flesh, so our Savior is the spiritual father of our born-again selves in mortality and our resurrected selves in eternity.

1. Are sons and daughters in my kingdom. Baptism, not judgment or resurrection, is the gateway into the kingdom of God (see 2 Nephi 31:17). When we accept the gospel and pass through the narrow gate of baptism, we also enter the kingdom of God, though only conditionally as long as we are in the flesh. The one condition is that we endure to the end on the path we have started (see Matthew 24:13; 3 Nephi 27:16)—that we stay faithful and stay put. Being a member of the Church in good standing is the same as being in the kingdom (see D&C 45:1; 72:1; 104:59; 136:41).

2. I will preserve thy life. This promise, based on her faithfulness, was literally fulfilled for Emma in the years following this revelation. Each time the mobs attacked Joseph, Emma and their children were also in great danger. The conflict in Missouri with its extermination order and winter exodus killed many of the Saints and proved very difficult for Emma, but through all these afflictions the Lord did preserve her life.

3. An elect lady. *Elect* does not mean "special" or "superior" but is a synonym for "chosen." For example, elected officials are not intended to be special citizens, but rather citizens chosen by vote of the people to serve the people. God's "chosen" people are those selected by God to serve him in doing his work upon the earth. Likewise, an elect individual is one chosen for God's work and service. Ultimately, *elect* or *chosen* refers to those who are chosen because of their faithfulness to bear the full burden of God's *work* for all eternity, and who will also then bear his glory (see Moses 1:39). Work *is* glory, and we cannot have celestial glory without undertaking celestial work. Thus, many are "called," or invited, to be exalted and continue God's work and glory, but few are "chosen," since comparatively few will accept the invitation and labor diligently for God and the kingdom (see D&C 121:34, 40).

In March 1842, the Prophet Joseph explained that Doctrine and Covenants 25:3–7 had been partially fulfilled by Emma's election to the presidency of the Relief Society, having previously been ordained to expound the scriptures.[2]

4. Murmur not. According to President Joseph Fielding Smith, "Emma Smith was human, possessing many of the characteristics which are found in most of us. Being the wife of the man whom the Almighty had blessed, she felt, as most women would have felt under like circumstances, that she was entitled to some special favors. It was difficult for her to understand why she could not view the plates, the Urim and Thummim, and other sacred things, which view had been given to special witnesses. At times this human thought caused her to murmur and ask the question of the Prophet why she was denied this privilege. In this revelation the Lord admonishes her and tells her that it is for a wise purpose to be made known in time to come, why she and the world were deprived of this privilege."[3]

6. Thou shalt go with him. When Joseph traveled, if possible, Emma was to accompany him.

6. Be a scribe for him. A literate and competent woman, Emma had already served as scribe for portions of the Book of

Mormon translation. The reference here is to her later service as a temporary scribe for the Joseph Smith Translation.

7. Ordained under his hand. As the Church has grown and become more developed in its structure, the members have also become more precise in their terminology. It was not so in the early Church, and the fine distinctions we insist upon today to avoid misunderstanding were often not observed back then. The word *ordain* was often used, as it was here, to describe the bestowing of the rights, authority, or commission, to work in some capacity in the Church, whether this was a priesthood capacity or not. Emma and her counselors in the Relief Society were certainly given the authority to function in their callings and were set apart for those callings but without receiving the priesthood. There are many kinds of legitimate authority in the Church that are not actually priesthood authority.

President John Taylor, the very person who "ordained" Emma's counselors at the organization of the Relief Society, explained what was meant back then by the term *ordain:* "I was in Nauvoo at the time the Relief Society was organized by the Prophet Joseph Smith, and I was present on the occasion. . . . [Emma] was elected to preside over the Relief Society, and she was ordained to expound the Scriptures. In compliance with Brother Joseph's request I set her apart, and also ordained Sister Whitney, wife of Bishop Newel K. Whitney, and Sister Cleveland, wife of Judge Cleveland, to be her counselors. Some of the sisters have thought that these sisters mentioned were, in this ordination, ordained to the priesthood. And for the information of all interested in this subject I will say, it is not the calling of these sisters to hold the Priesthood, only in connection with their husbands, they being one with their husbands."[4]

8. Thou shalt receive the Holy Ghost. At the time of this revelation, Emma had been baptized but not confirmed. She was later confirmed by her husband at a small, informal sacrament meeting held at the Smith farm in Harmony in early August.

9. Thou needest not fear. Apparently, Emma had been

concerned about how Joseph could support a family by farming if he spent his full time in building the Church. The answer was that Joseph *would* support her, but *not* by farming. The support would be in and through the Church for which he labored (see D&C 24:3).

11. A selection of sacred hymns. Emma was instructed to compile the first hymnbook of the Church. With the help of William W. Phelps, she fulfilled this charge and made a collection of hymns that was supposed to be printed in Missouri in 1833, but mobs there destroyed the Church's press before the hymnbook was printed. A revised collection was printed in Kirtland, Ohio, in February 1836. It included ninety hymns, of which thirty-four had been written by Latter-day Saints, primarily W. W. Phelps.[5] A second revised edition was printed in Nauvoo, Illinois, in 1841, containing three hundred forty hymns. A third edition was planned at Nauvoo but was never printed.

12. For my soul delighteth. Music and singing in the Church are not merely cultural accretions, for congregational singing and choral music have been part of the heritage of the people of God from the beginning and will be forever (see 1 Chronicles 15:27; Job 38:4–7; Mormon 7:7). Just before the greatest event of all time—Christ's suffering in Gethsemane—Jesus and his disciples sang a hymn together (see Matthew 26:30; Mark 14:26). Singing is an act of worship and of communion with God that delights him, and should delight us. It is not separate from the worship service, but is an integral part of it as much as prayer, to which it is compared here by the Lord. Like prayer, singing brings down the blessings of God on the faithful who worship him in this manner. Conversely, those who refuse to sing are in some degree refusing to worship, and thereby they lose divine blessings.

13. Cleave. Oddly enough, *cleave* means both "to split apart," as in cleaving firewood, and "to stick together" or "to adhere." Here the context makes it clear that Emma was being told to observe and keep, or adhere to, the covenants she had made.

14. Some things can be achieved only indirectly. When we focus on ourselves or seek to glorify ourselves, in pride and without meekness, we do ourselves a spiritual injury. But in our covenant relationship with God, if we lose ourselves and seek to do his work and to glorify him, because we are one with him this also brings glory to ourselves. In a marriage where two persons have truly become one, what glorifies one also glorifies the other. The practice of emphasizing one's own, separate identity apart from one's spouse is generally a step away from the goal of becoming one in the covenant of marriage. This is also true in the gospel covenant, in which we need to glory in God rather than in ourselves. While the advice given here is to Emma, a wife, it could just as well be given in another situation to a husband whose wife has achieved great things or has been called to prominent service.

15. Keep my commandments continually. Only those who keep the commandments, or who "seeketh so to do" (D&C 46:9), can receive a crown and go where God is. The "crown" figuratively spoken of here is the perfect righteousness we receive when we are justified by faith in Christ (see D&C 20:30).[6] Only Christ can bring us into the presence of God *perfectly* worthy and *perfectly* righteous. A crown also identifies those whose rightful place will be to rule, preside, or direct in the next life, as opposed to those who will merely minister, serve, or obey. Rulers wear crowns; servants and subjects do not.

16. My voice unto all. With the probable exception of verse 11, Doctrine and Covenants 25 can be applied or adapted to every member of the Church. Certainly large portions apply to all who would be "elect ladies"—or men—in the Church.

NOTES

1. See Smith, *History of the Church,* 1:103–4.
2. See Commentary on D&C 25:7; Smith, *History of the Church,* 4:552–53.
3. Smith, *Church History and Modern Revelation,* 1:125.
4. Taylor, *Journal of Discourses,* 21:367–68.
5. See Cook, *Revelations of the Prophet,* 36–37.
6. See also the commentary on D&C 20:30.

26

BACKGROUND

Joseph Smith offered no information in *History of the Church* about the circumstances under which Doctrine and Covenants 26 was received. We know, however, that it was received after his arrests and trials in New York, while he was working on his farm in Harmony, Pennsylvania, during July 1830. Section 26 was received at approximately the same time as sections 24–25 and was directed to Joseph Smith, Oliver Cowdery, and John Whitmer.

COMMENTARY

1. The church at Colesville. Colesville, New York, is about twenty miles north of Harmony, Pennsylvania. The branch of the Church there consisted mainly of the Joseph and Newel Knight families, but there were other interested persons in the area.

1. The next conference. Scheduled for 26 September 1830, this conference was held in Fayette, New York, which is northwest of Colesville and Harmony about a hundred miles (see D&C 30 heading).

2. Common consent. No person can hold a position of authority in the kingdom of God upon the earth without the consent of the members of the branch, ward, stake, or Church over whom they will preside (see D&C 20:65; 28:13). This principle of common consent is manifested in the sustaining vote asked of the members whenever someone is proposed for a position of authority over them. The Church is the Church "of Jesus Christ," and so, unquestionably, it belongs to him. But the Church is also "*of* Latter-day Saints," and so as members it is collectively our Church, too, and we have a sustaining voice.

One purpose for the practice of taking a sustaining vote is to protect the members against appointments made by leaders who may not be aware of pertinent facts concerning the individuals proposed. Sustaining also places the membership of the Church, collectively, in a position of governance and gives them a veto power when their voice is combined. No single individual can stop a proposed action without accurate information that raises serious questions of worthiness, but all objections will be heard and considered for merit. Should a majority of the Saints refuse to sustain a name or a proposed action, it must be withdrawn. As Elder Charles W. Penrose once stated: "The voice of the people should respond to the voice of the Lord. It is the voice of the Lord and the voice of the people together in this Church that sanctions all things therein. In the rise of the Church the Lord gave a revelation which said that 'all things shall be done by common consent.' And the Lord designs that every individual member shall take an interest therein, shall bear a part of the responsibility, and shall take upon him or her the spirit of the Church, and be an active living member of the body."[1]

The principle of common consent does not, however, create a democracy, for the members do not nominate individuals or propose actions. These are entirely prerogatives of priesthood leadership. But the Church must collectively agree to all that binds them and to all who preside over them. This is a basic law of heaven. "The priesthood selects, under the inspiration of our Father in heaven, and then it is the duty of the Latter-day Saints, as they are assembled in conference, or other capacity, by the uplifted hand, to sustain or to reject; and I take it that no man has the right to raise his hand in opposition, or with contrary vote, *unless he has a reason for doing so that would be valid if presented before those who stand at the head.* In other words, I have no right to raise my hand in opposition to a man who is appointed to any position in this Church, simply because I may not like him, or because of some personal disagreement or feeling I may have, but *only on the grounds that he is guilty of wrong doing, of transgression of the laws of the Church which would disqualify him for the position which he is called to hold.*"[2]

NOTES

1. Taylor, *Journal of Discourses*, 21:45–46.
2. Smith, *Doctrines of Salvation*, 3:123–24.

DOCTRINE AND COVENANTS
27

BACKGROUND

According to the account written by Joseph Smith in *History of the Church,* the revelation known as Doctrine and Covenants 27 was received by the Prophet in Harmony, Pennsylvania, in early August 1830, but was actually put into writing on two or, possibly three, separate occasions. The first four verses were written down in August of 1830, shortly after the recorded words were spoken by an angel. The rest was written down the following month, late September 1830, while Joseph was in Fayette, New York, in connection with a Church conference being held there.

Emma Smith and Sally Knight had been baptized on 28 June 1830, but a mob broke up the services and they were unable to be confirmed at that time.[1] Joseph Smith later explained that "Early in the month of August Newel Knight and his wife paid us a visit at my place in Harmony, Pennsylvania; and as neither his wife nor mine had been as yet confirmed, it was proposed that we should confirm them, and partake together of the Sacrament, before he and his wife should leave us. In order to prepare for this I set out to procure some wine for the occasion, but had gone only a short distance when I was met by a heavenly messenger, and received the following revelation [section 27], the first four paragraphs of which were written at this time, and the remainder in the September following."[2]

On the other hand, Newel Knight, Sally Knight's husband, recorded in his journal that the revelation was not just *written* on two occasions, but was actually *received* on two different occasions—verses 1–4 in August and the rest in September. This slight discrepancy is not terribly important, but present authors have accepted Joseph's account of the dates for all verses.[3] The 1833 Book of Commandments dates this revelation as 4 September 1830, but the 1833 version consisted only of verses 1–4, the first half of verse 5, verse 14, the first half of verse 15, and the words "and be faithful until I come" from verse 18.

The second half of verse 5 (from "and with Moroni") to verse 18 (ending with "ye ask of me"), excluding verses 14–15 and the words "and be faithful until I come" from verse 18, were first printed as part of section 27 in the 1835 edition of the Doctrine and Covenants. Nevertheless, these verses were identified in the 1835 edition, in *Manuscript History of the Church,* in Newel Knight's journal, and in other Church publications printed before Joseph's death as having been received in August or September of 1830.[4] Newel Knight's journal indicates that the original revelations, as written in August and September of 1830, included the full text of section 27 as it appeared in the 1835 Doctrine and Covenants, and therefore as we now have it—including verse 12.

Newel Knight also told us what happened in Harmony after the revelation was received: "In obedience to this revelation we prepared some wine of our own make, and held our meeting, consisting of only five persons namely, Joseph Smith and wife, John Whitmer, and myself and wife. We partook of the sacrament, after which we confirmed the two sisters into the Church, and spent the evening in a glorious manner."[5]

Frequently modern Saints, under the influence of a twentieth-century understanding of the Word of Wisdom, insist that "wine" in the scriptures means grape juice; most often this is incorrect. In this case, however, because the wine was made and used on the same day, it clearly *was* grape juice. Some congregations of the Saints continued to use wine for the sacrament until about the turn of the century, while most others used water. Since 1906 the Church has used water exclusively.[6]

COMMENTARY

1. Whose word is quick. See the commentary on Doctrine and Covenants 6:2.

2. It mattereth not. Because the emblems of the sacrament are symbolic rather than mystically connected to the physical body and blood of the Lord, any food or liquid may, with permission of priesthood leaders, be used as the emblems by which we remember him. Some Christians believe that the bread and the wine actually become the body and blood of Christ, which the believers then really eat and drink. This is the doctrine of transubstantiation, which the Church does not accept.[7] In the Latter-day Saint view, after the emblems have been blessed, the bread is still bread and the water is still water, although they have been consecrated for a particular use as symbols of Christ's flesh and blood, and in that capacity they are treated with respect.

3. Commandment. The commandment here is not against *using* wine for the sacrament, which practice continued for some time, but against *buying* sacramental wine from the enemies of the Church. If the Church used wine for the sacrament, it was to be wine of their own making and not purchased from their enemies.

4. New among you. This has reference to Joseph making sure the wine was pure and not tampered with by the enemies of the Church. Some have interpreted this as a commandment to use only grape juice rather than fermented wine for the sacrament, but this cannot be correct, because the Church continued to use fermented sacramental wine both in Kirtland and in Nauvoo.

5. I will drink of the fruit of the vine. When Jesus blessed the wine at the Last Supper, he told his disciples, "I will not drink henceforth of this fruit of the vine, until that day when I drink it new with you in my Father's kingdom" (Matthew 26:29; Mark 14:25; Luke 22:18). Most translators take "new" in this passage to mean "anew" or "again"; thus, as Elder John Taylor noted, "in partaking of the Sacrament we not only commemorate the death and sufferings of our Lord and Savior Jesus Christ, but we also shadow forth the time when he will come again and when we shall meet and eat bread with him in the kingdom of God."[8]

This great sacrament meeting, or perhaps this series of sacrament meetings, following the Second Coming is sometimes referred to as "the marriage supper of the Lamb" (Revelation 19:9; D&C 58:11; 65:3), and it may be similar to the sacrament meeting the resurrected Lord held with the Nephites when he visited them (see 3 Nephi 20:1–9).

Elder Joseph Fielding Smith wrote: "The Savior informed his Apostles on the night He ate the Passover that He will not drink of the 'fruit of the vine' with them again until He 'should drink it new with them in the kingdom of God.' (See Matt. 26:29; Luke 22:18) This was reiterated in the revelation to Joseph Smith wherein the Lord promised to eat and drink with His prophets and saints in His Father's kingdom which shall be built up on the earth."[9]

This could refer to several visitations that the Savior will make to the Saints as the time of the Millennium nears. For instance, there is the grand gathering at Adam-ondi-Ahman at which Adam will preside over his family (D&C 116). Perhaps there are other such meetings at which the sacrament of the Lord's Supper will be administered and the Savior will be present.

5. Fulness of my everlasting gospel. See the commentary on Doctrine and Covenants 1:23; 14:10; 20:9; 22:1; 42:12; 66:2.

5. The record of the stick of Ephraim. This refers to the Book of Mormon. The allusion here is to Ezekiel 37:15–19, where the Hebrew word translated as *stick* actually means "wood," referring to the wooden writing tablets of the time. Technically, the two "sticks" or "wooden tablets" are symbolic of the descendants or "houses" of Ephraim and of Judah who had divided into two separate kingdoms and were in Ezekiel's time bitter enemies. Ezekiel made this clear in 37:21–23. Thus, Ezekiel's prophecy, on one level at least, is about the gathering and reconciling of the house of Ephraim and the house of Judah, the northern and the southern kingdoms, which together would comprise all of Israel, including the lost ten tribes, the Book of Mormon peoples, and the Jews. Hence, since the house of Ephraim is the "stick," Moroni is correctly said here to hold "the keys of *the record of* the stick of Ephraim," that is, the record of the house of Ephraim, which is the Book of Mormon.

In contemporary LDS usage this fine distinction has been lost, and it is customary to speak of the Book of Mormon itself as the stick of Ephraim, rather than as *the record of* the stick of Ephraim. But on another level of meaning, the common interpretation, originally proposed by William W. Phelps,[10] is also correct, for the Bible and the Book of Mormon, as separate histories now joined, may themselves symbolize the two houses that have been separated but are soon to be joined as the union of their records foreshadows. Moreover, the term *sticks,* or writing tablets, makes no sense as a symbol for houses or descendants without some connection to their written records.

"The stick of Joseph, which is in the hand of Ephraim," another phrase from Ezekiel 37:19, may then refer to the Book of Mormon as restored in the latter days to the Prophet Joseph Smith, himself a descendent of Joseph through his son Ephraim (see D&C 113:4; 2 Nephi 3:6–9). The Nephite prophet Moroni holds the keys for all of God's work that involves the Book of Mormon, the record of the stick of Ephraim.

6. Elias. *Elias* is the Greek form of the Hebrew name *Elijah.* Therefore *Elias* and *Elijah* are really the same name, like *John* and *Juan* in English and Spanish, for example. *Elias,* however, is not always a proper name referring to the historical prophet of 1 Kings 17–2 Kings 2, but is also frequently used as a title or an office for a heavenly messenger who comes to prepare and restore. Elias can be anyone sent from God "in the spirit and power of Elias" (Luke

1:17). More than one person with a different proper name has also borne the title of *Elias,* and been so referred to in scripture. For example, Jesus identified John the Baptist as Elias (see Matthew 17:10–13). In Joseph Smith Translation John 1:28, John the Baptist referred to Jesus as Elias, partly because he restored all things in the meridian of time, but also because Jesus is the ultimate Elias who will restore the earth to its paradisaical glory and restore spirits and bodies to one another in the Resurrection.[11] Joseph Smith applied the title *Elias* to John the Revelator (see D&C 77:14).

Because the scriptures sometimes use Elias to designate the prophet Elijah specifically, and other times use Elias to designate other people who come in the *role* of an Elias (as in Luke 1:17), there can be a great deal of confusion if care is not taken to distinguish the two usages. The role of Elias—whoever might be referred to by that title or might function in that role—is to prepare and to restore. Thus, John the Baptist, for example, prepares the way before the Savior at both comings, and he restored the Aaronic Priesthood in the latter days. The historical prophet Elijah, who is also *an* Elias, besides preparing the way and restoring what has been lost, was also the last of the ancient Israelite prophets to hold the keys of the sealing power as they had been passed down to him (see D&C 27:9).

In verses 6–7 *Elias* is used as a title to designate some prophet whose own proper name is not given. President Joseph Fielding Smith stated that this Elias was Noah.[12] Joseph Smith indicated that Noah was the mortal designation for the individual who was known as the angel Gabriel in premortal life.[13] Finally, the Gospel of Luke explains that the heavenly messenger who came to Zacharias, the father of John the Baptist, was Gabriel. Thus, the loop is closed—the angel Gabriel came into the flesh, was known as Noah during his mortal life, and was also the angel who came as a disembodied spirit to Zacharias and to Mary, in the office of an Elias, to prepare them for the births of John and Jesus, themselves two of the most important Eliases that would ever be (see v. 7; Luke 1:19).

7–13. At the end of this dispensation, the representative heads of all previous dispensations of the gospel, as well as the faithful from all those dispensations, will drink the fruit of the vine with Christ at the marriage supper of the Lamb (see D&C 58:11; Revelation 19:9), whether that event consists of one session or of many.

10. Joseph and Jacob, . . . your fathers. Abraham, Isaac, Jacob, and Joseph are often called "the fathers" (see D&C 2:2) or "the patriarchs" (Greek for "first fathers" or "ruling fathers") because they are the ancestors by blood or by adoption of all the faithful Saints, the true house of Israel, who follow after them.

10. The promises remain. The promises that "remain" are the promises made to these patriarchs, the heads of the family, that: (1) a Savior would be provided for them and their posterity; (2) even though Israel would be scattered, they would eventually have a chance to hear the gospel and receive its blessings; and (3) Israel would someday be gathered together again, a righteous posterity to the patriarchs. Fulfillment of these promises is part of God's obligation to Abraham, Isaac, and Jacob's posterity under the terms of the Abrahamic covenant (see Abraham 2:6–11).

11. Michael, or Adam. Just as Noah's name in the premortal existence was Gabriel (Hebrew, "man of God"), so Adam's name in that existence was Michael (Hebrew, "who is like God"), the archangel (Greek, "ruling angel"). He is one of the angels of God's presence (see Isaiah 63:9; Abraham 1:15) who enjoyed the privilege of serving in the immediate presence of Jehovah and being one of his closest and most trusted associates among the spirits created by God the Father.

12. And of the same things which I revealed unto them. The language seems purposely vague here, perhaps because the reference may be to sacred ordinances.

13. The keys of my kingdom. These represent the authority to preside over the kingdom of God upon the earth, the Church, and to direct its activities here.[14]

13. Last times . . . fulness of times. "The last times" and "the fulness of times" both refer to our present dispensation as the last. The former phrase, however, emphasizes the character of this as the last in a series of many basically similar dispensations. The latter phrase emphasizes the unique nature of this dispensation as the one in which all things will be restored, the final gathering and restoration of Israel will take place, and all the words and promises of the Lord to other dispensations will be fulfilled.

14. Those whom my Father hath given me. Those who have entered into the gospel covenant and therefore through his Atonement belong to Christ at his coming (see D&C 45:4–5; 1 Corinthians 15:23; 1 Thessalonians 2:19).

15. Gird up your loins. In ancient Israel men wore loose robes or gowns held in place by a wide belt, or *girdle*. When preparing for any kind of physical exertion such as work, battle, or arduous travel, men would pull their robes up out of the way and tuck them in their belts. So the command to gird up one's loins is a command to pull ourselves together and get ready to work, fight, travel, or otherwise exert ourselves in the Lord's service. An equivalent modern expression might be "roll up your sleeves."

15–18. My whole armor. Verses 15–18a are of course a repetition of the very excellent exhortation of Paul found in Ephesians 6:13–17. Latter-day prophets have explained that the loins, heart, feet, and head represent those four parts of the body and four realms of human activity in which we are most at risk from evil influence. The loins symbolize procreative power. The heart symbolizes our conduct and what we love. The feet symbolize our course, our objectives, and our goals, and the head symbolizes our thoughts. When truth girds our loins, we are modest and virtuous, knowing the true significance and purpose of these powers. When the breastplate of righteousness covers our heart, our desires will be proper at all times and we will love righteousness. When our feet are shod with the preparation of the gospel of peace, we will walk in holy paths. And when our head is covered with the helmet of salvation, our thinking will be enlightened by knowledge of the Lord's great plan. In addition, the shield of faith will deflect the doubts that scoffers and critics will throw our way. Finally, our only weapon, and the only one we need, will be the sword of the Spirit, with which we can reach, touch, and cut to the quick those with whom we come in contact.[15]

16. Mine angels. The word *angel* (Greek *angelos* or Hebrew *malach*) in the Bible is simply the generic word for a messenger. So anyone authorized to bring a message from the presence of God is an "angel," whether they are spirits or translated or resurrected beings.

18. Ye shall be caught up. This is not the Protestant doctrine of the "rapture" per se, but refers to the righteous, both living and dead, who will be physically caught up from the earth before it is cleansed by fire at the second coming of Christ (see D&C 88:96–98; 1 Thessalonians 4:15–17). The purpose for being caught up is not to be taken away to heaven or anywhere else, but to avoid the conflagration that will consume the wicked who are not caught up and everything else that is telestial upon the earth. Christ is coming *here* to rule and reign upon a cleansed earth. Compare that to Matthew 6:10: "Thy kingdom *come.* Thy will be done *in earth,* as it is in heaven."[16] After the great cleansing by fire, mortal Saints will live out their appointed days upon the earth and then be changed to resurrected glory in the blink of an eye (see D&C 63:50–51).

According to Joseph Smith, "Christ and the resurrected Saints will reign over the earth during the thousand years. They will not probably dwell upon the earth, but will visit it when they please, or when it is necessary to govern it."[17]

NOTES

1. See Porter, "Study of the Origins of the Church," 203–4.
2. Smith, *History of the Church,* 1:106.

3. See Woodford, "Historical Development," 1:393–94.
4. See Woodford, "Historical Development," 1:393–98.
5. "Labors in the Vineyard," in *Classic Experiences and Adventures*, 63.
6. See Cook, *Revelations of the Prophet*, 127, n. 1.
7. See the commentary on D&C 20:75.
8. Taylor, *Journal of Discourses*, 14:185.
9. Smith, *Church History and Modern Revelation*, 1:132–33.
10. See "Tribe of Joseph," 1–2.
11. See the commentary on D&C 77:9.
12. See Conference Report, Apr. 1960, 72.
13. See Smith, *History of the Church*, 3:386.
14. See the commentary on D&C 65:2.
15. See Lee, *Feet Shod with the Preparation of the Gospel of Peace*, 2–7; Reeve, "Whole Armor of God," 193.
16. Emphasis added.
17. Smith, *Teachings*, 268.

28

⌒

BACKGROUND

During July and August of 1830, persecution of the Prophet and the Saints in the Colesville and Harmony areas continued to grow in intensity. Even Emma's parents turned against Joseph. Sometime in late August, two or three weeks after Doctrine and Covenants 27 was received, Father Peter Whitmer Sr. invited the Prophet and his family to come live with him again in Fayette, New York, about a hundred miles northwest of Harmony and near Manchester and Palmyra. Joseph, Emma, and Oliver had lived at the Whitmer farm once before, between June 1829 and June 1830, while the Book of Mormon was being translated and published and when the Church was being organized.

When the Prophet arrived in Fayette during the last week of August, he was grieved to discover that Hiram Page, one of the Eight Witnesses to the Book of Mormon and Father Whitmer's son-in-law, had been receiving "revelations" concerning Zion, Church organization, and other doctrines, by means of what Page believed to be a "seer-stone" into which he would gaze. These revelations contained many things contrary to the New Testament and also to the revelations given previously to Joseph Smith.[1] Many of the Fayette Saints had been deceived by these revelations and were accepting them as the word of God to the Church, including the Whitmers and even Oliver Cowdery, who actually supported Page in his activities. At this point in Church history, such an error is somewhat understandable, since the Church was only a few months old and the Lord had not yet given instructions as to who could or could not receive revelation for the Church. To many of the members it might have seemed logical that one of the Eight Witnesses of the Book of Mormon should be able to receive revelations for the Church and its members.

At first Joseph was going to wait for the conference scheduled for 26 September to address this problem. But when he realized how far the error had spread among the Saints, he decided to confront Hiram Page immediately—and was initially resisted very strongly by Oliver Cowdery. Finally, however, he was able to convince Oliver and the Whitmers privately that Page's revelations were not genuine. Then Joseph petitioned the Lord for further direction and received Doctrine and Covenants 28 in reply.[2] This revelation is directed through Joseph to the previously deceived Oliver Cowdery.

Newel Knight, who was an eyewitness to this affair, added a few notes of interest: "On my arrival [in Fayette for the conference] I found Brother Joseph in great distress of mind on account of Hyrum [Hiram] Page. . . . That night I occupied the same room that he did and the greater part of the night was spent in prayer and supplication."[3]

On 26 September the first item on the agenda for the conference was a discussion of the Hiram Page affair and the reading of Doctrine and Covenants 28. Perhaps Oliver had talked privately with Hiram Page before the conference, according to the Lord's command (see v. 11). At any rate, to Joseph's great relief, all present at the conference, including Hiram Page, renounced the stone and its "revelations."[4]

There are conflicting accounts of where Hiram Page's stone was located and what it looked like; perhaps more than one stone was claimed as Page's. An account cited in Robert J. Woodford's dissertation reported that in 1949 the stone was in the possession of the historical department of the RLDS Church in

Independence, Missouri, and described it as "a flat stone about seven inches long, four wide, and one-quarter inch in thickness," as being "dark gray in color with waves of brown and purple gracefully interwoven across the surface," and "a small hole has been drilled through one end of it as if a string had been threaded through it."[5] Alvin R. Dyer, however, reported that in June of 1955 the stone was in the possession of Mayme Koontz, a grand-daughter of Jacob Whitmer, and was a "light-grey, highly polished stone, about five inches by three inches, by one-half inch thick with two [large] round holes in [the center of] it."[6]

Given the conflicting accounts of its location and appearance, it would seem that the deception associated with this stone continues.

COMMENTARY

1. Oliver Cowdery and others sorely needed instruction on how revelation comes to the Church as a whole. Oliver's role was to be the "first preacher" to the Church by declaring and expounding the revelations given to Joseph, but Joseph, not Oliver, was the head appointed to receive the revelations. As a leading authority of the Church and an Apostle of the Lord, Oliver Cowdery had the right to be heard by the Church, but he did not have the right to receive revelation for the Church on his own authority. In the priesthood line of authority, Joseph stood between Oliver and the Lord (see D&C 30:7).

2. No one shall be appointed. The members already knew that the Prophet received revelation and that they were obligated to heed all his words as if from the Lord's own mouth (see D&C 21:4–5). They did not yet understand, however, that the Prophet was the *only* one who could receive revelation for the Church. Many of these Saints had been converted from churches with a very democratic structure, where church governance had been run more like a New England "town meeting"—from the bottom up—than by priesthood authority—from the top down. This background made it somewhat difficult for these Saints to learn the correct order of the priesthood and made them vulnerable to movements, proposals, and revelations that had no divine authority. Joseph Smith stated the principle this way, "It is contrary to the economy of God for any member of the Church, or any one, to receive instructions for those in authority, higher than themselves; therefore you will see the impropriety of giving heed to them."[7] Within six months, the new members in Kirtland had to be taught this same lesson all over again (see D&C 43:3–7), as have some new, inexperienced, or doctrinally naive Saints from that time to the present.

The acceptance of unauthorized "leaders" and other alternate voices has been a chronic failing of some Latter-day Saints in this dispensation, much as worshiping idols was a chronic failing of the children of Israel in former times. A First Presidency message to the Church in 1913 stated: "From the days of Hiram Page, . . . at different periods there have been manifestations from delusive spirits to members of the Church. . . .

"When visions, dreams, tongues, prophecy, impressions or any extraordinary gift or inspiration, convey something out of harmony with the accepted revelations of the Church or contrary to the decisions of its constituted authorities, Latter-day Saints may know that *it is not of God,* no matter how plausible it may appear. . . . The Lord's Church 'is a house of order.' It is not governed by individual gifts or manifestations, but by the order and power of the Holy Priesthood as sustained by the voice and vote of the Church in its appointed conferences."[8]

2–3. Even as Moses . . . even as Aaron. Joseph Smith and Oliver Cowdery were to the Latter-day Saints as Moses and Aaron were to Israel. Joseph was to receive the revelations, as did Moses; Oliver was to preach and make them known, as did Aaron (see D&C 21:12). "It was very necessary that Oliver Cowdery should receive this admonition, for he was inclined to take issue with the Prophet even in regard to matters of revelation. Much good came out of this unpleasant incident, for the members were taught that there was order in the Church and only one appointed to receive commandments and revelations for their guidance, and he was the one God had called."⁹

5. By way of commandment. Only Joseph commanded the Church in the name of the Lord. What Oliver said or wrote fell in the category of wise advice, because Oliver was not God's spokesman to the Church—Joseph was. At this point in Church history, Oliver was *Joseph's* spokesman as Aaron was Moses' spokesman (see Exodus 4:16, 30). Only Joseph was the Lord's spokesman, and therefore Oliver could not issue commandments to the Church on his own authority.

6. Thou shalt not command him who is at thy head. This was the second time Joseph and Oliver had been at odds on matters of authority and spiritual discernment. The previous month, while the Prophet was still in Harmony, Oliver had written to him that there was an "error" in the recorded wording of Doctrine and Covenants 20:37, which says: "And truly manifest by their works that they have received of the Spirit of Christ unto the remission of their sins." Oliver then *commanded* Joseph "in the name of God to erase those words, that no priestcraft be amongst us!"¹⁰ Joseph went to Fayette and convinced Oliver and the Whitmers that Oliver, and not the revelation, was in error. The wording in this verse, "thou shalt not command him who is at thy head," is perhaps a reference to this earlier exchange. Together with Oliver's errors in the Hiram Page affair merely a month later, these episodes foreshadow the future difficulties Oliver would have due to his tendency to follow his own judgment rather than the Prophet (see D&C 23:1).

8. Go unto the Lamanites. In the 1820s and 30s there were large numbers of native Americans living in the eastern and midwestern United States. Four months before Doctrine and Covenants 28 was received, on 28 May 1830, Congress had passed the Indian Removal Bill, which directed that all native Americans within the boundaries of the United States were to be relocated to the federal Indian Territory west of Missouri. Some of the tribes had already moved there, and it was clear that "the borders by the Lamanites" (v. 9) west of Missouri would be where the Church could most quickly reach the largest number of native Americans.

This relocation was far from complete, however, and Oliver's mission to the Lamanites would take him and his companions first to New York to the Catteraugus Indians, to Ohio and the Wyandots, and only then beyond Independence, Missouri, to present-day Kansas, the Indian Territory. Here, "on the borders by the Lamanites," the missionaries led by Oliver Cowdery taught the Shawnees and the Delawares. In all, the missionaries to the Lamanites covered about fifteen hundred miles, much of it on foot, in the winter of 1831. More information concerning this Lamanite mission and those who were to be Oliver's companions is recorded in sections 30 and 32.[11]

While traveling through Ohio, the missionaries stopped in Mentor, near Kirtland, to see Sidney Rigdon, a Reformed Baptist minister and a friend of Parley Pratt. Rigdon and more than 120 others in the Kirtland area were converted to the Church within a month's time, and a branch of the Church was organized there.[12]

9. Where the city Zion shall be built. Apparently, one of the topics addressed in Hiram Page's false revelations had been the location and development of Zion. Interest in this subject may have intensified at this time as a result of the revelation of Moses 7 to Joseph Smith, for this material in the Joseph Smith Translation seems to have led many in the Church to assume Zion was going to be established immediately. The Lord clarified in this verse that no one even knew at that time where the city of Zion would be built. This information would come later in Doctrine and Covenants 57:2–3.

10. By the voice of it. The Lord directed that Joseph would preside over the conference by the sustaining vote of the conference and that Oliver was to take Joseph's instructions.

11. Thy brother. The term *brother,* as used here, refers to the brotherhood of the gospel. Oliver Cowdery and Hiram Page did become brothers-in-law two years later when Oliver married Elizabeth Whitmer, sister to Hiram's wife, Catherine, but Hiram and Oliver were already very good friends in 1830.

11. Between him and thee alone. This is the correct procedure for reconciling a brother or sister who has offended. First Hiram Page was spoken to privately; then, since his error affected the Church, the details of his error were discussed openly at the conference, and his "seer-stone" and its revelations were renounced publicly by all present, including Hiram himself. Notice that Hiram Page was not evil, but he was mistaken and deceived, and it is the duty of the Brethren to correct those who would teach, preach, write, or otherwise spread false doctrine to the Church, even when those persons believe themselves to be in the right. Some in the modern Church who are deceived, as was Hiram Page, do not accept the correction and warning of the Brethren in the same humble spirit that Page did.

12–13. There are no self-appointed leaders or revelators, and no private or closed-door appointments or ordinations in the Church. Period. We are to follow only those leaders who have been publicly sustained by the Church collectively. No one may function in any position of authority over the members of the Church without the sustaining vote of the Church. This is the order of the kingdom and its scriptural defense against all claims of secret blessings or private ordinations (see D&C 26:2).[13] Elder Spencer W. Kimball counseled: "There are lines of defense for him who has been assailed by the deceivers. If the confused one is in doubt, let him ask of the pretending leader: Were you sustained and approved by the body of the Church? Early the Lord indicated this safeguard against impostors. Changes in policy, practice or doctrines will be approved by common consent of the Church."[14]

15. It shall be given thee. The itinerary for the coming Lamanite mission would be revealed to Oliver as he traveled. Oliver *was* entitled, like all the rest of us, to revelation for himself or concerning his own proper stewardship.

NOTES

1. See Smith, *History of the Church,* 1:109–10.

2. See Smith, *History of the Church,* 1:109–11.

3. Cited in Woodford, "Historical Development," 1:404–5.

4. See Smith, *History of the Church,* 1:115.

5. Cited in Woodford, "Historical Development," 406.

6. Dyer, *Refiner's Fire,* 256–57, with accompanying photo.

7. Smith, *History of the Church,* 1:338.

8. Smith, Lund, and Penrose, "Warning Voice," 1148–49; emphasis added.

9. Smith, *Church History and Modern Revelation,* 1:135.

10. Smith, *History of the Church,* 1:105.

11. See Gentry, "Light on the 'Mission to the Lamanites,'" 226–30.

12. See Pratt, *Autobiography of Parley Pratt,* 47–57.

13. See also the commentary on D&C 26:2.

14. Kimball, *That You May Not Be Deceived,* 11.

29

BACKGROUND

While the Prophet and his wife were living at Father Whitmer's farm in Fayette, sometime during September 1830, Joseph received another revelation from the Lord—Doctrine and Covenants 29. This was after receiving Doctrine and Covenants 28, but before the conference began on 26 September. The Prophet gave very little information about the historical setting of section 29, noting only that this revelation was given in September, in Fayette, and in the presence of six elders.[1] Elder Joseph Fielding Smith dates the revelation to shortly before the conference on 26 September.[2] Further, the *Far West Record* lists the elders who attended the conference, and there were only six besides the Prophet himself. Most likely these are the same six elders who were with Joseph when the revelation was given: Oliver Cowdery, David Whitmer, John Whitmer, Peter Whitmer, Samuel H. Smith, and Thomas B. Marsh.[3]

At the time section 29 was received, the little Church was barely five and a half months old. The first Church conference, held three months earlier on 9 June 1830, had been accompanied by such an outpouring of the Spirit that all the members were eager to attend the second conference on 26 September.

COMMENTARY

1. Voice of Jesus Christ. Again, it must be remembered that the "God" who is giving these revelations to Joseph Smith is specifically God the Son, Jesus Christ.

1. The Great I Am. This title refers to the name by which Jehovah, Jesus Christ, revealed himself to Moses on Mount Sinai: "I Am hath sent me unto you" (Exodus 3:14).

2. As a hen gathereth. When danger threatens, a hen gathers her chicks under her breast for protection by *calling* to them, and they come running to her. In just this fashion the Savior will call to his own when the dangers of the world and its imminent downfall threaten, and they also will come running to him.

3. Your sins are forgiven. All those who have entered into the gospel covenant and have been justified by their faith in Christ (see D&C 20:30)[4] have had their sins forgiven them, provided they have kept their covenants and have been faithful to Christ. Not everyone is fortunate enough to receive a direct reassurance like this one, but everyone who enters into the gospel covenant and endures in it may enjoy these same blessings.

5. Your advocate. An advocate is one who pleads your case. In a courtroom, an advocate is the defense attorney. As an advocate for the covenant people at their judgment, Jesus Christ will be their defense attorney, and he will never lose a case.[5]

5. His good will. The phrase "good will" is synonymous with grace.

7. The gathering of mine elect. All who will accept the gospel and live it faithfully are the Lord's elect, or chosen ones. Joseph Smith and the six elders with him were to participate in the gathering of the elect, who, like obedient chicks, will recognize the Lord's voice when he calls and will gather quickly to him. His voice includes the voices of those who speak for him: the prophet, the General Authorities, inspired missionaries, or the whisperings of the Holy Spirit. All who choose to hear and obey are elect.

8. Gathered in unto one place. Before the terrible tribulation and desolation that precede the Second Coming, the elect will be gathered together for instruction and protection, like the chicks gathered under their mother's breast in verse 2. At the time this revelation was given, the Saints did not know where the place for this gathering would be. Two months later, in December 1830, however, the Lord revealed that the Saints should gather temporarily to Ohio. And in June 1831, the Prophet received a vision identifying Jackson County, Missouri, as Zion and the central place where the final gathering would commence.[6]

Upon his arrival in Jackson County, Joseph received another revelation, Doctrine and Covenants 57, which designated the exact site of the center of Zion as being in Independence, Missouri. After their expulsion from Missouri in 1838, the Saints gathered to Nauvoo, Illinois, and after their expulsion from Illinois in 1846, they gathered to the Rocky Mountains. Today Latter-day Saints gather to Zion by coming into the stakes of Zion located throughout the world. Before the great tribulations of the Second Coming, the Saints will gather to many different places, in many different countries, but one of these places will be the city of Independence in Jackson County, Missouri—the center stake of Zion in the last days.

According to Joseph Smith: "The main object [of gathering] was to build unto the Lord a house whereby He could reveal unto His people the ordinances of His house and the glories of His kingdom, and teach the people the way of salvation; for there are certain ordinances and principles that, when they are taught and practiced, must be done in a place or house built for that purpose."[7] Since temples are now located throughout the world for these purposes, many Saints may gather to the stakes of Zion in their own lands and receive the blessings of the Lord's house there.

8. Desolation . . . upon the wicked. This and other scriptures sometimes talk of only two categories for humans—the righteous and the wicked. Sometimes "the Lord speaks of those who have not received the gospel as being 'wicked' as they are still under the bondage of sin, having not been baptized."[8] At other times, however, the scriptures state or imply the existence of a third category for those who are not "wicked" per se, but neither are they among the Saints who enjoy the gospel covenant. Those who are preserved at the last day will include, besides the faithful Saints, all those who are worthy of terrestrial glory; for example, the honorable men and women of the earth who, though not in the covenant, accept Christ on some less informed level and basically keep the biblical commandments. These people will also abide the coming of terrestrial glory to the earth, though they are not members of the Lord's Church (see D&C 76:72–80; 88:92–96).

9. When the earth is ripe. That is, ripe in the iniquity of its inhabitants.

9. I will burn them up. This does *not* refer, as many suppose, to burning the wicked in hell. Rather, it refers to the specific event on the last day of the earth's telestial existence when this physical earth shall be literally cleansed of all wickedness by being burned with fire in the brightness of the Lord's coming, so that the terrestrial Millennium may begin. "It is not a figure of speech that is meaningless, or one not to be taken literally when the Lord speaks of the burning. All through the scriptures we have the word of the Lord that at his coming the wicked and the rebellious will be as stubble and will be consumed."[9] Many have confused the description of this literal burning at the last day with the figurative fires of hell, to create a false picture of the ultimate fate of the wicked. Those who die by fire on that last day will go to hell—that part of the spirit world where Satan temporarily rules (see D&C 76:84–85)[10] —and they will suffer there for their sins (see D&C 19:17), but that spiritual hell comes to an end for most of them in a glorious, telestial resurrection at the end of the Millennium.

11. The hosts thereof. These are all the angels in heaven, many of whom will be faithful Saints from dispensations before Christ who were resurrected and freed from the spirit world at the time of Jesus' resurrection (see Matthew 27:52).

11. Dwell . . . on earth a thousand years. The seventh thousand years of the earth's temporal existence, whether that phrase is understood literally or not (see D&C 77:6–7), will be to the other six thousand-year periods as the Sabbath day is to the other six days of the week (see D&C 77:12). While temporal and profane activities may take place during the six days, the seventh day is sanctified and holy. So shall the seventh thousand-year period—the Sabbath Day of the earth's existence—be holy. The Latin word *millennium* means literally "a thousand years," and this period when the earth will be raised to a terrestrial, Eden-like condition and Christ will reign personally as king upon it is often called the Millennium. No wickedness will be allowed on earth during that time. Resurrected beings will interact with mortals, who will continue to be born, have children, and die, but their death will be an instantaneous transition from mortality to resurrected glory (see D&C 63:50–51; 1 Corinthians 15:52).

12. Mine apostles, the Twelve . . . , and none else. Jesus' original New Testament Apostles (except Judas) shall judge the righteous members of the house of Israel who have died in the Lord—in other words, those who were faithful covenant members when they died (see Matthew 19:27–28; Luke 22:30). Notice the delegation to these brethren of tasks we normally think of Jesus himself as performing.

13. A trump shall sound. At the second coming of the Savior there shall be what will sound like a trumpet blast announcing the resurrection of the righteous dead and the descent of the Lord to the earth. This was foreshadowed by a parallel event in the days of Moses when Jehovah, or Christ, descended to the earth on Mount Sinai (see Exodus 19:16–20, esp. 19).

13. The dead which died in me. To be "in Christ" is to be one with him in the gospel covenant. The dead in Christ are all the Saints who died faithful to their covenants but who have not yet been resurrected. This does not, however, exclude any children who may have died before accountability or any who would have accepted Christ and been faithful to him if only they had had the chance (see D&C 138:7–10).

13. To be clothed upon. To receive their resurrected bodies, their robes of righteousness and purity, and their celestial glory (see D&C 138:43; 2 Nephi 9:14; Moses 7:3; 2 Corinthians 5:1–4, 10).

14–21. The Prophet Joseph said, "I will prophesy that the signs of the coming of the Son of Man are already commenced. One pestilence will desolate after another. We shall soon have war and bloodshed. The moon will be turned into blood. I testify of these things, and that the coming of the Son of Man is nigh, even at your doors. If our souls and our bodies are not looking forth for the coming of the Son of Man; and after we are dead, if we are not looking forth, we shall be among those who are calling for the rocks to fall upon them."[11]

14. This great day. "Now brethren and sisters, the great day of the Lord is coming. It is going to be a terrible day. The wicked are going to be destroyed, and when I say the wicked I do not mean everybody outside the Mormon Church. There will be countless millions of people not of this Church spared because they are not ripe in iniquity and to them we will preach the everlasting Gospel and bring them unto Christ."[12]

14. The sun shall be darkened. Compare Doctrine and Covenants 45:42; Isaiah 13:9–11; Joel 2:31; 3:15; Matthew 24:29; Acts 2:20; Revelation 6:12. It is altogether likely that the sun, moon, and stars will still be there, but they will no longer be visible or will be only partly visible because of natural disasters upon the earth. Note the parallels at the end of the Nephite "world" prior to the Savior's arrival among them, which are described in roughly the same manner (see 3 Nephi 8:22).

14. Greater signs. According to Genesis 1:14; Moses 2:14; Abraham 4:14, the sun, moon, and stars were given as "signs" for human beings. Perhaps this means they serve as visible symbols for us of the celestial, terrestrial, and telestial glories, into which humanity will for the most part be divided. Or perhaps the existence of this creation implies existence of a Creator. At any rate, when these natural signs shall cease to give their accustomed light, they will be superseded by even greater signs in heaven and earth, signs that certainly will get our attention and will teach a stronger and more pointed message than their predecessors. Among these greater signs will be the pestilence and disasters that precede the Lord's coming, as described in verses 15–21. If humanity will not listen to the quiet voices of the natural signs we have already been given, the Lord will speak to us a little louder as the end approaches.

16. A great hailstorm. John the Revelator described this hailstorm in Revelation 16:21 and informed us that the hailstones will weigh about a talent each, or somewhere between 50 and 100 pounds. Because there were several different weights of talents in the ancient world, more information would be needed to give an exact weight, but these are the broad limits.

17. Vengeance upon the wicked. Vengeance is the application of punishment to wrongdoers. The Lord has said that "vengeance is mine" (Romans 12:19), and on this day he will take it in full measure. The Lord's vengeance is neither wrong nor unjust; it is the punishment the Lord metes out to satisfy the demands of justice so that the wicked may be forgiven and eventually receive some degree of glory. Note that the reason these people receive God's vengeance, when they could have received his grace instead, is that "they will not repent." In other words, they will bring it on themselves by their own free choice.

17. The cup of mine indignation. This cup symbolizes the accumulated iniquities of the wicked. After their death, justice will demand that the wicked drink that which they have prepared for themselves (see D&C 43:26; 103:3; Revelation 14:10). It is a bitter cup, full of the indignation, wrath, or anger of God at their sins. This indignation can be removed only by drinking the cup themselves and paying the full penalty for their sins (see D&C 19:15–17). Jesus Christ has already drunk for us this cup filled with the world's sins and with God's anger, and we can be spared the hideous experience if we will only repent (see D&C 19:18–19; Matthew 26:42).

17. My blood shall not cleanse them. There are only two possibilities for fallen and sinful humans: either they get clean or they stay filthy. The only way to get clean is through the blood of Jesus Christ. Thus, those in the gospel covenant are sometimes said to be "washed in the blood of the Lamb" (Ether 13:11; see also Alma 13:11; Revelation 7:14). Those few who refuse to repent and accept the atonement of Christ, either in this life or in the spirit world, will be raised up "filthy still" to stand before God at the final judgment, and will be cast out into outer darkness (D&C 88:35).

18. Flies upon the face of the earth. See Exodus 8:21.

19. See Zechariah 14:12 for another description of these events.

21. The great and abominable church. This is the only occurrence of this phrase in the Doctrine and Covenants, though it is probably to be identified with the churches built up "to get gain" in Doctrine and Covenants 10:56 and "the church of the devil" in Doctrine and Covenants 18:20. "The great and abominable church" does *not* refer to any particular denomination, neither Roman Catholics, nor Jews, nor Baptists, nor any other individual church. In its broadest definition, the great and abominable church is the collective term for all who oppose or fight against Zion (see 2 Nephi 10:16). It is also a general term for any manifestation of Satan's form of religion—religion practiced for money, gain, or pleasure, or religion that seeks to justify wickedness (see 1 Nephi 13–14; 22:13–14; 2 Nephi 6:12; 28:18).[13] For this reason the great and abominable church is called the whore of all the earth, because for her everything is negotiable (all values, standards, and principles) and because anything can be bought or arranged for with enough money. All who fight against Zion and all who practice priestcraft—religion for profit or temporal advantage—will be consumed at the last day.

21. Spoken by the mouth of Ezekiel. Ezekiel 38:18–22; 39:6, 17–20.

22. When the thousand years are ended. After the end of the Millennium, some mortals upon the terrestrial earth will once again rebel against God. This rebellion will be allowed to go on for a little while, but then there shall be another end of the world—this time the end of the terrestrial world. Other scriptures tell us that after the Millennium, Satan will again get power over mortals and will gather all his forces for one final contest, the battle of the Great God, which Satan will lose (see D&C 88:110–16; Revelation 20:7–21:1). This is sometimes called the battle of Gog and Magog (see Revelation 20:8; Ezekiel 38–39). Then the earth itself will experience a change comparable to death and resurrection, passing away as a terrestrial world and being born again or recreated as a celestial world (see D&C 88:26). "*A new heaven and a new earth* are promised by the Lord and recorded by the sacred writers. Or, in other words, the planetary systems are to be changed, purified, refined, exalted and glorified, in the similitude of the resurrection, by which means all physical evil or imperfection will be done away."[14]

24. All things shall become new. With the renewing of the earth to a celestial glory, all creation and everything in it will also be renewed or resurrected and become glorified, whether with a celestial, terrestrial, or telestial glory.

25. Not one hair. All things that now exist or have ever existed in this creation were created by God, down to the thinnest hair or the tiniest speck, or mote. And all that he created in the beginning, he will glorify in the end—every atom and molecule in its proper place and role.

26. Michael, mine archangel. This is Adam who was the first man created on the earth (see D&C 107:54; 128:21). Although Jewish and Christian tradition make Michael one of several archangels, the scriptures themselves refer specifically only to one—to Michael, *the* archangel (see D&C 88:112; 107:54; Jude 1:9). *Archangel* in Greek means "first angel," or "ruling angel," or "presiding angel." There may be many angels in positions of authority, but there is only one angel who presides over all the others, and that is Michael who was first of all the angels of God and who presides over all who came after him. Doctrine and Covenants 128:21 seems to give priority to Michael *the* archangel over Gabriel, Raphael, and other angels who were also in positions of authority in the premortal life. Christian tradition also credits Gabriel with the trumpet blast that will wake the dead and bring them to judgment—as in "Gabriel, blow your horn!"—but this verse tells us that Michael will sound that great blast.

26–29. The judgment scene alluded to here is the judgment from the great white throne (see Revelation 20:11–15) that occurs after the Second Resurrection. This is the only judgment that involves *all* the dead at once. The "wicked" spoken of here are those who still at that time stubbornly refuse to repent, even after suffering the pains of hell in the spirit world. These are they who cannot be given any glory, because they will not come to Christ. They are to be cast out with the devil and his angels into outer darkness—spoken of figuratively in verse 28 as "everlasting fire"—and are called sons of perdition (see D&C 76:36–37).

The "righteous," on the other hand, are all those who have repented, whether in mortality or in the spirit prison, and have turned to Christ to be saved. They include all who will be given some degree of glory, whether celestial, terrestrial, or telestial. For Jesus Christ saves and glorifies "all the works of his hands" (see D&C 76:43; see also v. 88). This is different from the earlier judgment scene at the Second Coming, where those on the Savior's right hand are limited to those who repented in mortality, or would have repented, given the opportunity, and who will inherit the celestial kingdom.

26. All the dead. Everyone who has ever lived on this earth will be resurrected. This includes the wicked and even those who will be cast into outer darkness at judgment. No one who has ever come to this earth and received a body will be denied resurrection.

30–32. The first shall be last. . . . First spiritual, secondly temporal. In the beginning God spiritually created man—Adam and Eve. This means on the one hand that he created their spirits, but it also refers to their physical creation in paradise or Eden, where they were not yet mortal and where they were governed by and in communion with him. With the Fall, humanity became mortal and temporal—physical, or "of the flesh," in the full sense. Being "in the flesh," or in mortality, they could also have children, and the great plan was set in motion. Thus, bringing humanity from its celestial, spiritual home down to a telestial, mortal world was the *beginning* of Christ's work.

At the *end* of his work, however, Christ will take fallen and temporal humanity and raise it back up again to glory in the Resurrection. The resurrected body is a spiritual body (not a spirit body) in the sense that it is immortal and is permanently infused with the spirit that governs it. This differs from our mortal condition in which our spirit is only a temporary tenant of our body and is often ignored. The beginning of Christ's work—*creation*—is to get us here, to bring us from the spiritual realm to the temporal; the end of Christ's work—*redemption*—is to get us home again, from the temporal realm back to the spiritual. So in this instance as in many others, the first will be last and the last will be first.

33. That you may naturally understand. That we may understand with our limited, natural minds. Actually, the reference points of "the beginning" and "the end" are artificial, given so that we mortals can make sense of things from our narrow, human perspective. From God's perspective, there is no beginning and no end. Likewise the division of things into temporal and spiritual is also an artificial human way of looking at things, for from God's perspective all things are spiritual, and all that God does and says has eternal, spiritual significance.

36. Because of their agency. All things eternal must be done voluntarily. This is the law of heaven. No one can be forced either to glory or to perdition. To have *agency* is to possess the power of self-determination, the power to decide, to accept or to reject. With the gift of agency God first bestows upon us the power to resist or to fight him, and then he works to win our love and *voluntary* obedience.

From this verse we know that God had given agency to his spirit children already in premortal life. "All men had a spirit birth, and, before the earth was created, lived in a pre-existent life, often called the first estate. In that existence, the spirit children of God, later to become the men and women of earth, possessed the faculties we enjoy here. They could learn, choose, grow or retrograde even as on earth. God, their Father, provided means for their development, but did not rob them of their free agency."[15]

36–39. From the second line in verse 36 to the end of verse 39—the material between the two dashes—there is a parenthetical interruption to the original line of thought, which expands upon the origin and function of the devil. The subject begun in verse 36, the temptation of Adam, resumes in verse 40.

36. The devil. From the Greek *diabolos,* meaning "one who separates or divides." "The devil" is one of Satan's titles and functions.[16] The devil indeed existed before Adam, but not necessarily before Michael, for Adam is the name of the physical or mortal person, and Michael is the name of that same person in premortality. Because God had already given agency to human beings in our premortality, the devil was able to convince a third part of our heavenly Father's children to rebel against him (see Revelation 12:4).

38. Hell. An ambiguous term in the scriptures. Generally, it means any place or any context where Satan rules over those who have chosen him, but it is used specifically to mean that place in the spirit world where the unrepentant suffer for their sins (see Psalm 16:10; Luke 16:23; 1 Nephi 15:35–36). *Hell* is also used for outer darkness, that cold, dark state or place where Satan, his angels, and the sons of perdition are cast forever and ever (see D&C 76:44–49; Revelation 20:14; Jacob 3:11). Hell is used occasionally to describe the whole of the spirit world (see Acts 2:27,

31),[17] and it is used for a state of spiritual anguish that can be suffered here in mortality (see Alma 26:13; 38:8). In the passage here it refers to outer darkness.[18]

39–40. "Some may regret that our first parents sinned. This is nonsense. If we had been there, and they had not sinned, we should have sinned. I will not blame Adam or Eve, why? Because it was necessary that sin should enter into the world; no man could ever understand the principle of exaltation without its opposite; no one could ever receive an exaltation without being acquainted with its opposite."[19]

40. Because he yielded unto temptation. Just as those who were tempted by the devil in premortality became his servants (see v. 37), so those who voluntarily yield to him in this life similarly become his servants and are subject to his will. We can either turn to Christ and be redeemed from Satan through the Atonement, or we will find ourselves under Satan's domination whether in this life, in the spirit world, or in eternity.

41. Spiritually dead . . . first death. The first death was the Fall, being cast, body and spirit, out of God's presence in the garden into mortality. Spiritual death does not mean that our spirit is destroyed or ceases to function, but rather that our spirit is separated from God. Through the Resurrection and the Atonement, Christ overcame this first death, the first separation from God, for all humanity who will accept him as Lord and Savior, whether they do so in this life or in the spirit world.

At the final judgment, which takes place at the end of the Millennium after all have been resurrected, some people will still not have repented. These "sons of perdition" will suffer the last death, the *second* death, which is being cast out again at judgment from the presence of God and from the kingdoms of glory into that outer darkness that is spoken of figuratively as everlasting fire. This second death is also spiritual because the spirit is again separated from that God who alone is life. From this second death there is no indication in scripture that there will ever be a redemption.

42. That they should not die. Apparently, the lives of Adam and his children before the Flood were lengthened so that no one died during this dispensation without first having had the opportunity to accept or reject the gospel (see 2 Nephi 2:21; Moses 5:58; 7:27). This longevity changed with the Flood (see Genesis 6:3), and it then became possible for people to die in ignorance. Perhaps that is why preaching the gospel to ignorant spirits in prison is often described as beginning with those "which sometime were disobedient, when once the long-suffering of God waited in the days of Noah" (see D&C 138:9; 1 Peter 3:20). Through the preaching of Adam, Enoch, Noah, angels from heaven, and even God himself (see Moses 5:58), no one who died before the Flood died in ignorance.

43. The days of his probation. This is also an ambiguous term. Usually it means the days of our mortal life, the acts of which will decide whether we suffer hell or paradise in the coming spirit world. The probation spoken of in this verse, however, is not just the days of our mortal lives but, at least for the wicked, also includes their time in the spirit world. For the wicked are still being tested in hell between death and resurrection, to see if they will yet believe and repent and receive some degree of glory. No one can be said to have utterly and permanently failed their test or probation until their resurrection takes place, when any change in glory is no longer possible and when those who have refused to repent will be "filthy still" and the Lord will command them to depart (see v. 28). For the purpose of avoiding the pains of hell in the spirit world, the days of our probation are the days of our mortal lives, but for the purpose of avoiding hell in outer darkness by repenting and receiving some degree of glory in the Resurrection, the days of our probation extend until resurrection.

44. Because they repent not. Notice that God does not condemn to outer darkness anyone who will repent. He doesn't *want* to cast out the unrepentant, but the decision is their own. They are cast out because they will not repent and will not allow Christ to redeem them.

45. Whom they list to obey. The phrase means "whom they choose, prefer, or want to obey." We choose whom we will work for, Christ or Satan, and then we receive from our chosen employer the appropriate wages of our service.

46. Little children are redeemed. "They are saved through the atonement and because they are free from sin. They come from God in purity; no sin or taint attaches to them in this life; and they return in purity to their Maker. Accountable persons must become pure through repentance and baptism and obedience. Those who are not accountable for sins never fall spiritually and need not be redeemed from a spiritual fall which they never experienced. Hence the expression that little children are alive in Christ."[20]

46. Redeemed from the foundation of the world. From the very beginning, the plan of salvation has made merciful provision for those who would die in infancy or who would be mentally handicapped.

47. They cannot sin. Sin and accountability require a knowledge of good and evil. Children, the ignorant, and the mentally handicapped cannot sin because they do not know enough to distinguish the good from the evil. All those who do have knowledge have been commanded by God to repent (see v. 49).

50. He that hath no understanding. President Joseph Fielding Smith explained that "The Lord has made it known by revelation that children born with retarded minds shall receive blessings just like little children who die in infancy. They are free from sin, because their minds are not capable of a correct understanding of right and wrong. Mormon, when writing to his son Moroni on the subject of baptism, places [mentally] deficient children in the same category with little children who are under the age of accountability: they do not require baptism, for the atonement of Jesus Christ takes care of them equally with little children who die before the age of accountability [Moroni 8:22].

"Therefore the Church of Jesus Christ of Latter-day Saints considers all . . . children with retarded capacity to understand, just the same as little children under the age of accountability. They are redeemed without baptism and will go to the celestial kingdom of God, there, we believe, to have their faculties or other deficiencies restored according to the Father's mercy and justice."[21]

NOTES

1. See Smith, *History of the Church*, 1:111.
2. See Smith, *Church History and Modern Revelation*, 139–40.
3. See Cannon and Cook, *Far West Record*, 3.
4. See also the commentary on D&C 20:30.
5. See the commentary on D&C 45:3.
6. See Smith, *History of the Church*, 2:254. The revelation alluded to in *History of the Church* might be identified as D&C 52 or D&C 54 (or both), or it might have been independent of them.
7. Smith, *History of the Church*, 5:423.
8. Smith, *Answers to Gospel Questions*, 1:110.
9. Smith, *Church History and Modern Revelation*, 1:238.
10. See also the commentary on D&C 76:84–85.
11. Smith, *History of the Church*, 3:390.
12. Charles A. Callis, in Conference Report, Apr. 1935, 18.
13. See Robinson, "Warring against the Saints of God," 34–39.
14. Pratt, *Key to the Science of Theology*, 60.
15. Widtsoe, *Evidences and Reconciliations*, 72. "Free agency" is a term never used in scripture.
16. See the commentary on D&C 76:28.
17. See Smith, *Teachings*, 310.
18. See Ludlow, *Encyclopedia of Mormonism*, 2:585–86.
19. Young, *Journal of Discourses*, 103.
20. McConkie, "Salvation of Little Children," 4.
21. "President Joseph Fielding Smith Answers Your Question," 81.

DOCTRINE AND COVENANTS

30

BACKGROUND

In the days immediately preceding the second Church conference in Fayette, New York, 26–28 September 1830, the Lord revealed sections 28–29. Of the conference itself Joseph Smith wrote: "At length our conference assembled. The subject of the stone previously mentioned [section 28] was discussed, and after considerable investigation, Brother Page, as well as the whole Church who were present, renounced the said stone, and all things connected therewith, much to our mutual satisfaction and happiness. We now partook of the Sacrament, confirmed and ordained many, and attended to a great variety of Church business on the first and the two following days of the conference, during which time we had much of the power of God manifested amongst us; the Holy Ghost came upon us, and filled us with joy unspeakable; and peace, and faith, and hope, and charity abounded in our midst. Before we separated we received the following"—Doctrine and Covenants 30–31.[1]

Doctrine and Covenants 30–31 were evidently given at the same time, at the close of the conference but before the participants had gone home. Section 30 was originally considered to be three separate revelations and was published in the 1833 Book of Commandments as chapters 30–32. In the 1835 Doctrine and Covenants these three were joined together to form one section.

The revelation to Thomas B. Marsh, section 31, remained separate, perhaps because it was considerably longer.

At the time sections 30–31 were received, Joseph Smith was living in the Whitmer home in Fayette. The three men addressed in section 30 were all Whitmers: David, Peter Jr., and John.

COMMENTARY

1–4. Hiram Page was married to David Whitmer's sister Catherine, and David had been convinced that his brother-in-law was receiving revelations through a "seer-stone" (see D&C 28:11–13).[2] David had been one of Hiram's chief supporters, and the Lord was displeased with this. David was, after all, one of the Three Witnesses of the Book of Mormon. He had stood in the presence of an angel and had heard a voice from heaven testify to him of the truthfulness of the book and the divine calling of Joseph Smith. Yet when the first counterfeit revelations came along little more than a year later, David Whitmer was among the first to be misled.

1. Feared man. This refers not to being frightened of someone, but rather to being too concerned about what people will think and too concerned with political or social consequences. David had given too much weight to the opinions and feelings of people around him, particularly Hiram Page. Our society generally worries too much about how our peers, colleagues, friends, neighbors, or family might react if we make a "big deal" of our religious convictions, yet we aren't concerned enough about how God will react if we abandon or adjust those convictions in order to "get along." The desire of some people to be considered broad-minded, flexible, or nondogmatic by the world is greater than their desire to be deemed faithful by the Lord—they cannot bring themselves to offend the idols of Babylon. On the other hand, people who are absolutely committed to the gospel are often also irritating to their more worldly neighbors—because they will not negotiate or compromise their beliefs for the sake of better relations with others.

2. Not given heed unto my Spirit. The two things that would have kept David (or any of us) from being deceived were the promptings of the Holy Ghost and the counsel of Church leaders, but he did not listen to either of these in the Hiram Page affair.

2. You have been called. See the commentary on Doctrine and Covenants 14:3–4, 11.

2. Whom I have not commanded. This means someone outside the priesthood line of authority. All those who are deceived by apostate groups or teachings have first, like David Whitmer, ignored the Lord's clear warnings by rejecting the promptings of the Spirit or the counsel of Church leaders, and have then allowed themselves to be "persuaded by those whom I have not commanded."

5–8. Peter Whitmer was called to serve as a missionary to the Lamanites in the capacity of a "junior companion." Along with Oliver Cowdery, Parley Pratt, and Ziba Peterson, Peter traveled by foot across New York, Ohio, Indiana, and Missouri to the federal Indian lands then beyond the borders of the United States. Peter remained faithful until his death in Missouri in 1836.

9–11. John Whitmer was called here to undertake a mission in his own neighborhood in Seneca County, New York. Sometimes it can be more difficult to undertake a mission among one's own friends and neighbors than in a foreign land.

10. Philip Burroughs. He was apparently a member of the Church in Seneca Falls, New York, which was just a few miles north of Fayette.[3]

11. Your whole labor shall be in Zion. Perhaps this is a foreshadowing of John Whitmer's still future call to replace Oliver Cowdery as Church historian (see D&C 47).

NOTES

1. Smith, *History of the Church,* 1:115.
2. See also the commentary on D&C 28:11.
3. See *Autobiography of Parley Pratt,* 42; Samuel H. Smith Journal 1831–32.

DOCTRINE AND COVENANTS

31

BACKGROUND

Doctrine and Covenants 31 was received immediately after Doctrine and Covenants 30, at the close of the Conference on 26–28 September 1830, in Fayette, New York.[1] This revelation was given through Joseph Smith to Thomas B. Marsh. Through the inspiration of the Spirit, Brother Marsh had been expecting a restoration of the true Church and was looking for it when the Spirit moved upon him to travel west from his home in Massachusetts to New York state. There, upon hearing of the Book of Mormon, he went to Palmyra in the fall of 1829, where the Book of Mormon was then being printed. At the printing office he met Martin Harris and acquired an early proof sheet of the book, containing only sixteen pages. On the basis of those sixteen pages, Thomas and his wife, Elizabeth, knew that the book was true. Shortly after hearing that the Church had been organized, he moved his whole family to the Palmyra area and stayed for a while with the Smith family in nearby Manchester. Thomas Marsh was baptized by David Whitmer in Cayuga Lake, one of the Finger Lakes near Fayette, on 3 September 1830, and "in a few days" (probably closer to three weeks) was ordained an elder by Oliver Cowdery.[2]

The speed with which Thomas was made an elder was perhaps an indication of his talents and spiritual promise. This

ordination must have taken place before the September conference began, since Thomas B. Marsh was listed as one of the elders
in attendance.[3]

Thomas Marsh, extremely talented and spiritual though he
was, apostatized from the Church in 1838, at which time he had
been President of the Quorum of the Twelve for more than three
years. He allowed a dispute between his wife and another sister
over the misappropriation of some cream to escalate into an issue
of family pride and refused to accept a series of fair judgments
against his wife. He was eventually excommunicated the following year (see v. 9). Eighteen years later, after the death of his wife,
Elizabeth, for whose sake he had left the Church, Thomas was
rebaptized at Winter Quarters in Florence, Nebraska. He went to
Utah and was received there in full fellowship on 6 September
1857. Had Thomas Marsh remained faithful after 1838, he would
have been senior to Brigham Young and might have succeeded
Joseph Smith as President of the Church when the Prophet was
murdered in 1844 (see D&C 112).

COMMENTARY

1. Your faith in my work. Thomas's great faith was displayed
in his willingness to move his whole family to New York on an
impression from the Spirit, and then move again to Palmyra based
on having read only sixteen pages of the Book of Mormon and
learning in a letter that the Church had been organized.

2. Afflictions because of your family. The reference here is
probably to Thomas's extended family rather than his immediate
family,[4] for at this time his wife was an enthusiastic believer in the
Restoration and their children were still quite small and unlikely
to offer their parents much affliction. He was promised that his
children would eventually join the Church although, like most
such blessings, this was conditioned upon continuing faithfulness (see D&C 58:31–33). Most of the blessings associated with
the gospel or pronounced upon the Saints under various

circumstances describe what will happen if, and only if, they remain faithful.

3. Your tongue shall be loosed. "As long as Thomas B. Marsh was faithful he was an eloquent speaker. At the time of the troubles in Clay County, Mo., he was elected a member of a committee to lay the grievances of the Saints before the authorities of the State. On that occasion he spoke so impressively that General Atchison, who was present, shed tears, and the meeting passed resolutions to assist the Saints in finding a new location."[5]

3. Glad tidings. The "good news" of the gospel.

4. Declare the things which have been revealed. So soon after the Hiram Page incident, it is reasonable that the Lord would remind the Saints to be mindful of the difference between what had been revealed to Joseph Smith and what had not.

4. Already to be burned. We might expect to read, "already to harvest" (see D&C 4:4), but shortly after the harvest comes the burning of the fields to remove all the leftover stubble and chaff. Thomas was to harvest those who would listen to the gospel so they will not be burned with the stubble and other useless debris (see D&C 86:7; Matthew 13:24–43). Here "already" should apparently be understood as "all ready."

5. Your sins are forgiven you. All who are keeping their covenants faithfully have this same promise of being justified, or made innocent, through the grace of Christ (see D&C 20:30).[6]

5. Sheaves upon your back. The "sheaves" of grain are the people Thomas would "harvest" by teaching them the gospel.

5. Your family shall live. Thomas was promised that though he was to spend his time in missionary service, his family would be provided for. The laborers, especially those with families who labor full-time for the Lord, deserve and will receive appropriate compensation for their services, whether in coin or in compensating blessings, or both. Not all of this compensation is temporal; not all will be paid in mortality, but sometimes it must be both immediate and temporal in nature.

6. Only for a little time. Thomas's family was dependent upon him for their support, therefore he was not required to be gone from them for very long.

7. Establish a church. That is, establish a branch of the Church.

8. They shall be gathered. The doctrine of the literal gathering of Israel, already known to the Church from the Book of Mormon, was taken very seriously right from the beginning of this dispensation. In the fall of 1832, Thomas led a group of Saints from Kirtland, Ohio, to Jackson County, Missouri, as part of that literal gathering to Zion.

9. Revile not against those that revile. To adopt Satan's methods, even in opposition to Satan, is to leave holy ground and fall under Satan's power. The end does *not* justify the means, and those who serve the Lord must employ the Lord's methods in doing so. Reviling and contending are Satanic behaviors, even when done in defense of the Church.

9. Govern your house in meekness, and be steadfast. Thomas Marsh did neither. It was largely his inability to govern his household that led to his apostasy between 1838 and 1857 (see D&C 112).

10. Physician unto the Church. Though Thomas was not a medical doctor, he was on occasion sought out to attend the sick.[7] His greater calling was, however, as a spiritual physician, for he solved problems, resolved conflicts, and answered many questions for the members of the Church until he became disaffected. When Thomas Marsh was faithful, he had a reputation for receiving frequent and specific revelations in answer to his prayers. His calling as "physician unto the Church" was primarily to help heal the hearts, minds, and spirits of the members rather than their bodies.

12. Pray always. Had Thomas only obeyed this commandment, it is unlikely that he would have "entered into temptation and lost his reward" as he actually did eight years after this revelation was received. No one is so "spiritual" or so "gifted" that they can ignore the often-repeated commandment to pray always and thus avoid temptation. Unless we communicate with the Lord regularly, through prayer on our part and through promptings of the Spirit on his, our relationship will diminish over time.

NOTES

1. See Background to D&C 30.
2. Marsh, "History of Thos. Baldwin Marsh," 18.
3. See Cannon and Cook, *Far West Record*, 3.
4. See Smith and Sjodahl, *Doctrine and Covenants Commentary*, 165.
5. Smith and Sjodahl, *Doctrine and Covenants Commentary*, 165.
6. See also the commentary on D&C 20:30.
7. See Marsh, "History of Thos. Baldwin Marsh," 18.

32

BACKGROUND

The exact date of this revelation cannot be determined, but it was received within about three weeks of the conference in Fayette on 26–28 September 1830. On 17 October 1830, all four men called to the Lamanite mission signed a statement of covenant concerning their coming labors, thus indicating that Doctrine and Covenants 32 had been received by that date.[1] Moreover, Parley Pratt reported that the mission commenced before the end of October.[2] Joseph Smith later stated that some time close to the September conference the elders manifested a great desire to know if additional missionaries couldn't be sent with Oliver Cowdery and Peter Whitmer Jr.,[3] so that the Lamanites might enjoy the blessings of the gospel all the sooner.[4] In consequence of their urging, Joseph inquired of the Lord and received in reply section 32, which added Parley Pratt and Ziba Peterson to the Lamanite mission. As soon as this revelation was received, Emma Smith and other sisters began collecting and making clothes and procuring other necessities for the four missionaries, since some of the four were not able to cover the costs themselves.[5]

The Lamanite mission was not a "mission" in the modern sense—an ongoing enterprise with geographical boundaries, a mission president, and a continuing flow of missionaries. A mission at that time consisted solely of the elders called to a particular area and lasted only as long as they stayed there. In this case, because of the harsh winter weather, the opposition of non-LDS missionaries to the Indians, and the small number of missionaries—five with the addition of Frederick G. Williams, a convert from Kirtland—the work was very difficult. Also, the federal Indian agent, likely with the encouragement of other Christian missionaries, decided to expel the Mormons from the Indian Territory altogether.[6]

Nevertheless, this missionary effort was hardly a failure. Amherst, Ohio, which had been the home of Parley Pratt for most of the four years prior to his joining the Church, was about fifty miles from Kirtland. Stopping in Mentor, Ohio, near Kirtland, on their way to Missouri, the missionaries visited Parley's former teacher, Sidney Rigdon, and others of his friends in the area. Within a month they had converted Sidney, Edward Partridge, Frederick G. Williams, and more than 120 others, thereby more than doubling the population of the Church and making the Kirtland area the largest concentration of Latter-day Saints anywhere at that time.

On this mission the elders presented copies of the Book of Mormon and taught the gospel to the Catteraugus Indians in New York, the Wyandots in Ohio, and the Delawares and Shawnees in the Indian Territory. On this mission also, Oliver Cowdery was able to familiarize himself with the lands around Independence, Missouri, where the Saints would soon settle, and made a small group of converts who served as the nucleus of the Church in Missouri.

Section 32, like section 17, was not printed in the Book of Commandments but was recorded in the *Kirtland Revelation Book,* and was included in the 1835 edition of the Doctrine and Covenants.

COMMENTARY

1. Parley Pratt. This is the first mention in the Doctrine and Covenants of Parley Pratt, one of the heroic figures of the early Church. While living in Ohio, Brother Pratt had been converted by Sidney Rigdon to the Reformed Baptist movement and was on a mission for that faith when he encountered the restored gospel and was baptized in September of 1830, about a month before this revelation was received. Parley then proceeded to Columbia County, New York, his family's home, and baptized his younger brother, Orson Pratt, on Orson's nineteenth birthday. Returning to Fayette in time for the September conference, he soon after received this call to the Lamanite mission. He was the only member of the Lamanite mission who was married.

1. Learn of me, and be meek. As a brand-new member of about one month called to be a full-time missionary, it would be necessary for Parley to learn a lot in a short period of time. Also, because he was an ordained Baptist minister and a missionary when he joined the LDS Church, it would perhaps have been natural for Elder Pratt to expect high standing in the new Church or to forget that Oliver Cowdery was his priesthood leader and Joseph Smith his Prophet. Throughout Parley's life of incredible service to the Church and in some of its highest offices, he remained for the most part "meek and lowly of heart."

2. Oliver Cowdery and Peter Whitmer, Jun. See the commentary on Doctrine and Covenants 28:8; 30:5–6.

2. Among the Lamanites. This reference by the Lord clearly established that native inhabitants of North America are descended from Lehi. According to Elder Spencer W. Kimball: "Wilford Woodruff, President of the Lord's Church, identified many of the larger [North American] tribes as 'Lamanites' . . . as have all the Presidents and leaders of the Church since. So we look upon the name as proper and dignified and fully acceptable. The Lord consistently called His people 'the Lamanites'"[7] (see D&C 30:6; 54:8).

3. Ziba Peterson. Ziba Peterson was also called to join the missionary elders. Brother Peterson had been baptized on 18 April 1830 by Oliver Cowdery, and now as a member for less than six months he was called to the Lamanite mission. Ziba left the Church in 1833.

3. Their advocate with the Father. See the commentary on Doctrine and Covenants 29:5; 45:3.

4. Pretend to no other revelation. Coming so soon after the affair of Hiram Page and his "seer-stone," in which even Oliver had been deceived, it seems reasonable that the Lord would warn the elders here to stick to the scriptures and make no pretense of receiving other revelations. Oliver Cowdery and Peter Whitmer were both special witnesses to the Book of Mormon, and their special calling was to witness to that book. Rather than seek new revelations, they were to pray for understanding of what had already been revealed.

4. Pray always. Over and over in the Doctrine and Covenants the Lord commands his people to "pray always." This is a more important principle than most of us realize and has been commanded of the Saints so far in these revelations five times, in order that we might conquer Satan and escape his servants (see D&C 10:5), have the Spirit poured out upon us (see D&C 19:38), avoid temptation (see D&C 20:33; 31:12), keep our reward (see D&C 31:12), and receive understanding of the scriptures (see D&C 32:4).

NOTES

1. See the full text of their statement in Cook, *Revelations of the Prophet,* 44.
2. See report to Bishop Edward Hunter in Woodford, "Historical Development," 1:446.
3. Called in D&C 28:8; 30:5–6, respectively.
4. See Smith, *History of the Church,* 1:118.
5. See Smith, *History of Joseph Smith,* 190.
6. See Gentry, "Light on the 'Mission to the Lamanites,'" 228.
7. Kimball, *Lamanites,* 3.

33

BACKGROUND

Ezra Thayre and Northrop Sweet were residents of Palmyra, New York, who were baptized in October of 1830 by Parley Pratt before Parley and the other Lamanite missionaries departed at the end of that month. Shortly thereafter, still in October, Ezra and Northrop visited the Prophet Joseph in Fayette, New York, to ask concerning the will of the Lord for them. In answer, they were instructed to preach the gospel, though it does not appear that they were called to leave Palmyra and their families to do so, in which case this call would be equivalent to being a modern stake missionary, or even to being missionaries in the sense that every faithful member is now obligated to be (see D&C 4; 11–12; 14–16).

Northrop Sweet did not last very long in the Church. He was ordained an elder within eight months after Doctrine and Covenants 33 was received, and he moved to Ohio in compliance with the commandment given in Doctrine and Covenants 37. Soon after arriving there, however, Northrop had false revelations instructing him to become the prophet for the Church. Before the end of 1831 he had left the Church and with others formed "The Pure Church of Christ," a venture which did not succeed.

Ezra Thayre, on the other hand, remained relatively faithful to the Church until after Joseph Smith's death. In May of 1831

Joseph received a revelation directing Ezra to prepare for a mission to Missouri, "even unto the borders by the Lamanites,"[1] which he was formally called to undertake a month later on 7 June (see D&C 52:22). Because Ezra delayed so long after receiving this call, he was finally instructed to stay behind in Ohio, and Selah J. Griffin was sent to Missouri in his place.[2] It is likely that Ezra Thayre's lack of diligence in obeying his call to Missouri grew out of his role in certain problems of the Thompson, Ohio, branch of the Church (see D&C 54, 56 headings). Ezra was at the time of his Missouri call already somewhat out of harmony with the Church and in need of repentance for pride, selfishness, and disobedience (see D&C 56:8). Apparently, Ezra Thayre later did repent and participated in Zion's Camp, eventually becoming a prominent Church member in Nauvoo. After the death of Joseph Smith, however, Ezra did not support Brigham Young and the Quorum of the Twelve, and eventually joined the Reorganized Church.

The Prophet Joseph Smith introduced Doctrine and Covenants 33 in *History of the Church* with the following few words: "The Lord, who is ever ready to instruct such as diligently seek in faith, gave the following revelation at Fayette, New York."[3]

COMMENTARY

1. Sharper than a two-edged sword. See the commentary on Doctrine and Covenants 6:2.

1. Discerner of the thoughts and intents of the heart. None of our words, thoughts, or motives are unknown to God. They are all known and will each have to be accounted for. Those that are evil will have to be paid for, whether by the Atonement if we repent or by our own suffering if we refuse to do so. "We may succeed in hiding our affairs from men; but it is written that for every word and every secret thought we shall have to give an account in the day when accounts have to be rendered before God, when hypocrisy and fraud of any kind will not avail us; for by our words and by our works we shall be justified, or by them we shall be condemned."[4]

2. A crooked and perverse generation. A generation such as this willfully twists away from the strait gate and narrow path. Without the atonement of Christ, all human beings are *natural* men and women, being still in their sins (see Mosiah 3:19). Therefore even those we think of as relatively "good people" by human standards are enemies to God and are crooked and perverse by the standards of heaven until they come to Christ. Still, God loves all his children, and he commands those who have entered the covenant, and are no longer natural men and women but who have been born again in Christ, to preach the gospel even to the crooked and perverse in the hope that they also may repent and be saved from suffering for their sins in hell—the spirit world between death and resurrection (see D&C 19:15–18; 76:84–89). Because of the Apostasy, the gospel must be preached to a generation that has never had the blessings of its ordinances.

3. The eleventh hour. A reference to the parable of the laborers in the vineyard (see Matthew 20:1–16, esv. 6). The day and night were each divided into twelve "hours" (see John 11:9–10). The working day in New Testament times normally extended from sunrise, the beginning of the first hour, to sundown, the end of the twelfth hour. In the parable, the lord of the vineyard hired whomever he could to bring in his harvest, even putting on an additional crew at the eleventh hour, even though they could work for only two hours or less. At the end of the day, the lord of the vineyard came to reward his laborers. The vineyard is the world; the grapes are those who can be converted to Christ; and the coming of the lord of the vineyard with the workers' pay is the Savior's second coming to reward his laborers. It is unlikely the parable of the ten virgins was originally alluded to here, since the bridegroom in that parable came at midnight, which in Jesus' time was the sixth hour, literally the middle of the night, and follows the eleventh hour only in modern reckoning.

In the history of the world, or "the Lord's vineyard," this

present dispensation is the last. Thus, it is the eleventh hour of the world's "day," and the last crew of laborers, such as Ezra Thayre and Northrop Sweet—or you and I—have been called.

4. My vineyard has become corrupted. The Lord's vineyard is the world; its fruits are the world's inhabitants. "Let me explain, when I use the term 'corrupt' with reference to these ministers of the gospel, that I use it in the same sense that I believe the Lord used it when he made that declaration to Joseph Smith, the prophet, in answer to the prophet's prayer. He did not mean, nor do I mean, that the ministers of religion are personally unvirtuous or impure. I believe as a class they, perhaps, in personal purity, stand a little above the average order of men. When I use the term 'corrupt' I mean, as I believe the Lord meant, that they have turned away from the truth, the purity of the truth, the beauty of the truth, and have turned to that which is false. A false doctrine is a corrupt doctrine; a false religion is a corrupt religion; a false teacher is a corrupt teacher. Any man who teaches a false doctrine, who believes in and practices and teaches a false religion is a corrupt professor, because he teaches that which is impure and not true."[5]

4. Priestcrafts. Priestcraft is religion practiced for money, power, prestige, or any motive other than the desire to serve God and do his will. Many non-LDS today are "corrupted," that is, they "err" or believe what is false, because of priestcrafts, because of false religions created, now or anciently, for money, power, prestige, and so forth. Even in the Church some members occasionally serve for rewards other than the Lord's—and will eventually be held accountable for it.

5. Called forth out of the wilderness. In scripture, cities and civilization are often equated with "the world" or "Babylon." It follows then that the wilderness, a place apart from the world, might symbolize "Zion." Thus, Joseph went into the woods, Moses up onto the mountain, and Jesus into the wilderness of Judea to encounter or commune with God. John the Baptist is a voice "that crieth in the wilderness" (Isaiah 40:3). The Saints are often called out of Babylon to go into the wilderness to avoid God's punishments upon the world, as was Israel under Moses, Lehi before the destruction of Jerusalem, and the modern Saints in their trek to the mountain West.

Here in verse 5, however, "the wilderness" symbolizes that place where the Church was kept during the great Apostasy. In the time after Jesus, the Church was metaphorically driven out of "the world" into "the wilderness" (see Revelation 12:6, 14; JST Revelation 12:5–7); that is, it was no longer found in the wicked and apostate world of men, but was taken to God. Thus, the Church being called forth out of the wilderness to take the gospel "into all the world" (D&C 18:28) here symbolizes the restoration of the true Church to the earth in the latter days.

6. Gather mine elect. See the commentary on Doctrine and Covenants 29:7–8.

6. From the four quarters of the earth. The lost and scattered of Israel are to be found everywhere upon the earth. The work of the Church in gathering Israel must eventually take place on a global scale, as it does now, because the dispersed of Israel, including the so-called lost ten tribes, will be found among every nation, on the isles of the sea, and in the four quarters of the earth (see 1 Nephi 22:4; 2 Nephi 10:8). For this reason the Church continually seeks to expand its missionary efforts into every corner of the earth.

8–10. Three times in these verses the Lord instructed these two missionaries to open their mouths and cry repentance. Silent witnesses are not worth much in building the kingdom of God, and the Lord promised that if these missionaries would open their mouths, their mouths would be filled.

8. You shall become even as Nephi of old. In 2 Nephi 1:27 Lehi stated that Nephi had the power of God with him when he taught his rebellious brothers. It was not Nephi who spoke, but "it was the Spirit of the Lord which was in him, which opened his mouth to utterance that he could not shut it."

8. In the wilderness. This is perhaps a reference to Ezra Thayre's later call to go "unto the borders by the Lamanites."[6]

9. Sheaves upon your backs. See the commentary on Doctrine and Covenants 31:5.

12. This is my gospel. We sometimes dismiss faith, repentance, baptism, and receiving the gift of the Holy Ghost as the "preliminaries" of the gospel and think of the principles we learn after baptism as the substance of the gospel. This is wrong. The gospel of Jesus Christ in its simplest and purest form consists of faith, repentance, baptism, and receiving the gift of the Holy Ghost. These constitute the "good news" or "glad tidings" we are to take to the world, and the rock upon which the Church is built (see D&C 11:24; 39:6; 2 Nephi 31; 3 Nephi 27:19–21; Articles of Faith 1:4).[7]

13. Rock. See the commentary on Doctrine and Covenants 11:24.

14. The church articles and covenants. The instructions and procedures found in Doctrine and Covenants 20.

15. You shall confirm . . . , and I will bestow. It is important to remember that those who lay their hands upon others to confirm them do *not* thereby bestow the Holy Ghost. They perform the ordinance of confirmation, but the Lord alone bestows or withholds the gift of his Holy Spirit.

16. Given . . . for your instruction. The holy scriptures—in the order given here: *first* the Book of Mormon and *then* the others—give specific training to missionaries and others concerning the fundamentals of the gospel. The Book of Mormon is first in this respect because it has the most to teach us about the nature and purpose of faith, repentance, baptism, and the gift of the Holy Ghost—the fulness of the gospel. Ezra Thayre and Northrop Sweet were told to remember, however, that it is the Spirit of the Lord that quickens all things—that makes all things live. The Spirit is also what makes the scriptures come to life in our hearts and minds. It is not enough simply to study; we must study by the light of the Spirit.

17. Praying always. Here it is again. This makes six times in thirty-three sections.[8] It would seem prayer is important.

17. Having your lamps trimmed and burning. In biblical times lamps were containers of oil with wicks in them. Necessary maintenance included cleaning the lamps, trimming the wicks, checking the oil level, and having enough extra oil on hand for every contingency—or else one ended up in the dark. It was also the custom in those times for the groom to have a celebration with his friends, and then with his friends go later at an indeterminate hour to the bride's home to complete the festivities and take her to his own home. The bride's guests, mostly girls her own age, had to be ready for his arrival with their lamps burning whenever he might show up. In the parable of the ten virgins, the five foolish virgins had lamps, wicks, and oil in their lamps, but they brought no *extra* oil in case the groom did not arrive early (see Matthew 25:1–13). When he did not come until the middle of the night, they were unprepared for such a long vigil and had run out of oil. Though they then tried to scramble for more oil, they ended up locked out—in the dark.

"In our lives the oil of preparedness is accumulated drop by drop in righteous living. Attendance at sacrament meetings adds oil to our lamps, drop by drop over the years. Fasting, family prayer, home teaching, control of bodily appetites, preaching the gospel, studying the scriptures—each act of dedication and obedience is a drop added to our store. Deeds of kindness, payment of offerings and tithes, chaste thoughts and actions, marriage in the covenant for eternity—these, too, contribute importantly to the oil with which we can at midnight refuel our exhausted lamps."[9]

18. I come quickly. *Quickly* does not necessarily mean "soon." It means completed from start to finish in a short time. In the parable, the bridegroom did not come as *soon* as the foolish virgins expected, but once he did come, there was not enough time for them to finally get organized. There will not be enough time between our perception of the Lord's imminent arrival and his actual arrival for us to get ourselves ready to meet him. It will all happen so "quickly" there will be no time for straightening up our lives. We must get ready *now* while there is still time; we must prepare *now,* forewarned by his apostles, prophets, and scriptures that he is almost here—or be left unprepared and without oil at his coming.

NOTES

1. Smith, *Kirtland Revelation Book,* 91–92.
2. See Marsh, "History of Thos. Baldwin Marsh," 18.
3. Smith, *History of the Church,* 1:126.
4. Taylor, *Journal of Discourses,* 24:232.
5. Hyrum M. Smith, in Conference Report, Oct. 1916, 43.
6. See Smith, *Kirtland Revelation Book,* 91–92; see full text in Cook, *Revelations of the Prophet,* 89.
7. See also the commentary on D&C 20:9; 42:12.
8. See the commentary on D&C 10:5; 31:12; 32:4; see also D&C 19:38; 20:33.
9. Kimball, *Faith Precedes the Miracle,* 256.

34

BACKGROUND

Shortly after Parley Pratt was baptized in Palmyra in early September 1830, he traveled to his family home in Canaan, Columbia County, New York, where some of his immediate family were sympathetic to the gospel message, though most were not. He did, however, convert and baptize his younger brother, Orson Pratt, on 19 September 1830, which was Orson's nineteenth birthday. Parley then hurried back to Fayette for the Church conference there on 26 September, at which conference he was called to the Lamanite mission.

About six weeks after being baptized, Orson Pratt also traveled to Fayette to meet the Prophet Joseph, and wrote the following concerning that meeting: "In October, 1830, I traveled westward over two hundred miles to see Joseph Smith the Prophet. I found him in Fayette, Seneca county, New York, residing at the home of Mr. Whitmer. I soon became intimately acquainted with this good man, and also with the witnesses of the Book of Mormon. By my request, on the 4th of November, the Prophet Joseph inquired of the Lord for me and received the revelation published in the Doctrine and Covenants, Section 34."[1]

COMMENTARY

1. My son Orson. Like his brother Parley, Orson Pratt was one of the more capable and faithful men in the early history of the Church. He served at least eleven missions to the eastern United States and seven to Britain and Europe, was part of Zion's Camp, and was called to the original Quorum of the Twelve Apostles. This revelation foreshadows his faithfulness and his life of service in the Church.[2]

1. Jesus Christ your Redeemer. Again we are reminded that the member of the Godhead who speaks to us through the Doctrine and Covenants is God the Son, Jesus Christ, and that faithful members have been born again as sons and daughters of Jesus Christ (see Mosiah 5:7; Ether 3:14).

2. This verse paraphrases John 1:5. Christ is the source of light and life for all this universe. All light or life that exists, exists only through him. The opposing principle, of course, is darkness, over which Satan is ruler.[3]

3. Who so loved the world. A paraphrase of John 3:16. Note that to be "sons of God" is equated here to having "everlasting life" in John 3:16. Also note that where other scriptures inform us that God the Father loved the world enough to give his Son, this passage informs us that God the Son also loved the world enough to sacrifice himself. "God" loved and loves us, in the persons of *both* the Father and the Son. "God so loved that *he gave*. Christ so loved that *he gave*. We are here on this earth to learn, after the example of the Father and the Son, to love enough to *give*—to use our agency unselfishly."[4]

3. Wherefore you are my son.[5] As a believer in the restored gospel and a baptized member of the covenant in good faith, Orson was truly "born again" a son of God, begotten of Christ through the life-giving power of the Atonement, as are all faithful members of the Church. As the sons and daughters of the Father spiritually and of the Son eternally, we have the promise that if we remain faithful, we will grow up to be like our heavenly parents, to be what they are and to have what they have.

4–5. These verses teach us that believing is good; in fact it makes us blessed, but preaching what we believe to those still in darkness makes us even more blessed.

6. Cry repentance unto a crooked and perverse generation. President Brigham Young taught: "I wish we had more Elders to go and preach just such sermons by the power of God, that is, 'I know that Joseph Smith is a Prophet of God, and this is the Gospel of salvation, and if you do not believe it you will be damned, every one of you.' . . .

" . . . When a man teaches that doctrine by the power of God in a congregation of sinners, it is one of the loudest sermons that was ever preached to them, because the Spirit bears testimony to it."[6]

Some Church members are embarrassed to teach the hard truth of the gospel straight on, fearing that it is offensive or untactful and thinking they will have better success if they "soften" the truth a little and teach it obliquely. But they forget the role of the Holy Ghost in conversion and in who bears witness to the truth as we have faith to preach it. The Holy Ghost will testify to the straight and undiluted truth with greater power and greater motivation for change than he will to modified truths taught "tactfully" by those weak in faith. The pure and undiluted gospel *is* offensive to the world; it always *has* been, and if we don't sometimes risk offending others with the hard, straight truth, we don't usually risk converting them either. In referring to the undiluted truth, we do not mean the deeper doctrines or the mysteries, which *should* be left alone when preaching, but to the "offensive" proclamations of the basic gospel: that Jesus Christ is the *only* way to salvation; that *all* must repent and be baptized in Christ or they cannot be saved; that baptism by proper priesthood authority is the *only* gate into the kingdom of God; and that *only* The Church of Jesus Christ of Latter-day Saints enjoys the fulness of the gospel and priesthood authority in these latter days.

7–10. "There are great things in the future, and we are sometimes apt to forget them. . . . These things have been sounded so long in the ears of the Latter-day Saints, that I have sometimes thought they have become like a pleasing song, or like a dream, and that they scarcely realize that these great events are at hand, even at the doors. But if we can depend upon the word of the Lord—if we can depend upon modern revelation which God has given—there is a time of tribulation, of sorrow, of great judgment, of great wrath and indignation, to come upon the nations of the earth, such as has not been since the foundation of the world. . . . I know that these things are true."[8]

10. Therefore prophesy, and it shall be given. Orson Pratt possessed the gift of prophecy to an extraordinary degree throughout his life. Verse 10 records the beginning of that tremendous gift and the Lord's promise that whatever Orson prophesied would come to pass.

12. Quickly. See the commentary on Doctrine and Covenants 33:18.

NOTES

1. Cited in Woodford, "Historical Development," 1:461.
2. See the commentary on D&C 34:3.
3. See the commentary on D&C 88:6–13.
4. Marion D. Hanks, in *Ensign*, Nov. 1990, 39.
5. See the commentary on D&C 11:30; 25:1; 76:24.
6. Young, *Journal of Discourses*, 4:298–99.
7. See Orson Pratt, in Conference Report, Apr. 1880, 86; see also the commentary on D&C 2:1; 29:14; 45:40, 45.

35

BACKGROUND

When the missionaries to the Laminites arrived in the area around Kirtland, Ohio, in late October or early November 1830 (see D&C 32), they went to see Sidney Rigdon, Parley Pratt's teacher, friend, and former associate in the Reformed Baptist movement. Sidney was the minister to several congregations of Reformed Baptists in the Kirtland area, and had been greatly influenced by the early teachings of Alexander Campbell, a famous Protestant theologian and minister who was a leader of the Reformed Baptist or Disciple movement.[1] These Protestant "Disciples," eventually to be called "The Disciples of Christ," in 1832, were ardently looking for a restoration of the New Testament gospel. When Sidney Rigdon formed a communal Christian society called "the Family" in August of 1830, however, it caused a break between Sidney and Alexander Campbell. When Sidney joined with the Latter-day Saints and accepted the Book of Mormon as inspired scripture, the break between them became irreparable.[2]

The missionaries had presented Sidney with a copy of the Book of Mormon, which he studied carefully for about two weeks. At the end of that time he concluded the book was of God, and he was baptized on 14 November 1830, in Mentor, Ohio.

Through Sidney Rigdon, scores of others in his several congregations were also eventually converted.

When the Lamanite missionaries continued on their way to Missouri, they ordained several elders in Kirtland, but apparently they left no single individual to preside over the new Saints. This may have contributed to some of the spiritual confusion that developed among these members before Joseph Smith arrived in February, though John Whitmer had been sent from Fayette, New York, to preside over the Church in Kirtland.[3] In the meantime, Lyman Wight had acted as leader, since the other elders had returned to their various homes and Sidney Rigdon together with Edward Partridge, a sincere investigator from nearby Painesville, Ohio, had traveled to New York to see the Prophet Joseph Smith and inquire concerning the Lord's will for them. Doctrine and Covenants 35 was received in response to their inquiry in Fayette, New York, sometime in early December 1830.

Two early versions of Doctrine and Covenants 35 were printed in the *Ohio Star,* on 5 January 1832, and in the Painesville *Telegraph,* on 17 January 1832. These both give the date of this revelation as 7 December 1830. Lucy Mack Smith, however, states that Sidney and Edward Partridge arrived at the Smith's new home in east Waterloo, near Fayette, the day before Edward was baptized. Since Partridge was baptized on 11 December 1830, Lucy's account has them arriving on 10 December, thus conflicting with the 7 December date. The date of section 35 in all LDS printings has been given simply as December 1830.

At the time Doctrine and Covenants 35 was given, Joseph Smith had already begun his inspired translation of the Bible, the Joseph Smith Translation. In September of 1830, however, his main scribes, Oliver Cowdery and John Whitmer, were called on missions (see D&C 28:8; 30:9–11), leaving Joseph in need of a scribe when Sidney Rigdon arrived in December.

COMMENTARY

1. The beginning and the end.[4] The beginning of all things is Christ because he is the Creator of all things. The end of all things is also Christ, for he is the judge of all and the Savior of all who come to him.

1. One eternal round. See the commentary on Doctrine and Covenants 3:2.

2. Crucified for the sins of the world. Christ did not suffer and die only for the sins of the righteous who would accept the gospel in this life. He died also for the sins of the "world" or of Babylon, *including* the wicked who, whether they know it or not, will also be blessed by the atonement of Christ. For example, even the most wicked individuals will be resurrected through the power of his atonement, and the vast majority of them will eventually repent in the spirit world and will turn to Christ in some degree. They will then be redeemed from the devil, also through Christ's atonement, and will receive a degree of glory appropriate to their less valiant behavior. Even this lesser glory is made possible only through Jesus' suffering in their behalf (see D&C 76:41–43).

Christ's work is for both the righteous and the wicked—for the sins of the *whole* world. Those who believe on his name in *this* life, however, or who would have if they had been given the opportunity, may become his sons and daughters and be one with him and the Father in the celestial kingdom.

2. As I am one in the Father. See Doctrine and Covenants 93:3.[5]

3. Prepared thee for a greater work. The good Sidney Rigdon did as a Baptist minister in imparting to many people a preparatory understanding of faith, repentance, and baptism by immersion was a "great" work in the eyes of the Lord in preparing souls for the fulness of the gospel. The work he was called to here, however, to preach the fulness of the gospel, was an even "greater work."

4. John . . . and . . . Elijah. Sidney's work as a Baptist minister was compared by the Lord to that of John the Baptist among the ancient Jews. Sidney had some understanding, but not a fulness. This passage gives one of several reasons why ministers and members of other churches cannot be labeled as "apostates" or even necessarily as opponents. This is because many of them have some gospel light with which, as servants of God, they prepare the world for greater light to come—even though they may not accept the fulness of the gospel themselves.

In many foreign lands the LDS Church now reaps the harvest sown by non-LDS missionaries who sometimes gave their lives to bring a little light to those who did not know Christ at all. Those noble souls will not lose their reward. In Sidney Rigdon's case, his preaching as a Protestant minister had prepared scores of people to recognize the restored gospel when it arrived in Ohio with the Lamanite missionaries. Sidney's groundwork also preceded the coming of Elijah the prophet to the Kirtland Temple in 1836 to restore the keys of the sealing power, and he prepared many Saints to receive the blessings of the temple. Those Latter-day Saints who can see other Christian churches and their members only as adversaries do not understand the difference between having some light and having the fulness thereof, and they apparently disregard the witness of Doctrine and Covenants 35.

5–6. Though Sidney's labors as a Protestant minister had been a positive thing and pleasing to the Lord, it had also been without authority. Now, as a priesthood holder in the restored Church, Sidney would baptize with authority and be able to lay hands on those baptized, and they would receive the gift of the Holy Ghost.

7. Great work in the land. The work of the Restoration performed by Joseph Smith, Sidney Rigdon, and others would not be the end but the beginning of God's work in the latter days. That work is described in the following verses. Those who believe will witness miracles; the fulness of the gospel is to be taught among the Gentiles, and Babylon will be destroyed.

7. Even among the Gentiles. The present dispensation will consist largely, and up until the present time has consisted entirely, of what the Lord has called the times of the Gentiles (see D&C 45:25–30), a period during which every nation, kindred, tongue, and people will have the opportunity to hear and accept the gospel of Jesus Christ. Now is their time to hear and obey the word of the Lord. When the times of the Gentiles are over, this dispensation will be near its end. According to Joseph Smith Translation Luke 21:25, 32, the generation in which the times of the Gentiles are fulfilled will be the generation that witnesses the signs in the sun, moon, and stars (see D&C 29:14; 34:9; 45:40–44).[6]

8. Arm is not shortened. God's arm is symbolically his power or ability. Thus, to say his arm is not shortened is to say that his power has not declined or become limited in any way.

8. Miracles, signs and wonders. Only the faithful will see the miraculous works of God in the latter days. Those without faith either will not see them at all or will not see them as miraculous until the unmistakable signs of the end, when it may be too late.

9. Compare Matthew 11:5; Luke 7:22; Moses 3:5. When the gospel is restored, those who believe will share all the gifts of the Spirit enjoyed by saints in other dispensations. This does not mean that *every* devil will be cast out, or that *every* sick person will be healed. It does mean that these miracles will at times be manifested among the faithful.

11. The wine of the wrath of her fornication. Babylon, or Satan's world, is a prostitute from whom anything can be bought for money. She willingly desecrates whatever is holy for carnal satisfaction or temporal reward. Making the sacred things of God—religion, standards, values, and ethics—commodities to be bought or sold or desecrated for carnal lusts constitutes her "fornication," for like a whore she sells or betrays for money that which is most sacred.

The "wrath of her fornication" is God's anger at Babylon's behavior. "The *wine* of the wrath of her fornication" is the bitter cup or the punishment prepared for her and her partners to drink in order to answer the demands of God's justice: destruction in this life, and the pains of hell in the life to come. Babylon makes all nations drink of this bitter cup by seducing them to be her guilty partners in whoredom—in her buying, selling, or desecrating what is sacred for money, power, immorality, or other carnal rewards (see D&C 88:94; Revelation 17:2; 18:3). For example, the drug industry, pornography industry, or abortion industry are promoted to the nations of the world by Satan and his servants with the promise of money and power to those who sell and with the promise of unhindered physical or sexual gratification to those who buy. But such abominations will bring down the wrath of God upon this and every nation that becomes partners with Babylon in promoting or allowing these things to exist.

12. None that doeth good. What humans consider good and what God defines as good are often different. Since God "cannot look upon sin with the least degree of allowance" (D&C 1:31), then *good* or *just* from his celestial perspective must mean "perfectly good," "absolutely innocent," or "completely just and worthy." Because humans can become completely just and worthy, absolutely innocent, or perfectly good only through the atonement of Christ, it then follows that the "good" can be only those who have entered into the gospel covenant or who are looking for it. Conversely, the "bad" are those who reject Christ or his covenant, however admirable their habits might be by relative human standards. Without the Atonement, no one's behavior qualifies as "good" before a perfect Lord. With the cleansing power of the Atonement, however, anyone can be made "good" (see D&C 76:69; 3 Nephi 27:16).

13. The weak . . . , unlearned and despised. Since this world is in league with Babylon, it frequently happens that those who are most successful in the world are also partners with Babylon. On the other hand, those who most adamantly refuse to cooperate with Babylon will often be unsuccessful by the world's standards. The world's motto is: You go along to get along. The world's heroes are usually the strong or the rich who acquire the world's goods, the educated who acquire the world's reasoning, or the popular who acquire and reflect the world's values and desires. As society ripens in iniquity, these heroes are often killers, thieves, adulterers, nihilists, and others whose popularity and standing as heroes is primarily based on their wickedness.

13. To thrash the nations. *Thrash* is the same as *thresh*. God will use the powerless, the unqualified by Babylon's standards, and those whom the world hates to do his great work among the Gentiles. Certainly, the Church is unpopular in much of the world, yet the gospel restored by the unlearned Joseph Smith has spread to the four corners of the earth. Certainly, most LDS missionaries have no clout, have no degrees, and get little appreciation from the larger population among whom they labor, yet the Saints are gathered and the kingdom rolls forth. The testimony of such as these will thresh the nations—it will cut through all arrogance, pretense, and deception like a threshing machine to separate the grain that is gathered from the stubble and chaff that is left behind to be burned.

14. Buckler. *Buckler* (Hebrew *magen*) is a synonym for "shield." It also means "defense."

15. The poor and the meek. These are those who are unimportant in Babylon, who have no money or no inclination to force their will on others (see Isaiah 29:19). "Poor" may also refer to those who are poor in spirit or poor in self-adulation as well as those who are poor in money. The poor and the meek are not usually so distracted by this world that they lose their place in the better one that is coming.

16. The parable of the fig-tree. Compare Matthew 24:32–33; Joseph Smith—Matthew 1:38–39. The poor and the meek, undistracted by Babylon and its concerns, will be able to see and recognize the signs of Christ's coming, just as discerning gardeners can tell by the leaves on the fig-trees what time of year it is. It is not yet the fall harvest for us, but is still the summer of work.

17. In weakness have I blessed him. Joseph Smith accumulated little money or formal education, and he never became a popular figure in the eyes of the world. But by this time in 1830, he stood at the head of the last dispensation, the dispensation of the fulness of times, and alone of all the earth's inhabitants held the keys of the kingdom of God. These he will hold forever.

18. Keys of the mystery of those things which have been sealed. Joseph Smith holds with these priesthood keys control over what God has hidden from the world. He can at his discretion and as allowed by the Spirit make any of these things known to individuals, to the Saints, or to the world in the latter days. Joseph Smith, as head of the dispensation of the fulness of times, holds the responsibility and authority to direct the revealing of all the knowledge and light that is to come to the world in this dispensation. One exercise of these keys was the translation of the Book of Mormon, of the Joseph Smith Translation, and of the book of Abraham. Another was the revelation of the ordinances of the temple, and a third was the revelations now found in the Doctrine and Covenants—"the things which shall come from this time until the time of my coming." Moreover, Joseph and no other will enjoy these keys for as long as he is faithful and abides in Christ, and his control of these things continues even now, as from the other side of the veil he continues to direct the work of this dispensation and the mysteries to be revealed from heaven to the earth (see D&C 90:3).

19. Watch over him. Sidney was given charge to look out for Joseph's spiritual welfare by faith and prayer and to give him advice, counsel, and strength as directed by the Holy Ghost. Even prophets need the counsel of their priesthood brethren and the love, support, and service of those over whom they preside.

20. Thou shalt write for him. Joseph's two scribes, Oliver Cowdery and John Whitmer, had been called on missions (see D&C 28:8; 30:9–11), and he needed a reliable scribe. Sidney Rigdon was called to fill that need, and he was a major scribe for the Joseph Smith Translation of the Bible.

20. The scriptures shall be given, even as they are in mine own bosom.[7] The reference here is to the Joseph Smith

Translation of the Bible, which will render the Bible to the Church as it is in God's own understanding. This does not necessarily mean that the Joseph Smith Translation will simply restore the original texts of the biblical books; it goes beyond that. The texts will be rendered as God himself wants us to understand them—corrected, adapted, edited, revised, and supplemented especially for use of the Saints in the latter days. In the Joseph Smith Translation, Joseph sometimes corrected and added to what had been originally written to give us a more complete understanding than was possible even with the original text. For essentially the rest of his life, at different intervals the Prophet Joseph, with Sidney's help, continued to work on the Joseph Smith Translation.

21. They will hear. The elect are promised that they will hear and see the Lord, will not be caught asleep or unprepared when he comes, and will survive the great and terrible day of the Lord.

21. For they shall be purified. By the atonement of Christ through justification by faith in Christ (see D&C 20:30). As the faithful become one with Christ in the gospel covenant, they become part of him, and they share his purity. Obedience to the gospel makes the faithful as pure as Christ is, vicariously at first and then ultimately in actual fact.

22. Tarry with him. Sidney is not to return home to Ohio, but is to remain with Joseph Smith.

23. There is no doubt that Sidney is better educated and more experienced than Joseph Smith. There is also no doubt that despite these differences Joseph is the Lord's anointed Prophet. Sidney was warned, as was Oliver Cowdery (see D&C 28:2–7), that he was to use his talent to sustain Joseph and not to try to control or to eclipse him. It was Sidney's calling to support the Prophet and to preach and expound upon the things Joseph received and to use the Bible to support Joseph's teachings.

25. Israel shall be saved. In the narrow sense, Israel is the infant Church that will survive and thrive to be caught up at the Savior's coming. In the broader context, Israel is all the posterity of Jacob, including the Jews, the Book of Mormon peoples, the lost tribes, and the Gentiles who are adopted into the family. All these who believe shall be led to salvation by the keys of the priesthood held by the apostolic leaders of the latter-day Church.

26. Lift up your hearts and be glad. Is this perhaps the most disobeyed commandment among faithful Latter-day Saints? Often even the most faithful members have difficulty obeying the commandment of the Lord to rejoice, be glad, and fear not. Whether through lack of understanding or lack of faith, they resist the joy that should already be theirs, and they continue to fear for their place in the kingdom.[8] If you are worthy to partake of the sacrament, or if endowed to go to the temple, then reread the assurances of verses 26–27, and be glad!

27. Fear not . . . the kingdom is yours. Not "may be yours" or even "will be yours," but rather "*is* yours" (see D&C 25:1).[9] As long as Church members are faithful, they should know that the kingdom is *already* theirs, even before it comes physically upon the earth. The physical reality is not here yet, but it is coming, and the faithful Saints already own a piece of it.

27. I come quickly. See the commentary on Doctrine and Covenants 33:18.

NOTES

1. Often referred to, for that reason, as Campbellites.
2. See Bushman, *Joseph Smith and the Beginnings of Mormonism,* 173–74, 180–83.
3. See headnote to D&C 41; *History of the Church,* 1:146–47, 154.
4. See the commentary on D&C 19:1.
5. See also the commentary on D&C 93:3.
6. See also the commentary on D&C 45:21, 25, 28–30.
7. See the commentary on D&C 38:4.
8. See the commentary on D&C 35:27.
9. See also the commentary on D&C 25:1.

DOCTRINE AND COVENANTS

36

BACKGROUND

The setting for Doctrine and Covenants 36 is almost identical to that for Doctrine and Covenants 35. At roughly the same time as section 35 was given to Sidney Rigdon, Joseph Smith received section 36 for Edward Partridge. Edward was a successful and much respected hatmaker in Painesville, Ohio, near Kirtland. When he left with Sidney Rigdon to visit Joseph, he was not yet convinced of the truth of the Restoration, but wanted to investigate further. He, like Sidney, had first been introduced to the gospel by the missionaries to the Lamanites as they preached in the Kirtland area. Apparently, Edward Partridge was so well respected by others in his congregation that he was asked to investigate the claims of the Restoration for them as well. He was so honest and humble, they felt, that he would not be deceived in spiritual things.

Concerning the visit of Sidney Rigdon and Edward Partridge, Lucy Mack Smith later recorded: "In December of the same year [1830], Joseph appointed a meeting at our house. While he was preaching, Sidney Rigdon and Edward Partridge came in and seated themselves in the congregation. When Joseph had finished his discourse, he gave all who had any remarks to make, the privilege of speaking. Upon this, Mr. Partridge arose, and stated that he had been to Manchester, with the view of obtaining further information respecting the doctrine which we preached; but, not finding us, he had made some inquiry of our neighbors concerning our characters, which they stated had been unimpeachable, until Joseph deceived us relative to the Book of Mormon. He also said that he had walked over our farm, and observed the good order and industry which it exhibited; and, having seen what we had sacrificed for the sake of our faith, and having heard that our veracity was not questioned upon any other point than that of our religion, he believed our testimony, and was ready to be baptized, 'if,' said he, 'Brother Joseph will baptize me.'

"'You are now,' replied Joseph, 'much fatigued, brother Partridge, and you had better rest to-day, and be baptized tomorrow.'

"'Just as Brother Joseph thinks best,' replied Mr. Partridge, 'I am ready at any time.'

"He was accordingly baptized the next day" on 11 December 1830.[1] If Lucy's record is correct, then sections 35–36 were received after 10 December 1830.[2]

In his own account of the reception of Doctrine and Covenants 35–36, Joseph Smith called Edward Partridge a "pattern of piety, and one of the Lord's great men. Shortly after the arrival of these two brethren, thus spake the Lord: [section 35].

"And the voice of the Lord to Edward Partridge was: [section 36]."[3]

COMMENTARY

1. The Mighty One of Israel. This is one of the titles of Jehovah in the Old Testament and early Book of Mormon (see Isaiah 1:24; 30:29; 1 Nephi 22:12), an equivalent phrase to the one "strong and mighty," who is also Jesus Christ (Psalm 24:8; see also Psalm 89:6–8, 13). "The mighty one," or the "mighty God," or the God with a "mighty hand" or "strong hand" are all common designations for Jehovah-Christ in the ancient scriptures (see Genesis 49:24; Joshua 14:11; Isaiah 9:6; 10:21; 28:2–17; Mosiah 13:34). He was and is the Lord of Hosts, Jehovah, the Mighty God of Israel.

1. Your sins are forgiven you. Edward's sins were forgiven because he had exercised faith in Jesus Christ, had repented of his sins, had just been baptized by immersion, and had received the remission of sins that comes thereby (see Articles of Faith 1:4; Acts 2:38).

2. I will lay my hand upon you. Edward Partridge was actually confirmed a member of the Church by Sidney Rigdon. This verse taught Edward a very important concept: the hands of the authorized servant, in this case Sidney, are as the hands of the Master. When a worthy individual who holds the holy priesthood lays hands upon someone, it is as if God himself has done it (see D&C 1:38). "Do you get the significance of that? When one is ordained by authority it is as though the Lord Himself were laying also his hand upon that person by the hand of His authorized servant, for them to receive the gifts and the endowments of the Spirit"[4] (see D&C 84:12).[5]

2. Comforter. See the commentary on Doctrine and Covenants 21:9.

2. The peaceable things of the kingdom. These are the blessings of the kingdom—the doctrines, ordinances, gifts, promises, assurances—that bring spiritual peace to an individual. Although the Church and its members exist in a world of turmoil, the gospel brings peace to those who obey its precepts and causes them in turn to become men and women of peace.

3. Hosanna, blessed be the name. See the commentary on Doctrine and Covenants 19:37.

4. Concerning all men. The verses following are for the Church leadership rather than just for Edward Partridge and concern Church policy in dealing with all men (see v. 7).

5. This calling and commandment. The calling is the one just given to Edward in verse 1 "to preach my gospel." The commandment is the commandment in verse 3 to declare the kingdom "with a loud voice, saying: Hosanna." In other words, whoever wants to be a missionary and preach the kingdom of God may, from this time on, be ordained and sent out by Church leaders—provided they are worthy.

6. This untoward generation. The language here cites the King James translation of Acts 2:40 where the Greek word *skolia*—translated "untoward"—means "crooked" or "perverse." Something that is crooked or perverse will not go straight *toward* its proper object, and is therefore *untoward*.

6. Hating even the garments spotted with the flesh. This is an allusion to Jude 1:23. Both Jews and Jewish Christians in Jesus' day, largely due to rules in the law of Moses, had a tremendous aversion to bodily fluids and discharges (see Leviticus 13:47–59; 15). Garments spotted by disease or by the reproductive organs and their discharges were considered unclean and had to be either washed, torn, or burned depending upon the source and circumstances of the pollution.

Similarly, in the gospel covenant our aversion to moral disease or pollution ought to be so strong that we respond sharply and negatively to even the slightest indication of it. "Garments spotted with flesh are garments defiled by the practices of carnal desires and disobedience to the commandments of the Lord."[6]

7. See Commentary on verses 4–5. Even in Joseph Smith's day, every worthy, male member of the Church had at least some obligation to enter missionary service and preach the gospel of Jesus Christ.

8. Gird up your loins. See the commentary on Doctrine and Covenants 27:15.

8. I will suddenly come to my temple. There was no temple in the Church at this time, nor has there been any mention of a temple before this verse. The Lord was perhaps foreshadowing here the construction of future temples in Kirtland and Nauvoo, where he came "suddenly" to bestow great blessings upon the faithful of his people.

NOTES

1. Smith, *History of Joseph Smith,* 191–92.
2. See Background to D&C 35.

3. Smith, *History of the Church,* 1:128.
4. Lee, "Priesthood in Mission Field Emphasized," 5.
5. See also the commentary on D&C 84:12.
6. Smith, *Church History and Modern Revelation,* 1:163.

37

BACKGROUND

When Sidney Rigdon received a revelation from the Lord in early to mid-December 1830, he began immediately, in obedience to the commandment given in that revelation (see D&C 35:20), to act as scribe for the Prophet Joseph in his work of translating the Bible. The book of Moses in the Pearl of Great Price was part of that Joseph Smith Translation. Other parts are simply referred to collectively as the Joseph Smith Translation; many of these can be found on pages 797–813 in the appendix to the LDS scriptures.[1]

Before the end of December 1830, Sidney had written down, at the Prophet's dictation, the words of Enoch, which now comprise Moses 7 in the Pearl of Great Price. Soon after this was done, and still in December of 1830, less than three weeks after Sidney and Edward Partridge had arrived in Fayette from Kirtland, the Lord gave to Joseph and Sidney the revelation now known as Doctrine and Covenants 37.

Unknown to Joseph and Sidney, opposition to the Church in New York had reached the point where at least some of their enemies seem to have actually conspired to kill the Saints (see D&C 37:1; 38:13, 28–29). To save their lives, the Lord commanded Joseph and Sidney to stop the work of translating and to strengthen the branches of the Church in New York. Then they were to move the Church to Kirtland, Ohio, where there were at that time, due to the success of the Lamanite missionaries, almost three times as many Saints as in New York.

COMMENTARY

1. The Ohio. This refers to the entire area now called the state of Ohio rather than to the Ohio River, which does not run anywhere near Kirtland. In 1831 this area was not yet a state of the Union and was commonly referred to as the Western Reserve, or the Ohio.

1. Because of the enemy. Opposition to the Restoration had become so intense that the Saints were in great danger (see D&C 38:13, 28–29, 31).

2. My gospel in those parts. They were to preach in New York one last time and strengthen the branches there, particularly Colesville, where the members had been faithfully praying for help and where the persecution of the Saints and the schemes against them were the most severe.

3. A commandment I give unto the church. This is the first "gathering" of the Saints in the latter days, when the Lord commanded those who had accepted the gospel to assemble themselves near Kirtland. Some of the New York Saints looked on this exodus as a repetition of those of Lehi or Moses.[2]

3. Against the time that my servant Oliver Cowdery shall return. Oliver Cowdery was still the second elder of the Church and was a more important figure in its organization at this time than we sometimes acknowledge. The Church was genuinely looking forward to his return. Oliver was at this time in or near Jackson County, Missouri, on his Lamanite mission.

Here the New York Saints are instructed to move to Kirtland in anticipation of Oliver's return there. Oliver did not arrive in Kirtland, however, until 27 August 1831—more than ten months after he left Fayette for Missouri, and about eight months after this revelation was received. Oliver, obedient to the Lord's command, did not leave Missouri until Joseph went there in the summer of 1831 (see D&C 28:8–15) and, at the instruction of the Lord, personally accompanied Oliver back to Kirtland (see D&C 58:58).

4. Let every man choose for himself. We cannot choose for ourselves what will *be* right or what will *be* wrong—the Lord has already made those designations clear. But all of us must choose for ourselves whether *to do* right or wrong. Even when the will of the Lord is clear and unambiguous, the principles of agency and common consent are still operative. All obedience to the commandments and all participation in the kingdom of God is and must be voluntary—even when the right and wrong paths have been made perfectly obvious. We may not coerce righteousness, for where obedience or participation are not voluntary, they have no merit.

NOTES

1. See Matthews, "Plainer Translation"; this is the definitive work on the Joseph Smith Translation.
2. See Smith, *History of Joseph Smith,* 196, 203.

38

BACKGROUND

Merely eight months after the organization of the Church and sometime during December of 1830, while engaged in his translation of the Bible with the newly arrived Sidney Rigdon, Joseph had received the revelation now recorded in the Pearl of Great Price as Moses 6–7. The story of Enoch recorded there describes the establishment of Zion by Enoch in the period before the Flood. Revelation of the Enoch material was followed almost immediately by Doctrine and Covenants 37, received during what we would call the Christmas holidays in mid to late December of 1830. In this revelation the Lord commanded the members of the Church to leave their homes and farms in New York and gather to Ohio to prepare to establish a Zion like Enoch's in their own day. When the Church met in its scheduled general conference in Fayette the day after New Year's 1831, the members desired more information from the Prophet concerning this "gathering" of the Saints and the establishment of Zion.

Joseph described the conference very briefly in his historical writings: "The year 1831 opened with a prospect great and glorious for the welfare of the kingdom; for on the 2nd of January, 1831, a conference was held in the town of Fayette, New York, at which the ordinary business of the Church was transacted; and in addition, the following revelation was received"—Doctrine and Covenants 38.[1]

No official minutes of this conference were recorded,[2] but fortunately some journal accounts exist describing the proceedings and the reception of Doctrine and Covenants 38. One is by John Whitmer: "The time had now come for the general conference to be held. Which was the first of January 1831. and according to this appointment the saints assembled themselves together. After transacting the necessary business, Joseph the Seer addressed the congregation and exhorted them to stand fast, looking forward considering the end [i.e., the object or goal] of their salvation. The solemnities of eternity rested on the congregation, and having previously received a revelation to go to Ohio [D&C 37], they desired to know somewhat more concerning the matter. Therefore, the Seer enquired of the Lord in the presence of the whole congregation, and thus came the word of the Lord saying: [D&C 38].

"After the Lord had manifested the above words, through Joseph the Seer, there were some divisions among the congregations, some would not receive the above as the word of the Lord: but that Joseph had invented it himself to deceive the people that in the end he might get gain. Now this was because, their hearts were not right in the sight of the Lord, for they wanted to serve God and man; but our Savior has declared that it was impossible to do so.

"The conference was now closed, and the Lord had manifested his will to his people. Therefore they made preparations to journey to the Ohio, with their wives, and children and all that they possessed, to obey the commandment of the Lord."[3]

A second, although brief and anonymous, account of this conference on 2 January 1831 found in the *Journal History of the Church* reads: "The Saints manifested unshaken confidence in the great work which they were engaged, and all rejoiced under the blessings of the gospel. Considerable business was transacted for the Church.

"It was at this conference that we were instructed as a people, to begin the gathering of Israel, and a revelation was given to the prophet on this subject."[4] It would seem that, as is usually the case, the majority of the members gladly accepted this revelation which had been so dramatically delivered to Joseph in the presence of them all, while a small minority were shocked at the prospect of leaving their homes and their livelihoods and accepted the commandment to do so only grudgingly or not at all.

COMMENTARY

1. In Doctrine and Covenants 38 the Lord gave the Saints assurance and understanding about their gathering to Ohio in three ways: by reminding them whom they were dealing with (see vv. 1–7), by revealing the conspiracies that made it necessary for them to leave New York (see vv. 13, 28–31), and by informing them of the great blessings he would give them as they established Zion (see vv. 16–21, 31–32, 39).

1. The Great I Am.[5] The Lord seems to be emphasizing that this revelation came not from Joseph Smith, as some were thinking,[6] but from himself. Moreover, the phrase "the Great I Am" reminded the Saints that the God who spoke to them and desired to lead them by Joseph's hand out of New York is the same God who led the children of Israel out of Egypt to a promised land by the hands of Moses and Aaron. Jesus Christ, the God of the Doctrine and Covenants, is Jehovah, God of the Old Testament and the Book of Mormon, who has led his people "out of Egypt" to establish "Zion" many times in the past. The Saints who gathered to Ohio viewed their journey as an "exodus" from New York.

1. Wide expanse of eternity. Besides this verse, the term *expanse* appears in scripture only in chapter 4 of the book of Abraham and in Facsimiles 1 and 2. In every case it is associated with the firmament, or the boundary marking the limits of this creation. God the Creator, before the Creation took place, looked upon the vast expanse of space where creation was to be.

1. Seraphic hosts of heaven. *Seraph* is the Hebrew verb "to burn." The seraphim, or "burning ones," are the angels who dwell in glory in the presence of God. They are near the immense power and glory of God himself, and their description as "burning ones" shows that God does indeed dwell in everlasting burnings.[7] Before our world was created, Jehovah, or Christ, looked upon or reviewed or inspected all these seraphic hosts, which included the pre-earth spirits of some men and women who would dwell on the earth (see D&C 109:79). Isaiah also saw seraphim in his vision of God (see Isaiah 6:2–7; 2 Nephi 16:2–7). That God who reigns over all the angelic hosts now commanded his mortal people to gather in Ohio.

2. Knoweth all things. God knows everything. Every fact that ever has existed, now exists, or ever will exist is *already* known to God. The scriptures repeatedly declare there is nothing that God does not know (see D&C 88:6, 41; 130:7; 2 Nephi 2:24; 9:20; Alma 7:13; Moroni 7:22; Moses 1:6). Human reasoning leads some to deny this plain declaration of scripture and maintain that God does *not* know all things, but human reasoning is limited, particularly by the element of time. God's perspective is not limited by time, for "all things are *present* before mine eyes."[8] Just because we cannot in mortality comprehend *how* God's knowledge could be unaffected by time or avoid infringing on our freedom of choice, this does not justify us in denying that it is so, nor in insisting that God must also suffer under our mortal limitations, especially in view of the clear, unambiguous declaration of the scriptures to the contrary.

Joseph Smith taught that even before the Creation "the past, the present, and the future were and are, with Him [Jehovah], one eternal 'now;' He knew of the fall of Adam, the iniquities of the antediluvians, of the depth of iniquity that would be connected with the human family, their weakness and strength, their power and glory, apostasies, their crimes, their righteousness and iniquity."⁹ God functions in a great, eternal now and perceives all existence simultaneously—while we mortals can perceive only the present, and very little of that. We function in bits and pieces of time that must be carefully bordered for us with beginnings and endings tied together with threads of time. Even so we forget the past and cannot see the future.

A God who is ignorant of *some* things could never know exactly what he doesn't know, or how those things of which he is ignorant might affect what he *thinks* he knows. How could we trust such a being? If there were limits to God's knowledge, then Satan could have been right that maybe there *was* a better plan than God's—maybe God left something out, or didn't do enough research. If he could have missed *anything,* who knows what it might be or how important it might prove.

You will see at once that we cannot have saving faith in an ignorant God. If he doesn't know *everything,* he can't guarantee *anything,* and we couldn't trust him. As the Prophet Joseph Smith taught in the *Lectures on Faith:* "Without the knowledge of all things God would not be able to save any portion of his creatures. For it is by reason of the knowledge which he has of all things, from the beginning to the end, that enables him to give that understanding to his creatures by which they are made partakers of eternal life; and if it were not for the idea existing in the minds of men that God has all knowledge it would be impossible for them to exercise faith in him."¹⁰

3. The same which spake, and the world was made. This verse clarifies yet again that Jesus Christ is the Creator of the world. Moses was told that God made the earth by the power of his Only Begotten Son (see Moses 1:32–33).

4. Into mine own bosom. "To be 'in the bosom' of someone is a Hebrew idiom derived from the fact that anciently a man's clothing consisted of large flowing robes wrapped around his person and fastened with a sash, forming a spacious repository above the waist in which things, including children, were often carried. . . . So the phrase 'to be in the bosom of another' implied a very close and favored relationship (see 2 Samuel 12:8; Luke 16:22; John 1:18)."[11]

4. The Zion of Enoch. From the beginning to the end of this temporal world, one of God's purposes and a main objective of his Saints has been to establish Zion. The term *Zion* refers to a society of Saints who have successfully gathered together to live the laws of the celestial kingdom among themselves here on the earth, who have actually succeeded in making God's will "be done in earth, as it is in heaven" (Matthew 6:10). Moses 7:18 explains some conditions that must be met for the Saints truly to establish a Zion: (1) they must be of "one heart and one mind," (2) they must dwell "in righteousness," and (3) there must be "no poor among them." According to the scriptures, Enoch, the seventh generation from Adam, was able to establish a Zion with those he converted to the gospel. It is called the City of Holiness in the scriptures but is often referred to as the City of Enoch by Church members (see Moses 7:16–21).[12]

Between Enoch and the Flood those who accepted the gospel were gathered to Zion, and eventually Enoch's Zion itself was physically taken up from the earth into heaven, or "into mine own bosom." According to Joseph Smith Translation Genesis 14:32–36, Melchizedek, who blessed Abraham and accepted his tithing, was also able to establish Zion with his people. The people of Nephi were able to establish Zion after the visit of the Savior among them. In time to come, the Latter-day Saints will establish Zion on the American continent, which Zion will be called the New Jerusalem (see Articles of Faith 1:10; Ether 13:1–12). Then, at or near the beginning of the Millennium, God will bring the Zion of Enoch physically back to the earth to be joined together with the "New Jerusalem" Zion of the Latter-day Saints (see D&C 133:24; Moses 7:62–64).

These references to Enoch and Zion in Moses 7, received in mid-December 1830, and in Doctrine and Covenants 38, received a couple of weeks later on 2 January, clearly anticipate what the Saints themselves did not really know yet—that they were going to be invited to establish Zion, the New Jerusalem, in Missouri in their own lifetime.

4. By the virtue of the blood. What gives Christ the right to plead our case before God? It is the virtue or power of the blood he voluntarily spilt for us in Gethsemane and upon the cross. His innocent body torn and his innocent blood spilt for us are the invincible arguments that ultimately secure our salvation (see D&C 45:4–5). Without that sacrifice for us and our acceptance and reception of it by being joined to him in the gospel covenant, even a perfect being like Christ could not protect us from the demands of justice.

5. The residue of the wicked have I kept in chains. In the period between Enoch and the Flood those who repented and accepted the gospel gathered to the Zion of Enoch. Later, when Zion had been taken up to heaven, converts were still taken physically from the earth and translated to Zion. This meant that the humanity they left behind was constantly becoming more wicked, stubborn, and rebellious as the more righteous individuals were slowly being taken away (see Moses 7:27). Those wicked and rebellious souls who were left behind were like the "residue" left in a pan as the liquid is boiled off. When these wicked and rebellious dregs, who had had every chance to accept the gospel, perished in the Flood, their spirits were consigned to hell to suffer there until the Resurrection. At that time they will have to answer for themselves before God—having rejected the advocate Jesus Christ who would have pleaded their case for them. Still, even these hard cases may be redeemed through Christ and receive some degree of glory if they will repent.

5. At the end of the earth. At the end of the Millennium when all the remaining dead will be resurrected and brought to judgment.

8. Veil of darkness. This is the barrier that separates us both physically and spiritually from the presence of God. This vast expanse of darkened space is not what it seems to us, and will somehow be removed or pulled back from the earth all at once at the second coming of Christ, like pulling the cover off a bird-cage.

8. He that is not purified shall not abide. The only way to become pure is to be washed in the blood of the Lamb. All who have refused to be purified in this manner will be destroyed with all other impurities at the last day when the Savior returns to the earth.

9. The kingdom is yours. Notice again the present tense (see v. 15).

10. Ye are clean, but not all. Taken together, the Church on 2 January 1831 was approved by the Lord and worthy to abide his coming. There was a percentage, however, for whom, because of their own sins and rebellion, the cleansing of the Atonement was not at that time effective in their lives. No doubt the reference here includes those members who questioned the integrity of the Prophet Joseph, rejected his revelations, and accused him of trying to profit at their expense (see v. 14).[13]

11. All flesh is corrupted. Due to the fall of Adam, all flesh has become fallen and therefore corrupted before the Lord. The only cure for this corruption, which is our carnal nature, is the atonement of Christ that purifies all who have faith in Christ, repent, and are baptized by proper priesthood authority. Since most of earth's inhabitants have not accepted the gospel, the world is still corrupt, and it is natural that the powers of darkness and corruption should prevail over earth's inhabitants in such circumstances.

12. All eternity is pained. One often hears the ignorant blame God for the way things are, but God is more pained than we are at the evil of this corrupt world. The cause of the evil is not God, but *us*—and the powers of darkness we allow to prevail over us. Both individually and collectively, humanity insists on the right to disobey, the right to exercise their agency for evil. And then humanity generally blames God for the terrible consequences of human disobedience.

12. The angels are waiting the great command. This is a reference to the parable of the wheat and the tares, when the angels who have been anxious to gather the righteous and punish the wicked are finally given permission to proceed. "In the time of harvest I will say to the reapers, Gather ye together first the tares, and bind them in bundles to burn them: but gather the wheat into my barn" (Matthew 13:30). Compare Doctrine and Covenants 86:1–7, where the order is reversed: first the gathering of the wheat and then the burning of the tares (see also JST Matthew 13:29).

12. The enemy is combined. As in a secret combination (see 3 Nephi 7:6–9; Moses 5:51). In other words, the enemies of the Church had combined together secretly to plan and work for the destruction of the Saints.

13. Bring to pass even your destruction. The Lord revealed in very clear terms that the enemies of the Church had joined together in secret to plan the destruction of Joseph and the Saints (see also vv. 28–29). It appears from the historical record that the center of this activity was the area around Colesville, New York. Sidney Rigdon had preached a strong sermon there just prior to the date of this revelation, and it had greatly increased the intensity of both pro- and anti-Mormon feelings.[14] The existence and intent of the secret combinations, however, were still unknown to the Saints.

15. The kingdom is yours. Notice yet again the present tense. We become heirs of the kingdom of God on earth at baptism, which is the strait and narrow gate through which we enter God's kingdom (see 2 Nephi 31:17). The kingdom remains ours until we rebel and reject Christ. As long as we honor our covenants and remain loyal to Christ, the kingdom remains ours.

16, 32. Commandment. There is a long passage between the mention of the commandment in verse 16 and the defining of it in verse 32, but the commandment is to gather in Ohio. The reasons for such a commandment are to save the Saints from those who plot their deaths, to answer the prayers of the poor and provide for their temporal needs, to give the Saints God's law, and to endow them with power from on high.

16–17, 25–28. The gathering in Ohio would have several results. Among the most important was the temporal and spiritual salvation of the Saints. But the manner in which this would be accomplished was surprising. As the Saints learned to love each other as themselves, they shared their goods with one another, thus living the celestial laws of sacrifice and consecration. As the Saints lived these laws—and as we live them—the poor would be saved temporally, which was their immediate need, and the rich would be saved spiritually, which was their ultimate need. God had heard the prayers of the poor Saints and was not pleased with the gap between the rich and the poor in the world.

These celestial laws were later taught to the Saints in Ohio (see D&C 42:30–40). Note that the prayers of the poor Saints coming up to Jehovah from New York were parallel to the prayers of the afflicted Israelites going up to him from Egypt (see Exodus 3:7). His solution in both cases was the same: to gather his people together to a place where he could give them his law and thereby save them both spiritually and temporally.

It should be noted that the problem in all this was not the well-to-do Saints, and that this was not a dispute between the rich and poor members. The oppressive evil is the noncelestial, competition-based, economic systems of the world—whether Egypt, Babylon, or New York—that always create rich and poor. The Lord's system works on cooperation based on love rather than competition based on greed.

18. Those Saints faithful enough to gather to Ohio were promised that they would be given "a land of promise, a land flowing with milk and honey" (compare Exodus 3:8). Again this strikes the Exodus motif. Symbolically, Joseph and Sidney may be understood to represent Moses and Aaron, and the Saints as the new Israel. The "law" to be given in Ohio would be like a new law from Sinai, only better (see section 42).

18. No curse when the Lord cometh. Without the keys of the priesthood and of the sealing power, and therefore without the work that they make possible, the earth would be "utterly wasted"

(D&C 2:3) or smitten "with a curse" (Malachi 4:6) at the Lord's second coming. Much of the earth, wherever evil prevails, *will* be cursed and destroyed at his coming, but not Zion. For the Saints in Zion, however, the day of the Lord's coming will be "great" rather than "dreadful" (D&C 2:1).[15]

19. The land of your inheritance. This phrase has meaning at two levels. On the one hand it describes that specific land, later to be identified as Jackson County, Missouri, that the Saints were to receive in mortality if they were faithful—just as the promised land of their inheritance for the children of Abraham was Canaan, or the promised land for Lehi was in the new world. These temporal promised lands, however, are themselves symbols for the ultimate promised land—the land of our inheritance in eternity, which shall be for the faithful this celestialized earth upon which the Father and the Son may dwell and which those Saints who are truly Saints may inherit forever and ever.

20. My covenant with you. The terms of this covenant are that if the Saints will truly seek their inheritance with all their hearts and continue faithful, they will establish Zion and receive a temporal inheritance there, and they will also receive an inheritance in the celestial Zion, this earth dressed in its celestial glory.

21. No king nor ruler. *In time*—not now, but after the Saints establish Zion—they will have no other ruler than Christ the King. At his coming all other rule and authority will be swept away entirely, and during the Millennium he will rule personally as king upon the earth in a divine monarchy (see Articles of Faith 1:10).

22. Ye shall have no laws but my laws. Note the important qualifier "when I come." By the second coming of Christ, the Saints will have established Zion, so that when he comes they will be ready to live under and observe no laws but his throughout the Millennium. While it is right to attempt to observe all the commandments of God, it would be premature for anyone to think that the Saints may cease observing the laws of the land before that great day. Christ is our lawgiver, not Moses, Joseph,

Congress, or anyone else, and when he comes we will live under his law and no other.

23–27. In order to prepare the Saints for the celestial law of consecration about to be given them, the Lord commanded that they teach each other, within the scope of their callings, that they learn to care about their fellow Saints as much as they did themselves, and that they practice virtue and holiness. Note the repetition of the commandment to esteem their brother as themselves in verse 25, for this is the key. For example, if I truly love you as I love myself, then I cannot be happy if you are in want, and your well-being becomes a condition of *my* well-being. This is the attitude the Saints had to develop if they were going to be able to live the Lord's celestial law when they got to Ohio and Missouri.

26. Having twelve sons. Not all the parables of Jesus are in the New Testament. This parable of the twelve sons is found in the scriptures only here. By this parable the Lord revealed his feelings about some of his beloved children arbitrarily having more than they need when others of his children, our brothers and sisters, are in want.

27. Be one. Through the covenant of the gospel we as individuals become one with Christ and therefore one with each other in Christ. If we truly are his and have truly become one with him, it is a mathematical necessity that we are also one with everybody else who has become one with him. If I am one with Christ and you are one with Christ, then we must be one with each other. If A equals B and A also equals C, then B and C must be equal. A, the middle ground, that which is common to both and makes them one, is Christ. If B, however, will *not* be equal to C, if you or I will not be one with each other, then neither you nor I nor both are really one with the Savior or genuinely in the gospel covenant. Hence, "if ye are not one ye are not mine."

29. Ye hear of wars in far countries. The Saints could read newspapers and discern what was going on in Europe or in other places around the world, but they did not know that the people across town, or around the corner, or down their own street, were conspiring together to put them to death.

29. Ye know not the hearts of men in your own land. At the time of this revelation, as now, many citizens of the United States felt they were immune from the civil disturbances that plagued other countries. But even then, there were evil men hatching evil plans for the country generally and for the Saints in particular. The Civil War was one result of this hidden evil for the nation as a whole, while the expulsion from Missouri and Illinois out into the wilderness was one result for the Saints in particular.

30. A voice louder. The Lord told the Saints of the plots against them in a calm and collected manner. The enemies of the Church would have informed the Saints of their plans eventually—with bullets and death. There are few sounds louder than a pistol going off in your ear. The lesson, of course, is that we can learn by heeding the still, small voice of God or by suffering the louder and harsher voice of experience.

30. If ye are prepared ye shall not fear. We must be prepared by our own efforts, by heeding the warnings of God through his Spirit and through his leaders, and by keeping the commandments. Then we need not fear the plans and schemes of the opposition or even of the adversary himself.

32. Go to the Ohio. The commandment is given clearly and unambiguously—go to Ohio. The Lord then explained that he would there give the Saints his law and endow them with power. In Ohio the Saints would build a temple, the Kirtland Temple, a place where the Lord could converse openly and directly with his Saints and give them sacred, celestial teachings and sacred, celestial blessings. Such a temple, necessary for the further preparation and training of the Saints, could probably not have been built in New York at that time because the opposition was too strong and too well-established. All the Saints could hope to do by this time was to escape from their enemies to Ohio (see v. 31) and continue their preparations there.

32. The Ohio. See the commentary on Doctrine and Covenants 37:1.

32. I will give unto you my law. This promise was fulfilled on 9 February 1831, by the Church's receiving Doctrine and Covenants 42 in Kirtland, Ohio, through the Prophet Joseph Smith.

32. Endowed with power from on high. Originally from the Greek verb *enduo,* meaning "to be clothed," the word *endow* has come in contemporary English to describe bestowing a gift of great proportions. If one sends a $50 contribution to one's alma mater, for example, that is a gift; but if one sends $50 million dollars, that is an *endowment.* God intended to give his Saints certain gifts of staggering proportions when they gathered in Ohio (see D&C 6:13). Part of this endowment would "clothe" the Saints with power from the celestial worlds, including first the fulness of the keys of priesthood power generally, and later personal power in the priesthood individually. Between January and May of 1836 before, during, and after the dedication of the Kirtland Temple, the Saints in Ohio also received a tremendous outpouring of the Pentecostal gifts of the Spirit (see Acts 2:1–21).

34. Certain men . . . shall be appointed. Note the interesting parallel in verses 34–36 to Acts 6:1–4, when the ancient Church was faced with similar needs at a parallel point in its history.

37. Farms that cannot be sold. Many of the Saints left their lands in New York and traveled to Ohio. Some, however, retained claim upon their lands and rented or leased them, to sell at a later date. An example of the latter was Joseph Knight Sr., who did not sell his land when he moved to Ohio, but did so later when he got a better price.[16]

39. Riches of eternity. These are the spiritual riches the Father can give the Saints, but only through the temple. These riches are endowments of spiritual things to the members, including the revelation of celestial laws and principles (see D&C 42), the fulness of the priesthood, and the ordinances of exaltation. Receiving these make us the richest people in the world, our temporal financial status notwithstanding.

39. Riches of the earth. These are mostly up to God. He bestows them on some of the Saints and not on others, as he sees fit. But he desires to give *all* faithful Saints the riches of eternity.

39. Beware of pride. Wealth in itself is not evil, and the Lord is not automatically displeased with the wealthy, for he himself has blessed them with their riches. It is, however, the *natural* course of things for the rich, or perhaps for their children or grandchildren, to become first proud and then unfaithful. If the rich take no measures to keep this from happening, or if they just don't give it much thought, it *will* happen, just as surely as an untended garden will become overgrown with weeds. Therefore, wealthy Saints must be aware of the natural effect wealth has on people and must work actively and creatively to keep those weeds from their gardens. The natural progression, whether in one generation or the next, is to pride, then to unfaithfulness, and thence to wickedness and destruction.

41. The warning voice. The gospel is a warning to the world of its fallen state and of its need of repentance and of a Savior in order to escape the judgments of God, both at the Second Coming when the wicked will be burned and at the Resurrection when those who are "filthy still" will be cast out with Satan and his angels (see 2 Nephi 9:16; D&C 88:102). Without faith in Christ, repentance from sin, and baptism by immersion, all who have reached the age of accountability are doomed to suffer for their sins, whether in mortality, in hell, or in eternity. We sometimes forget this necessary element of warning as we preach and teach the gospel. We are not, however, to pound the pulpit and preach "hellfire and damnation" in the usual sense, or to loudly condemn or put down nonmembers, but to sound a warning to our neighbors "in mildness and in meekness."

42. Save yourselves. Although we are totally dependent upon the atonement of Jesus Christ for our salvation and exaltation in the kingdom of God (see Alma 22:14), we can "save ourselves" from the wickedness, wars, and natural disasters that will precede the end of this world. This we do by choosing to leave the "world" and gathering to Zion where the land will not be cursed or wasted at the Lord's coming.

42. Be ye clean that bear the vessels of the Lord. This is probably an allusion to the ancient priest who carried the holy vessels or implements used in the tabernacle from place to place as Israel went out of Egypt and traveled to the promised land. As Latter-day Saints we also are a "kingdom of priests" (Exodus 19:6), and we also have responsibility for bearing sacred things such as the priesthood of God, the truth of his gospel, the witness of the Spirit, our stewardships, our families, our very selves. Therefore we also must be clean and worthy in order to bear these sacred "vessels" as we come out of the world of a secular "Egypt" or "Babylon" to establish Zion (see D&C 133:5; Isaiah 52:11; 3 Nephi 20:41).

NOTES

1. Smith, *History of the Church,* 1:140.
2. See Cannon and Cook, *Far West Record,* 5.
3. Whitmer, *Early Latter-Day Saint History,* 32–34; see also Woodford, "Historical Development," 1:491.
4. Cited in Woodford, "Historical Development," 1:490–91.
5. See the commentary on D&C 19:1; 29:1; 35:1.
6. See Background.
7. See Smith, *Teachings,* 347.
8. Emphasis added.
9. Smith, *History of the Church,* 4:597.
10. Smith, *Lectures on Faith,* 51–52; see also Dahl and Tate, *Lectures on Faith in Historical Perspective,* 77.
11. *Doctrine and Covenants Student Manual,* 76.
12. This is not to be confused with the other city of another Enoch in Genesis 4:17; Moses 5:42.
13. See Background.
14. See Whitmer, *Early Latter-Day Saint History,* 31–32.
15. See also the commentary on D&C 2:1.
16. See Porter, *Study of the Origins of the Church,* 296–322.

DOCTRINE AND COVENANTS

39

BACKGROUND

Shortly after the Church conference of 2 January 1831, at which Doctrine and Covenants 38 was received in front of the entire congregation, Joseph Smith had an interview with a Baptist minister that he later described in these terms: "Not long after this conference of the 2nd of January closed, there was a man came to me by the name of James Covill, who had been a Baptist minister for about forty years, and covenanted with the Lord that he would obey any command that the Lord would give to him through me, as His servant, and I received the following"— Doctrine and Covenants 39.[1]

Despite his individual revelation, James Covill quickly rejected the gospel and the Prophet Joseph and returned to his former life and beliefs among the Protestants (see D&C 40).

COMMENTARY

1. The Great I Am. See the commentary on Doctrine and Covenants 38:1.

2. The light and the life of the world. Light and life are divine qualities; all light and all life, even that enjoyed by the wicked, come from God. Christ is the creator of all things. It is his light or energy that permeates matter and causes it to obey physical laws, thus making all subsequent creation possible, and it is his power that gives life to all living things (see D&C 88:15; John 1:1–5). In this creation, there is no source of life or energy outside of Jesus Christ.

3. Meridian of time. See the commentary on Doctrine and Covenants 20:26.

4. Gave I power to become my sons. Notice the combination of grace and works described here. God *gives* us by his grace the power to become his children, but we then must perform what he has put within our power. Without God's gracious gift, no sonship. Without our faithful response, no sonship.

5. Receiveth my gospel. To receive Jesus Christ is to receive his whole gospel; it is a package deal. The doctrine of Christ cannot be separated from the person of Christ, nor can one accept Christ without believing and obeying his doctrine. Jesus cannot be treated like a mascot or a good-luck charm. For those who invoke Jesus because they want God on their side "for luck," but who refuse to submit their will to his and believe his doctrine, there shall be no benefit.

6. This is my gospel.[2] James Covill was reminded of the basics as presented both in the Bible and the Book of Mormon (see Acts 2:38; Hebrews 6:1–3; 3 Nephi 27:19–21), although faith in the Lord Jesus Christ is apparently assumed here, probably because of Covill's life as a Baptist minister.

7. My servant James. James Covill[3] was almost seventy-five years old when he met Joseph Smith, and he had been a Baptist minister for about forty years.[4] Though not yet baptized, the Lord referred to Covill as "my servant," perhaps because of the preparatory ministry he had performed as a Baptist (see D&C 35:4),[5] and the Lord had already blessed him greatly for his service in the past (see D&C 39:8).

8. Notice the heavy qualifiers used here: "now" and "at this time." Since Covill did not obey the commandments he was given here, and the Lord knew he would not, it is understandable why this endorsement of Covill was qualified so carefully. When the revelation and commandments were given, Covill's heart was right, but once he had received them, he had second thoughts and turned away.

9. Thou hast rejected me many times. Nonmembers can and do know Christ to some considerable degree through the Bible, the light of Christ that permeates all things, and the occasional inspiration of the Holy Ghost. James Covill had been a Baptist minister for forty years. He knew Christ in some degree, but had wavered in the past between faithfulness to what he knew and his pride and care for the things of the world. Here he was given the opportunity to know Christ to the fullest degree possible, but the price was everything he had, including his pride and his temporal concerns. Unfortunately, for Covill the price proved too high. Covill was not an investigator seeking to know the truth; he had already received a spiritual witness that the gospel was true, but it cost too much, and he rejected Christ yet again.

10. The days of thy deliverance are come. James Covill could be delivered from the false doctrines and pride that had disrupted his life. If he humbled himself before God and entered into the covenant of baptism, then his sins would be forgiven, and he would be apportioned an inheritance with Israel.

11. If thou do this. Most of the promises given by God to mortals are conditional; if we meet the conditions, then the promises of God are fulfilled (see D&C 82:10). If James Covill obeyed the conditions laid upon him, in this case by being baptized and moving to Ohio (see vv. 10, 14), then the Lord would endow him with true power and send him forth to preach and baptize.

11. A greater work. Note particularly that the work Covill had previously done as a Baptist minister to teach Christ was here by implication a "great work." Now if he would be baptized and obey the Lord's commands, he would be given an even *greater* work to do, which is to preach the fulness of the gospel to the world in the power of the priesthood and by the gift of the Holy

Ghost. Though coming from circumstances similar to Sidney Rigdon's and dealt with by the Lord in the same manner, Covill presented a foil or contrast to Rigdon's humility and obedience when presented with the same choices and offered the same blessings (see D&C 40).[6]

11. The covenant. The new and everlasting covenant (see D&C 22:1), by which the righteous descendants of Israel will be gathered back into the family, as will those adopted into Israel by their faith in Christ.

12. Power shall rest upon thee. Likely a reference to the Holy Ghost and the Melchizedek Priesthood.

13–14. Note the parallels here to Isaiah 52:7–12.

14. The eastern countries. The eastern parts of New York where Covill was from. He would apparently have preferred to go back there, but he was called with all the other Saints to gather to Ohio in the West.

15. A blessing such as is not known. The blessings of the keys of the sealing power and other ordinances requiring a temple had not yet been restored to the earth, but they would be restored when the Saints gathered to Ohio as commanded (see D&C 110:11–16).

16. Thinking I will stay my hand in judgment. The new converts in Ohio were praying that the Lord would change his plans to destroy the wicked prior to his Second Coming. But God must be just as well as merciful, and all his words must be fulfilled (see D&C 1:37–39). Thus the prayers of the Ohio Saints, though fervent, faithful, and sincere, were in vain on this point. This is exactly why Latter-day Saints are commanded to take the gospel to the world, for the only way to save the wicked is to preach repentance to them, to convert them, and bring them into the new and everlasting covenant. All humanity must repent and accept the gospel or suffer death at Christ's coming and hell until the Resurrection. It is this we are called to warn the world about and to save them from.

17. See the commentary on Doctrine and Covenants 24:19; 33:3.

18. Become sanctified. This means to become Saints, sanctified ones, through the atonement of Christ and his gospel of faith, repentance, baptism, and receiving the Holy Ghost.[7]

19. The kingdom of heaven is at hand. Viewed from the perspective of the world's total history, "at hand" could mean just a few centuries, and, of course, the kingdom was already upon the earth in a preliminary way as The Church of Jesus Christ of Latter-day Saints. That the kingdom of heaven was at hand was also the declaration of both John the Baptist and Jesus (see Matthew 3:2; 4:17).

19. Hosanna. See the commentary on Doctrine and Covenants 19:37.

21. The time is at hand. A vague indication.[8]

21. The day or the hour no man knoweth. Though we are encouraged to watch for the signs, the scriptures tell us that "no man knows" when Christ will return. Anyone who would venture such a prediction should be understood as contradicting the scriptures, an act which should be avoided as a snare and a hazard.

22. In time and in eternity. Time is a mortal limitation; thus "time" refers to our present mortal lives. "Eternity" is that which extends beyond this present life. Thus, "in time and in eternity" is another way of saying both in this life and in the next.

23. Looking forth for the signs of my coming. This is perhaps an under-observed commandment among the Saints. The "signs of my coming," however, are not to be discovered or explained in the writings of self-appointed authorities, for this is a favorite subject of false teachers past, present, and future. For some reason, when some contemporary Saints approach the subject of the end-time, they lose all balance, discernment, and judgment. The "signs of my coming" that had been revealed before Doctrine and Covenants 39 was given consisted basically of Doctrine and Covenants 29, 38, Matthew 24, Mark 13, the book of Revelation, and some statements of the Prophet. Today the only reliable guides on this subject are still limited to the scriptures and the prophets; other teachings or teachers upon this topic should be taken very lightly or, better yet, ignored altogether.

Notes

1. Smith, *History of the Church,* 1:143.
2. See the commentary on D&C 33:12.
3. Spelled *Covell* in non-LDS sources.
4. See Cook, *Revelations of the Prophet,* 56–57.
5. See also the commentary on D&C 35:4.
6. See also the commentary on D&C 35:3.
7. See the commentary on D&C 20:31.
8. See the commentary on D&C 39:19.

DOCTRINE AND COVENANTS

40

BACKGROUND

The background to Doctrine and Covenants 40 is much the same as for Doctrine and Covenants 39. James Covill, the Baptist minister who had received a conviction that Joseph was indeed a prophet and who covenanted with God to obey any command given him through Joseph Smith, had violated his covenant and had apostatized from the Church. On reconsidering the personal cost of obedience to the commandments he had received (see D&C 39:10, 14), Covill chose not to be baptized and, rejecting the new and everlasting covenant, returned instead to his former residence and income and to his former Baptist beliefs.

Covill's behavior greatly puzzled Joseph Smith and Sidney Rigdon, for they had judged Covill's commitment to be genuine. Joseph recorded concerning the reception of section 40: "As James Covill rejected the word of the Lord, and returned to his former principles and people, the Lord gave unto me and Sidney Rigdon the following revelation, explaining why he obeyed not the word"—Doctrine and Covenants 40.[1] Section 40 was the last of the revelations now recorded in the Doctrine and Covenants to be received in New York or Pennsylvania.

COMMENTARY

1. The heart of my servant James Covill was right. The tragedy of James Covill is that he knew what he was doing. He had received a conviction of the truth of the restored gospel and had voluntarily made a binding covenant with God to obey any commandment given him. He was, at that time, right in his desires, but later lost his resolve, when he realized how much he would lose if he became a Latter-day Saint. Doctrine and Covenants 40 reminds us that God will hold us responsible for those proper individual promises and "deals," or covenants, that we make with him and then do not keep.

2. Received the word with gladness. The Lord applied to Covill his description from the parable of the sower of those who receive the word in stony places (see Matthew 13:20–21). The seed of the word had genuinely taken root in Covill's heart, but he could not stand up in the long run against the threat of personal loss or persecution.

2. Fear of persecution. In Doctrine and Covenants 39:9 James Covill was informed by the Lord that because of pride and care for the things of the world, he had rejected the Lord many times in the past. To this list of weak spots in his life, the Lord now added another: fear of persecution. It could not have been an easy decision for James Covill, a seventy-four-year-old Baptist minister, to join the Church, give up his minister's income, and begin at his age to learn the gospel. Yet, in much the same circumstances, Sidney Rigdon, though much younger than Covill, had followed his conscience and the Spirit of God and had joined the Church. As a result, he converted scores from his own congregations and scores more as a Melchizedek Priesthood holder. Again, the contrasting responses of James and Sidney are instructive.

3. James Covill had not just failed to join the Church; he had made an actual covenant with the Lord, which the Lord had accepted, and then James had broken it. Since Covill had made his covenant to obey of his own free will, God had accepted it and had given him the commandments he sought (see D&C 39). Covill will be judged of God for the covenant he violated. Thus it will be with each of us.

NOTE

1. Smith, *History of the Church,* 1:145.

DOCTRINE AND COVENANTS

SOURCES

Anderson, R. L. "The Mature Joseph Smith and Treasure Searching." *BYU Studies,* Fall 1984, 489–560.

———. "The Organization Revelations." In Robert L. Millet and Kent P. Jackson, eds. *The Doctrine and Covenants.* Vol. 1 of *Studies in Scriptures.* Salt Lake City: Deseret Book, 1989.

Backman, Milton V., Jr. *Joseph Smith's First Vision.* 2d ed. Salt Lake City: Bookcraft, 1971.

———, ed. *Ohio.* Regional Studies in Latter-day Saint Church History Series. Provo, Utah: Brigham Young University, 1990.

Backman, Milton V., Jr., and Richard O. Cowan. *Joseph Smith and the Doctrine and Covenants.* Salt Lake City: Deseret Book, 1992.

Benson, Ezra Taft. "'Strengthen Thy Stakes.'" *Ensign,* Jan. 1991, 2–5.

———. *A Witness and a Warning: A Modern-Day Prophet Testifies of the Book of Mormon.* Salt Lake City: Deseret Book, 1988.

Brown, Colin, ed. *The New International Dictionary of New Testament Theology.* Grand Rapids, Mich.: Regency Reference Library, 1986.

Brown, S. Kent. "Book Review of *April Sixth.*" *BYU Studies,* Summer 1982, 375–83.

Brown, S. Kent, Donald Q. Cannon, and Richard H. Jackson, eds. *Historical Atlas of Mormonism.* New York: Simon and Schuster, 1994.

Bushman, Richard L. *Joseph Smith and the Beginnings of Mormonism.* Urbana, Ill.: University of Illinois Press, 1984.

Cannon, Brian Q. "Priesthood Restoration Documents." *BYU Studies* 35, no. 4 (1995–96), 162–207.

Cannon, Donald Q., and Lyndon W. Cook, eds. *Far West Record: Minutes of The Church of Jesus Christ of Latter-day Saints, 1830–1844.* Salt Lake City: Deseret Book, 1983.

Carmack, John K. "Fayette: The Place the Church Was Organized." *Ensign*, Feb. 1989, 14–19.

Carter, Jared. Journal. Harold B. Lee Library, Special Collections, MSS Sc 547, Brigham Young University, Provo, Utah.

Clark, James R., comp. *Messages of the First Presidency of The Church of Jesus Christ of Latter-day Saints*, 6 vols. Salt Lake City: Bookcraft. 1965–75.

Clark, J. Reuben, Jr. *Our Lord of the Gospels.* Salt Lake City: Deseret Book, 1954.

Conference Report of The Church of Jesus Christ of Latter-day Saints. Salt Lake City: The Church of Jesus Christ of Latter-day Saints, 1880–1969.

Cook, LyndonW. *Joseph Smith and the Law of Consecration.* Provo, Utah: Grandin, 1985.

————. *The Revelations of the Prophet Joseph Smith: A Historical and Biographical Commentary of the Doctrine and Covenants.* Salt Lake City: Deseret Book, 1985.

Cowdery, Oliver. "Dear Brother." *Messenger and Advocate*, Oct. 1834, 13–16.

Crawley, Peter. "A Bibliography of The Church of Jesus Christ of Latter-day Saints in New York, Ohio, and Missouri." *BYU Studies*, 12, Summer 1972, 485.

Dahl, Larry E., and Charles D. Tate, Jr. *The Lectures on Faith in Historical Perspective.* Provo: Brigham Young University, 1990.

The Doctrine and Covenants Student Manual. Church Educational System, Religion 324–325 student manual, 1981.

Dyer, Alvin R. *The Refiner's Fire: The Significance of Events Transpiring in Missouri.* 2d ed. Salt Lake City: Deseret Book, 1968.

Ferguson, Everett, ed. *Encyclopedia of Early Christianity.* New York: Garland Publishing, 1990.

The Five Gospels. Edited by Robert Funk, et al. New York: Macmillan, 1993.

Fyans, Thomas J. In Conference Report, Korea Area Conference 1975.

Gentry, Leland H. "Light on the 'Mission to the Lamanites.'" *BYU Studies* 36, no. 2 (1996–97), 226–30.

Gunnell, Wayne Cutler. "Martin Harris—Witness and Benefactor to the Book of Mormon." Master's thesis, Brigham Young University, 1955.

Howard, Richard P. *Restoration Scriptures: A Study of Their Textural Development*. Independence, Mo.: Reorganized Church of Jesus Christ of Latter-day Saints, 1969.

Jenson, Andrew, ed. "The Three Witnesses." *The Historical Record,* May 1887.

Jessee, Dean C. "Joseph Knight's Recollection of Early Mormon History." *BYU Studies,* Autumn 1976, 29–39.

———. *The Papers of Joseph Smith.* 2 vols. Salt Lake City: Deseret Book, 1989–92.

———. *The Personal Writings of Joseph Smith.* Salt Lake City: Deseret Book, 1984.

Journal of Discourses. 26 vols. London: Latter-day Saints' Book Depot, 1854–86.

Kimball, Spencer W. *Faith Precedes the Miracle.* Salt Lake City: Deseret Book, 1972.

———. "The False Gods We Worship." *Ensign,* June 1976, 3–6.

———. *Integrity.* In Brigham Young University Speeches of the Year, 25 Feb. 1964.

———. *The Lamanites: Their Burden—Our Burden.* In Brigham Young University Speeches of the Year, 25 Apr. 1967.

———. *The Miracle of Forgiveness.* Salt Lake City: Bookcraft, 1969.

———. *That You May Not Be Deceived.* In Brigham Young University Speeches of the Year, 11 Nov. 1959.

King, Arthur Henry. "A Man Who Speaks to Our Time from Eternity." *Ensign* 19 (March 1989): 12–16.

Kirkham, Francis W. *A New Witness for Christ in America: The Book of Mormon.* Salt Lake City: Utah Printing, 1960.

"Labors in the Vineyard." In *Classic Experiences and Adventures.* Salt Lake City: Bookcraft, 1969.

Lane, William. *The Gospel According to Mark.* Grand Rapids Mich.: Eerdmans, 1974.

Lee, Harold B. *Feet Shod with the Preparation of the Gospel of Peace.* In Brigham Young University Speeches of the Year, 9 Nov. 1954.

———. "Priesthood in Mission Field Emphasized." *Church News,* 8 July 1961, 5.

———. "The Way to Eternal Life." *Ensign,* Nov. 1971, 9–17.

Lefgren, John C. *April Sixth.* Salt Lake City: Deseret Book, 1980.

Ludlow, Daniel H., ed. *Encyclopedia of Mormonism.* 5 vols. New York: Macmillan Publishing, 1992.

Marsh, Thomas B. "History of Thos. Baldwin Marsh." *Deseret News,* 24 Mar. 1858, 18.

Matthews, Robert J. *"A Plainer Translation," Joseph Smith's Translation of the Bible: A History and Commentary.* Provo: Brigham Young University Press, 1975.

Maxwell, Neal A. "The Doctrine and Covenants: The Voice of the Lord." *Ensign,* Dec. 1978, 4–7.

McConkie, Bruce R. "The Keys of the Kingdom." Address to Wilford Stake priesthood meeting, 21 Feb. 1955.

———. *Mormon Doctrine.* 2d ed. Salt Lake City: Bookcraft, 1966.

———. *The Mortal Messiah: From Bethlehem to Calvary.* 4 vols. Salt Lake City: Deseret Book, 1979–81.

———. *A New Witness for the Articles of Faith.* Salt Lake City: Deseret Book, 1985.

———. "The Salvation of Little Children." *Ensign,* Apr. 1977, 2–7.

McKenzie, John L., trans. *The Anchor Bible: Second Isaiah.* Garden City: Doubleday, 1968.

"The Mormon Creed." *Telegraph,* 19 Apr. 1831.

Murdock, John. Autobiography. Typescript, Harold B. Lee Library, Special Collections, Brigham Young University, Provo, Utah.

Oaks, Dallin H. "Sin and Suffering." In *Brigham Young University 1989–90 Devotional and Fireside Speeches,* 5 Aug. 1990, 145–53.

Ohio Star, 2 Oct. 1831.

Parkin, Max H. "A Preliminary Analysis of the Dating of Section 10." In *Seventh Annual Sidney B. Sperry Symposium.* Provo: Brigham Young University, 1979.

Perkins, Keith W. "'Thou Art Still Chosen.'" *Ensign,* Jan. 1993, 15–19.

Peterson, H. Donl. "Moroni: Joseph Smith's Teacher." In Larry C. Porter,

Milton V. Backman Jr., and Susan Easton Black, eds. *Regional Studies in Latter-day Saint Church History: New York.* Provo: Brigham Young University, 1992, 49–70.

Peterson, Paul H. "Book Review of *Inventing Mormonism: Tradition and the Historical Record.*" *BYU Studies* 35, no. 4 (1995–96), 209–27.

Phelps, W. W. "The Saints." *The Evening and the Morning Star.* Independence, Mo., May 1834, 158–59.

———. "The Tribe of Joseph." *The Evening and the Morning Star.* Independence, Mo., Nov. 1832, 1–3.

Porter, Larry C. "Dating the Restoration of the Melchizedek Priesthood." *Ensign,* June 1979, 5–10.

———. "The Restoration of the Priesthood." *Religious Studies Center Newsletter.* Provo: Brigham Young University, May 1995.

———. "A Study of the Origins of the Church of Jesus Christ of Latter-day Saints in the States of New York and Pennsylvania, 1816–1831." Ph.D. dissertation, Brigham Young University, 1971.

Pratt, Orson. "Explanation of Substituted Names in the Covenants." *The Seer* 2 (March 1854): 228.

Pratt, Orson, Sr., and Joseph F. Smith. "Report of Elders Orson Pratt and Joseph F. Smith." *Millennial Star,* 9 Dec. 1878, 753–73.

Pratt, Parley P., ed. *Autobiography of Parley Pratt.* Classics in Mormon Literature series. Salt Lake City: Deseret Book, 1985.

———. *Key to the Science of Theology.* 9th ed. Salt Lake City: Deseret Book, 1965.

Reeve, Rex C., Sr. "The Whole Armor of God." In *Brigham Young University 1981–82 Fireside and Devotional Speeches,* 8 Aug. 1982, 189–97.

Roberts, B. H. *Outlines of Ecclesiastical History: A Text Book.* Classics in Mormon Literature series. Salt Lake City: Deseret Book, 1979.

Robinson, James M., trans. *The Nag Hammadi Library in English.* Brill: Leiden, 1988.

Robinson, Stephen E. "Eternities That Come and Go." *Religious Studies Center Newsletter.* Provo: Brigham Young University, May 1994.

———. "Warring against the Saints of God." *Ensign,* Jan. 1988, 34–39.

Shipps, Jan, and John W. Welch, eds. *The Journals of William E. McLellin, 1831–1836.* Provo: Brigham Young University, 1994.

Smith, Hyrum M. *The Doctrine and Covenants Commentary.* 1919.

Smith, Hyrum M., and Janne M. Sjodahl. *The Doctrine and Covenants Commentary.* Rev. ed. 1972.

Smith, Joseph. "History of Joseph Smith." *Times and Seasons,* 1 July 1842, 832; 15 July 1842, 853.

————. *History of The Church of Jesus Christ of Latter-day Saints.* 7 vols. 2d ed. rev. Edited by B. H. Roberts. Salt Lake City: The Church of Jesus Christ of Latter-day Saints, 1932–51.

————. *Kirtland Revelation Book.* Salt Lake City: Modern Microfilm, 1979.

————. *Lectures on Faith.* Salt Lake City: Deseret Book, 1985.

————. *Teachings of the Prophet Joseph Smith.* Selected by Joseph Fielding Smith. Salt Lake City: Deseret Book, 1976.

Smith, Joseph F., Anthon H. Lund, and Charles W. Penrose. "A Warning Voice." *Improvement Era,* Sept. 1913, 1148–49.

Smith, Joseph F., John R. Winder, and Anthon H. Lund. "'One Mighty and Strong.'" *Improvement Era,* Oct. 1907, 929–43.

Smith, Joseph Fielding. *Answers to Gospel Questions.* 5 vols. Compiled by Joseph Fielding Smith, Jr. Salt Lake City: Deseret Book, 1957–66.

————. *Church History and Modern Revelation.* 2 vols. Salt Lake City: Deseret Book, 1953.

————. *Doctrines of Salvation.* 3 vols. Compiled by Bruce R. McConkie. Salt Lake City: Bookcraft, 1954–56.

————. "President Joseph Fielding Smith Answers Your Question Concerning the Status of Retarded Children." *Improvement Era,* Feb. 1959, 80–81.

Smith, Lucy Mack. *History of Joseph Smith.* Edited by Preston Nibley. Salt Lake City: Bookcraft, 1958.

Smith, Samuel H. Journal 1831–32. Archives of The Church of Jesus Christ of Latter-day Saints, Salt Lake City, Utah.

Talmage, James E. *Jesus the Christ.* 3d ed. Salt Lake City: The Church of Jesus Christ of Latter-day Saints, 1916.

Taylor, John. "The Blessing of Children." *Millennial Star,* 15 Apr. 1878, 235–36.

Tuttle, A. Theodore. *Spirituality: The Challenge of Today.* In Brigham Young University Speeches of the Year, 28 Mar. 1967.

Whitmer, David. *An Address to All Believers in Christ.* Richmond, Mo.: David Whitmer, 1887.

Whitmer, John. *An Early Latter-day Saint History: The Book of John Whitmer, Kept by Commandment*. Edited by F. Mark McKiernan and Roger D. Launius. Independence, Mo.: Herald Publishing House, 1980.

Whitney, Newel K. Collected papers. Harold B. Lee Library, Special Collections, MSS 1–2, Brigham Young University, Provo, Utah.

Widtsoe, John A. *Evidences and Reconciliations*. 3 vols. in 1. Arranged by G. Homer Durham. Salt Lake City: Bookcraft, 1960.

Woodford, Robert J. "The Historical Development of the Doctrine and Covenants." 2 vols. Ph.D. dissertation, Brigham Young University, 1974.

DOCTRINE AND COVENANTS

INDEX

Justice: law of, 20–21, 114; demands of, 201, 240, 259, 272
Justification, 40, 133, 136, 173, 196; by works, 225; by faith, 243

Keys: of mysteries of kingdom, 1, 242; priesthood, 25, 30–31, 61, 91, 244, 266; of sealing power, 31, 262; apostolic, 129–30; authority and, 183–84
Kimball, Spencer W., 129; and the Doctrine and Covenants, 1; on deception, 193; on the Lamanites, 221
Kindness, 229
Kingdom: millennial, 42; of God, 244, 261
Kirtland, Ohio, Church to move to, 250–51
Kirtland Revelation Book, 98, 220
Kirtland Temple, 238, 265–66
Knight, Joseph, Sr., 53, 86–87, 111, 123, 266; on organization of the Church, 148; revelation to, 158–61; commanded to pray vocally, 160; and confrontation with mob, 162
Knight, Newel, 87, 177, 188; Joseph arrested at home of, 162–63
Knight, Sally, 177–78
Koontz, Mayme, 189

Lamanites, 39, 75, 153, 191–93; mission to the, 213, 219–20, 235–36, 245
The Latter-day Saint Messenger and Advocate, 7, 9, 11–12
Laws, celestial, 262
Leaders, self-appointed, 193
Leadership, prerogative of priesthood, 175
Lectures on Faith, 10, 12–13
Lee, Harold B., 27, 127, 129
Lehi, descendants of, 39–40
Levi, sons of, 91
Liahona, 39, 99

Life: waters of, 77; eternal, 94; light and, 269
Light: loss of, 26; Christ as, 269; of Christ, 271
Lineage, 159
Literary Firm, 4–5, 7
Loins, girding up, 184
Lord: great and dreadful day of the, 32; service to, 42–43; tempting the, 72; words of the, 96; arrival of the, 124. *See also* Jesus Christ
Lord's Preface, the, 18
Love, 24–25, 43, 87, 106

Malachi, 3
Man, nature of, 134
Manifestations, contrary to Church authorities, 190
Manuscript, lost pages of, 72–73
Marriage, 173; new and everlasting covenant of, 151, 229; supper of the Lamb, 180, 183
Marsh, Thomas B., 195; revelation to, 212, 214; ordination of, 214–15; apostasy of, 215; excommunication of, 215; rebaptism of, 215
Martyrdom, foreshadowing of, 49, 57
McConkie, Bruce R., 129
McLellin, William E., 4, 131, 155
Meek, the poor and the, 241
Meetings, commandment to attend, 141, 229
Melchizedek Priesthood, 89, 91, 150; restoration of, 103; power of, 272
Mercy, 272
Merits, Jesus Christ's, 40
Messenger and Advocate. See The Latter-day Saint Messenger and Advocate
Messiah, Christ as, 90–91
Methodists, 107
Michael, 183, 203–4, 206
Might, 43

Peterson, Ziba, 213, 219, 221–22
Peter the Apostle, 59–61, 84, 103
Phelps, William W., 181; and
    publication of the revelations,
    3–6, 18; to assist in preparing the
    Doctrine and Covenants for
    publication, 9
Pixley, Reverend, 6
Plates, gold, 37; and record of
    Nephites, 25; Moroni and,
    29–30; Joseph Smith receives,
    34; taken from Joseph, 35, 41, 70
Poor, the meek and the, 241
Pornography, 240
Pratt, Orson: and revelation
    manuscripts, 2; chairs
    publication committee, 13; and
    D&C 2, 31; and D&C 22, 154;
    baptism of, 221; revelation for,
    231–34; and gift of prophecy,
    234
Pratt, Parley, 192, 213, 219;
    conversion of, 221; as missionary,
    223, 231
Prayer, 71, 172, 217–18, 222; vocal,
    122, 160; importance of, 229
Preachers: self-appointed, 82; called
    by authority, 83
Preaching, 77–78, 119
Premortality, 206
Preparation, 265
Preparedness, oil of, 229
Presidency, 130; keys of the, of the
    Church, 61; power of, in Aaronic
    Priesthood, 90
Pride, 159, 267
Priestcraft, 76, 202, 226
Priesthood: restoration of the, 24,
    42; keys of the, 25, 30–31, 61,
    244; duties of the, 140;
    ordination to the, 140; line of
    authority, 213. See also Aaronic
    Priesthood; Melchizedek
    Priesthood
Prince of Peace, 77
Printing: of Book of
    Commandments, 6

Prison, spirit, 32
Privileges, 38
Probation, days of, 208
Promises, 39–40, 183, 271
Prophecy, 149
Prophets, 149–50; voice of, 27–28;
    and signs of Second Coming, 274
Publication, need for, of revelations,
    17–18
Punishment, 48; unbelieving are
    sealed to, 20
Pure Church of Christ, the, 223
Purification, 243, 260
Purse nor scrip, 166

Quorum of the Twelve Apostles,
    108, 150

Rebaptism, 144
Rebellious, the, 20, 203
Rebirth, spiritual, 48
Reconciliation, 193
Records, retention of, 56
Redeemer, Christ as, 112
Reflector, 110
Reformed Baptist movement, 221,
    235
Relief Society, organization of, 171
Religion, false, 226
Repentance, 130, 133, 228, 267;
    forgiveness and, 20; crying, 54;
    and renewing commitments, 83;
    calling world to, 105, 227; Christ
    provided opportunity for, 106;
    rewards of, 107; revelation
    regarding, 111–12; or suffering,
    114; and resurrection, 116–17;
    preaching, 119–20, 233
Repetition, 37, 53
Responsibility, blessings and, 108
Rest, 97
Restoration: Doctrine and Covenants
    capstone of, 1–2; of all things,
    92; of priesthood keys, 104; of
    true Church, 227; as beginning,
    238

Sin(s): accounting for, 20, 117;
unrepented, 26; inquiry
regarding, 90; children and, 142;
forgiveness for, 196; suffering for,
in hell, 225; Christ crucified for,
of world, 237; and Atonement,
240
Sjodahl, Janne M., 39
Smith, Emma Hale, 34, 162; as
scribe, 41–42, 52–53, 170–71;
baptism of, 168; revelation to,
168; as elect lady, 169–70;
confirmation of, 171, 177–78;
and missionaries to Lamanites,
219
Smith, Hyrum, 53, 57, 80, 86, 129;
as son of Jesus Christ, 84; letter
to, 103; and organization of the
Church of Christ, 127; revelation
to, 158
Smith, Hyrum M., 39
Smith, John, 9
Smith, Joseph, Jr.: revelations to, 1,
23, 80, 158, 174, 214, 231;
copying of revelations by, 2–5;
corrections by, 4–5, 59; and
committee to arrange revelations,
8; compiles revelations, 17; and
First Vision, 29; and keys of
sealing power, 31; receives gold
plates, 34; and Urim and
Thummim, 34–36, 69–70; gold
plates taken from, 35, 41, 70;
transgressions of, 37–38;
foreordination of, 38; calling of,
as witness, 46; generation of, 47;
receives Aaronic Priesthood, 48,
90–91, 103; death of,
foreshadowed, 49, 57; on the
spirit of revelation, 63; role of,
64; labors of, 71; warned of
conspiracy, 72; validity of,
72–73; Satan's plan to discredit,
73; on love, 87; on sacrifice, 92;
and testimony of Three
Witnesses, 99–100; ordination
of, to office of elder, 104; mission

of, 105; on the end of the world,
113; on preaching the Gospel,
123; on organizing the Church,
126; organizes the Church of
Christ, 127; on reference to
years, 128; and Melchizedek
Priesthood, 129–30; sins of, 130,
163; on section 21, 147–48; as
seer, 149; arrest of, 162–63;
tarring and feathering of,
attempted, 163; Saints to
support, 163–64; on the
Millennium, 185; as Moses,
190–91; on gathering, 197; on
signs of Second Coming, 200; on
sections 30 and 31, 211; and
section 32, 219; blessed by the
Lord, 241–42; receives revelation
for Edward Partridge, 245; on
knowledge of Jehovah, 256–57;
and section 42, 266; interview
with Baptist minister, 269; and
James Covill, 275
Smith, Joseph, Sr., 42, 52
Smith, Joseph F.: and the Doctrine
and Covenants, 1
Smith, Joseph Fielding, 54, 92; on
Oliver Cowdery, 159; on Emma
Smith, 170; on Elias, 182; on
D&C 29, 195; on mentally
handicapped, 209–10
Smith, Lucy Mack, 36, 41, 236; on
Emma Smith, 53; on meeting
with Edward Partridge, 245–46
Smith, Samuel, 52, 80, 195; and
organization of the Church of
Christ, 127; revelation to,
158–60; death of, 160
Sons: of Perdition, 117, 204, 206–7;
of God, 232, 270; and daughters
of Christ, 237
Spirit: striving of the, 26; prison, 32;
confirmation of the, 67–68;
recognizing the, of God, 82;
denying the, 84; world, 90, 116,
206–8; contrite, 138–39; of
Christ, 139; that quickens, 228

Standard works, 77–78
Stewardship, 70–71, 153
Strength, 43
Striving of the Spirit, 26
Study by the Spirit, 228
Stupor of thought, 67
Success, temporal, 164
Suffering, 114–15, 117; in body and spirit, 118
Sweet, Northrop, 223
Sword: imagery of the, 21, 54; of Laban, 99
Symbols, bread and wine as, 143, 179

Taylor, John, 12–13, 171, 180
Teachers, duties of, 140
Teaching, home, 229
Telegraph, 127, 236
Telestial salvation, 95, 116
Temperateness, 87–88
Temple: ordinances of the, 23; symbolic, 150; coming of the Lord to, 248
Temptation, 72; of Christ, 134–35
Tenets, 123
Ten Tribes, 60
Terrestrial salvation, 95, 116, 198
Testimony of Eight Witnesses, 102
Thayre, Ezra, 223–24
Thoughts, God's knowledge of, 55–56
Three Witnesses to Book of Mormon, 47, 49, 95, 98–99, 108, 132
Time, meridian of, 135
Times and Seasons, 31
Times, fulness of, 184
Torment, endless, 114–15
Transgressions, 37
Translated beings, 60
Translation: New, of the Bible, 8, 17, 31; of Book of Mormon, 24, 34, 52–53, 66, 93; gift of, 38, 46; and Oliver Cowdery, 62; process, 62; nears completion, 98

Translator, 149
Transubstantiation, 179
Trials, patience in, 164
Tribes, lost, of Israel, 61, 227
Truth: revelation reflects, 138; expedient, 140
Twelve Apostles, Quorum of: testimony of, 11

Unbelieving, the, 20
Unrepentant: destruction of, 48; punishment of, 117; suffering of, 118; and outer darkness, 208
Urim and Thummim, 37, 39, 130; Moroni and the, 29–30; Joseph Smith receives, 34; taken from Joseph, 35, 69–70; returned to Joseph, 36, 69; description of, 70; as instrument of the Lord, 82; revelation received through, 94, 98; witnesses to see, 99

Validity, seeking, 72–73
Vessels, 268
Vineyard: prune, for last time, 166–67; parable of laborers in, 225–26
Voice: still, small, 265; warning, 267
Vote, sustaining, 175, 192

Warning, voice of, 19
Wars, 264–65
Wasting of the earth, 32–33
Water, 143
Waters of life, 77
Wayne County Sentinel, 110
Weakness, 24–25
Wealth, 267
Whitmer, David, 94, 195, 212; as witness, 47, 95, 98–99, 101; revelation to, 53; and Oliver Cowdery, 56, 93; and organization of the Church of Christ, 127
Whitmer, John, 178, 195; copying of revelations by, 2, 5; appointed